The Life and Thought of Louis Lowy

RELIGION, THEOLOGY, AND THE HOLOCAUST

Louis Lowy, ca. 1964. Photographer unknown.
Courtesy of Edith Lowy.

The Life and Thought of
Louis Lowy

Social Work Through the Holocaust

Lorrie Greenhouse Gardella

Foreword by Joachim Wieler

To Terri,

Lorrie G Gardella

April 17, 2015

SYRACUSE UNIVERSITY PRESS

∞ The paper used in this publication meets the minimum requirements of the American National Standard for Information Sciences—Permanence of Paper for Printed Library Materials, ANSI Z39.48-1992.

For a listing of books published and distributed by Syracuse University Press, visit our Web site at SyracuseUniversityPress.syr.edu.

ISBN 978-0-8156-0965-0

Library of Congress Cataloging-in-Publication Data

Gardella, Lorrie Greenhouse.
    The life and thought of Louis Lowy : social work through the Holocaust / Lorrie Greenhouse Gardella. — 1st ed.
        p. cm. — (Religion, theology, and the Holocaust)
    Includes bibliographical references and index.
    ISBN 978-0-8156-0965-0 (cloth : alk. paper)
    1. Lowy, Louis.   2. Jews—Czech Republic—Prague—Biography.   3. Jews, Czech—United States—Biography.   4. Jewish refugees—Germany—Deggendorf—Biography.
5. Social workers—Massachusetts—Boston—Biography.   6. Holocaust survivors—Massachusetts—Boston—Biography.   I. Title.
    DS135.C97L694 2011
    940.53'18092—dc23
    [B]   2011031737

Manufactured in the United States of America

For Ditta

Lorrie Greenhouse Gardella is professor of social work and associate dean of the School of Graduate and Professional Studies at Saint Joseph College, Connecticut. She is the co-author, with Karen S. Haynes, of *A Dream and A Plan: A Woman's Path to Leadership in Human Services* (2004).

Contents

Illustrations

Photographs

* By permission of the United States Holocaust Memorial Museum. The views or opinions expressed in this book, and the context in which the images are used, do not necessarily reflect the views or policy of, nor imply approval or endorsement by, the United States Holocaust Memorial Museum.

Maps

Chart

Foreword

JOACHIM WIELER

THIS BOOK IS ABOUT REMEMBERING, about diving into the abyss of the Holocaust and coming out of it, as Louis Lowy and others have shown us. This thoroughly researched and well-written book is also one of the first to explore the relationship between surviving the Holocaust and forming a professional identity as a social worker.

Lorrie Greenhouse Gardella allows Louis Lowy to speak for himself, and she involves other closely related people who tell of their own experiences, confirming similarities but also adding their own memories. The author weaves individual experiences into living dialogues and institutional contexts and puts everything into a larger historical framework. We are reminded of the generic approach in formulating social histories in social work by moving from personal concerns and very concrete experiences to social and institutional connections and on to structural contexts, including the micro, mezzo, and the macro levels. This account is a tangible enactment of social work philosophy.

We encounter in this book some of the last eyewitnesses to the Holocaust. It must have been very painful for these witnesses to relive some of their horrifying experiences through inquiries and narrative interviews, and I join the author in thanking them for opening their lives and for making this moving eyewitness report possible. Let me also congratulate the publisher. Without books on social work history and Holocaust history, we deny the past, and how can there be a future if there is no past? Critical acknowledgment, constructive analysis, and alternative action as demonstrated in this book will lead to a renewed future for the social work profession.

Remembrance is the foundation of reconciliation. This wisdom, based on the Talmud and on other basic religious and humanistic teachings, has many implications. Remembrance and acknowledgment seem to be a prerequisite and the most important key for any kind of research. For Holocaust research it has a particular meaning. Remembrance is the foundation, but not reconciliation as such. It is a necessary precondition, and if acknowledged, it might lead to reconciliation.

I live in Weimar/Germany, where the first democratic constitution led to the Weimar Republic and, ironically, where the Nazi Concentration Camp Buchenwald casts a lasting shadow. Every year, when we have commemorated the liberation of Buchenwald and other concentration camps, former inmates have come back to help us remember. Every year, there are fewer and fewer eyewitnesses who return. Nonetheless, there is considerable emphasis on turning these terrible places into memorials for a different future. This book is another sign post in that direction.

It has taken a long time for scholars in social work and other fields to reflect critically and constructively on the horrors of the war and the Holocaust. However, some professionals, including social workers, made immediate efforts to alleviate loss, pain, and destruction. Louis Lowy participated in those efforts long before his formal training and before he called himself a professional social worker. Likewise, in the archives of several American schools of social work along the East Coast, I have found master's degree theses from the 1940s and 1950s that dealt with various groups of European war refugees and survivors. They focused on practical issues for specific groups, such as unaccompanied minors, mothers with children, and survivors from various professions. A wealth of information on Holocaust survivors in social work remains available.

Realistically speaking, however, the chances for life encounters with survivors are diminishing, and soon we will have to rely entirely on secondary sources or on written and otherwise recorded testimony. This impressive account of Louis Lowy's life might be a stimulus for continuation, for further remembrances, and thus for adding to this kind of research into social work history and the Holocaust. It certainly is a challenging invitation!

Preface

THIS IS THE STORY OF LOUIS LOWY, the international social worker and social work educator, who remembered surviving the Holocaust as the beginning of his career. The early life and thought of Louis Lowy are also a part of a larger story, the story of social work history, Jewish history, and the meaning of the Holocaust in the development of the social work profession.

Holocaust research today is flourishing as never before. More than sixty-five years after the end of the Second World War, archives in Eastern Europe are opening to the West, once classified materials in the West are becoming accessible to the public, and recently established Holocaust museums and memorials throughout the world are posting their collections online. An outpouring of eyewitness testimonies is being preserved in audio and video recordings, and written memoirs are being published or prepared for posthumous publication, even as survivors and their children continue, incredibly, in their search for information about lost family and friends.[1] In the academy as in the family, among artists, historians, philosophers, political scientists, scientists, social scientists, theologians, and others, younger generations are discovering the Holocaust even as the older generations and their memories are passing away.

Unfortunately, social work, with its pragmatic eye, rarely focuses on its past. Relatively few American social workers are engaging in Holocaust research, even though the rise of National Socialism, which effectively destroyed the social work profession in Central Europe, had profound effects on social work in the United States. Prominent social workers who were exiled from Germany and Nazi-occupied territories in the 1930s fled to the United States, and they were followed after the war by younger survivors who chose social work as a career.[2] As discovered by the German social work historian Joachim Wieler,[3] the roster of social work exiles and survivors reads like a *Who's Who* of twentieth-century American social workers, including, to name a few, Werner Boehm, Hans Falck, Sophie Freud, Alex Gitterman, Gisela Konopka, Henry Maier, Kurt Reichert, Maria Hirsch Rosenbloom, and Louis Lowy, who, in his long and eminent international career, never spoke publicly about his activities during the war.

In the last year of his life, however, Louis Lowy broke his silence. At the age of seventy and in failing health, he decided to record an oral narrative that would explore how his experiences during the Holocaust had led to his becoming a social worker. From October 1990 through April 1991, with the assistance of his friend and colleague Leonard Bloksberg, Louis recorded sixteen hours of testimony during nine interview sessions. Louis planned to use his oral narrative as the basis for an article called, "The Making of a Social Worker," but he died before completing the work.

Twelve years later, in 2003, Louis Lowy's colleagues from Boston University, Leonard Bloksberg, Arthur Eisenberg, and Julianne Wayne, decided to continue the project that Louis had begun. In consultation with Joachim Wieler and with Louis's wife, Ditta, they invited me to use the oral narrative as the basis for a book on Louis Lowy's life and thought. Lenny Bloksberg lent me the audiotapes that he and Louis had recorded, and Ditta gave me access to Louis's published and unpublished writings, including books, hundreds of lectures and articles, boxes of personal papers and correspondence, and some issues of the *Deggendorf Center Review,* the newspaper of the Deggendorf Displaced Persons Center.

On the basis of these sources, I believe that Louis Lowy remembered his imprisonment in the Terezín ghetto and his leadership of the Deggendorf Displaced Persons Center as times when he appreciated the values of individual human worth, community self-determination, and the interdependence of generations. In Terezín, where he had cared for orphaned youth, Louis resisted the Nazis by illegally teaching and preparing Jewish children for a future. Emerging as a community leader and social statesman after the war, he organized the Jewish self-government of the Deggendorf Displaced Persons Center, where he tried to instill hope by engaging people in social participation and learning.

Louis later incorporated the values and roles that he had learned in these "early professional activities" into his identity as a social worker. It was as a social worker, Louis believed, that he could help repair "the break in time" that was the Nazi era by promoting human and social development, democracy, and the future of a human community. After establishing himself professionally at Boston University School of Social Work, Louis returned to Germany every year for more than twenty years to help restore social work education in Germany and in other countries.[4]

Eyewitness testimonies such as Louis Lowy's oral narrative are often the most credible historical source materials available in Holocaust research, particularly when one person's testimony corresponds with the testimonies of others.[5] In recovering Louis Lowy's story, I did not need to rely on his memories alone. It was only after interviewing three other witnesses that I learned the significance of Louis's work as a youth leader in the Terezín ghetto and as a community leader in the Deggendorf Displaced Persons Center.

Edith "Ditta" Jedlinsky was deported from Vienna to the Terezín ghetto when she was fifteen years old, and she met Louis Lowy as one of his pupils in the Youth Home in Building L414. Louis and Ditta were separated when Ditta was deported to Auschwitz, but they were reunited and married in the Deggendorf Displaced Persons Center after the war. I conducted an oral narrative interview with Ditta during two sessions in her home in Newton, Massachusetts, on August 12 and 19, 2004. I also viewed the Holocaust testimony that Ditta had recorded in 1994 for the Fortunoff Video Archive for Holocaust Testimonies.[6]

Werner "Vern" Drehmel arrived in Terezín from Hamburg at the age of fourteen, and he looked upon Louis Lowy as a father figure who protected him throughout the war. Louis and Vern were together in Terezín, in Auschwitz-Birkenau, in the Gliewitz III labor camp, in the death march and their escape from the death march, and in the Deggendorf Displaced Persons Center. They remained close friends after Vern's immigration to Boston as a Jewish war orphan. I conducted an oral narrative interview with Vern in two formal sessions during a visit to his home in Sea Ranch, California, on January 11 and 12, 2007.

Reinhard Frank was also fourteen years old when he was deported from Berlin to Terezín. He met Louis when he joined the cast of one of the plays that Louis directed in the attic of L414. Together with Louis and Vern, Reinhard endured Terezín, Auschwitz-Birkenau, Gleiwitz III, the death march, and the escape across Europe, and he witnessed Louis's work in the Deggendorf Displaced Persons Center. I interviewed Reinhard at his home in Cambridge, Massachusetts, on November 4, 2006.

Inevitably, there were internal inconsistencies within Louis Lowy's own oral narrative as well as discrepancies among four independent eyewitness accounts of incidents that had occurred nearly seventy years ago. My goal in reconciling Louis Lowy's oral narrative with those of the other survivors was to present as accurate a picture as possible of Louis Lowy's activities, and, in keeping with oral history methodology, to let the witnesses speak for themselves with minimal editorial interference.[7] In some cases, I was able to reconcile discrepancies, such as those of dates, by reference to external sources. In other cases, I presented several versions of events in the witnesses' own words. In addition, I tried to provide just enough historical background to allow readers to follow the stories as they were being told.

Louis Lowy's story might easily have been forgotten. The meaning of his work to the communities of Terezín and the Deggendorf Center might have been lost in the postwar "conspiracy of silence" about the Holocaust that enveloped survivors, researchers, and health and human services providers in social work and other fields. Jewish war refugees of the 1940s and 1950s found that Americans, by and large, could not listen to or comprehend their experiences. Jewish communal agencies that were charged with providing resettlement services were often unprepared and overwhelmed by their task. Tangible assistance from the American Jewish community, though generous, was sometimes also tainted by prejudice, suspicion, and disbelief.[8] Professionals and war refugees spoke different languages, literally and figuratively, and social workers and psychiatrists, lacking knowledge of trauma, posttraumatic stress, or the particular traumas that survivors had endured, did not know how to help them build new lives upon the broken foundations of their pasts. As described by the Swedish psychiatrist Leo Eitinger: "None of those who were supposed to help the survivors knew much about the traumas they had suffered. When they learned what had happened, they couldn't easily believe it. The survivors did not want to be considered liars, so they remained silent."[9]

Before they had begun their new lives in the United States and elsewhere, however, Jewish survivors in the displaced persons camps had anticipated the danger of forgetting their pasts. Louis Lowy and other leaders of the *She'erit Hapeletah,* "the surviving remnant" of European Jews, had come together from displaced persons camps throughout Bavaria to establish the Central Committee of Liberated Jews, an organization that advocated for the self-determination of the Jewish community. In November 1945, the Historical Commission was formed to gather evidence of Jewish life before and during the war.[10] The Historical Commission sought not only to document war atrocities, but also to preserve the memory of Jewish communities, now destroyed, before their few survivors were scattered around the world. Newspapers in Jewish displaced persons camps called for written materials such as diaries, correspondence, official documents, and photographs, and oral materials, such as folklore, idiomatic expressions, humor, and songs.[11] Above all, the Historical Commission sought volunteers to record oral narrative histories. This book is one response to that call.

The significance of Louis Lowy's work transcends his particular message to the children and youth of Terezín, to the displaced community in the Deggendorf Center, or to students of social work and gerontology. Just as Louis Lowy valued the interdependence of generations, so I hope that social workers will increasingly value historical research, for without the guidance of our forbearers, we lose sight of our purpose and the possibilities for achieving it.

January 2011

Acknowledgments

THIS BOOK BEGAN when Louis Lowy recorded an oral narrative history during the last months of his life. It was a critically important yet exhausting undertaking for Louis, made possible thanks to the assistance of his friend and colleague Leonard M. Bloksberg, who listened to and recorded the story. I am very grateful to Lenny and to Arthur Eisenberg and Julianne Wayne, all friends of Louis Lowy from Boston University School of Social Work, and to Louis's wife, Edith "Ditta" Lowy, for inviting me to write this biography and for trusting me with the work. Ditta, Vern Drehmel, and Reinhard Frank, who had lived through the war with Louis Lowy, participated in oral narrative interviews, lent me historical documents and photographs, and reviewed multiple drafts of the manuscript, despite the costs of remembering. Vern Drehmel's wife, Grace R. Robbin, kindly welcomed me to their home in Sea Ranch, California, where I interviewed Vern.

Many others extended their help. Professor Maria Hirsch Rosenbloom, a survivor and social work educator, told me about her work with Jewish war refugees. Amy Aldefer, a librarian with the United States Holocaust Memorial Museum, guided me toward archival materials throughout the world. The staff of the Fortunoff Video Archive for Holocaust Testimonies at Yale University Library located testimonies related to the Terezín ghetto. Professor Donna Wagner provided a copy of Louis Lowy's last professional presentation, an audio-recording that was generously restored by Kyle Evans of National Public Radio. Professors Nancy Billias and Edgar Schick assisted with German-to-English translations. Joseph W. Stoll of the Syracuse University Cartographic Laboratory drew historical maps. Professors Alex Gitterman, Lawrence Langer, and Joachim Wieler offered encouragement and comments on the manuscript. Remaining errors of fact or judgment are mine alone.

I am grateful to Dean Wilma Peebles-Wilkins and Boston University School of Social Work for a research grant and to Saint Joseph College for a sabbatical leave. Billye W. Auclair, vice president for academic affairs/ dean, and faculty colleagues Robert G. Madden and Raymie Wayne made the sabbatical possible. Lynnette Colón-Ayala, Kelly A. Joslyn, and Debbie Scheinblum gave technical assistance, and Peter Lowy prepared photographs for publication.

Rabbi Benjamin E. Scolnic and Temple Beth Sholom of Hamden, Connecticut, offered spiritual sustenance throughout this project. My husband, Peter Gardella, the true historian in our family, did not let me lose heart. Our son, William G. Gardella, on his visits home from college and law school, reviewed the manuscript with the patience and wisdom that Louis Lowy called "filial maturity."

Finally, I thank Annelise Finnegan, D. J. Whyte, and the editorial staff at Syracuse University Press, who believed in the project and helped bring it to fruition.

It is a sad postscript that Vern Drehmel died on November 1, 2008, at the age of seventy-nine, and Reinhard Frank died on December 12, 2010, at the age of eighty-two. They did not live to see the publication of this book.

The Life and Thought of Louis Lowy

Bedrich Fritta, Painting of the Vltava River in Prague Drawn from a Photograph by Theresienstadt Prisoner Bedrich Fritta. Photograph #44154. By permission of the United States Holocaust Memorial Museum.

1

A European Childhood

AT THE END OF HIS LIFE, Louis Lowy told a story that he had never tried to tell before, the story of his return from the Holocaust. In an oral narrative that he recorded from October 1990 to April 1991, Louis remembered his survival as the formative experience of his career as a social worker. Among his professional papers and publications, however, Louis left only one essay that dealt with the Holocaust explicitly, an address at a local synagogue on the occasion of Yom HaShoah, Holocaust Remembrance Day of 1978. It was in this essay, "Reflections on the Holocaust," that Louis asked the question that determined his life's work, "What do I think I personally have learned?"

I have learned that human beings are neither good nor evil, neither angels nor devils, but that people are engaged in a struggle between what Freud called the "id forces" and the dictates of the superego and a mediating agent, the ego, and that the struggle is very much affected by cultural, social, economic and political conditions. The strength of our moral fiber affects very much how we respond to such eternal conditions and how we act towards other people in various situations.

I have learned that everybody has a breaking point in life and there-fore it behooves us to be cautious about making glib judgments about people. We must differentiate between people and their behavior and avoid simple-minded characterizations which inevitably lead to stereo-typing and ultimately to the loss of an individual's identity.

I have learned that in the face of existential survival people can be brutally selfish and also magnificently altruistic. May people be spared such extreme tests! In the concentration camps, under conditions of severe stress, many people showed dignity and integrity, sharing their sorrow and their bread. Even as a captive one can preserve a space of inner freedom, and still exercise a measure of control over one's thoughts and feelings and cherish memories of joy and grief. In my wife's and my own experiences we found it indispensable to preserve such an inner space and to fill it with either religious or ideological beliefs and with feelings of love and affection for another person. . . .

I have also learned that survival is not the greatest good if it comes at the cost of one's soul or at the cost of somebody else's well-being. As peace at any price ends up in a peace not worth having, so survival at any price ends up as not worth surviving. There are times when death is preferable to living. I can tell you there were days and nights when I would have preferred to die, to be relieved of the agony of living. Ever since, dying for me has never held the dread that it once did. At the same time I have learned that there must be continuity in living and in life and therefore there had to be a new family for us that would provide such continuity. My wife and I had to make a new beginning in a new land and our children-to-be were to form a link in the chain of a family that had ceased to exist but had to be created again.

I have learned that the temptation to hate, to seek revenge, had to be conquered, because one cannot build a new life on hatred. A new life must come to terms with all residual feelings in order to start anew. This meant overcoming the temptation to ascribe collective guilt to all Germans. The concept of collective guilt avoids holding individual persons accountable and responsible for their actions and blames guilty and innocents alike, thus perpetuating injustice and prejudice. And so I had to come to terms with the German people and with Germany after the war, especially with a new generation. It was not easy, but I managed to go over there to teach in my field and to contribute my modest share to the education of young people in that tragic land, with what success I do not know.

I have also learned that what happened there can happen anywhere, to Jews and non-Jews, to white and black, to young and old. Therefore, I have asked myself, "What can I, what can we do to forestall this dreadful possibility?" As an individual, I have to be involved in the affairs of the Jewish as well as the non-Jewish community, to be engaged and not disengaged, to be vigilant and fight against all forms of racism, anti-Semitism and prejudice. . . . We have to fight against bigotry and be willing to take unpopular positions whether it involves a stand against capricious, unjust bureaucratic organizations and arbitrary decisions by government or other administrators (even in a university).

We must be engaged in fighting for the survival and growth of Israel (without arrogating ourselves a mandate to meddle into their internal affairs based on what we think is good for Israel) because Israel's exis-tence is vital for the Diaspora and a viable, strong Diaspora is vital for Israel. We must foster the solidarity of Jews everywhere, to seek ways to help them when and where needed, and avoid a repetition of the tragedy of omission of the thirties.

We must be ready to defend our democratic institutions in this country and examine whether we should be increasingly engaged in the "the pursuit of happiness," primarily through materialistic gratification, or whether we should rather be engaged in the "pursuit of social justice and human rights," in the spirit of one of the greatest legacies of Juda-ism to the world, the concept of *Tsedakah,* i.e. distributive social justice. What do we do in our daily lives to practice it?

Before the War, I was a student in Prague, studying philology and philosophy. After surviving the Holocaust, I decided to become a social worker, because I found in this field an opportunity to work on behalf of social justice and to cope with social issues. In addition, I always had an urge to be a teacher; I am fortunate enough to be able to combine both roles. However, all of us must be teachers about the Holocaust and communicate to others the lessons to be learned for ourselves and for our children.

Those few of us who were fortunate enough to survive have a special obligation to bear witness to what happened, to inform, to speak out and to try to convey our experiences to others as best as we can. We have to remind the world that civilization can be a thin veneer, that man's inhu-manity to man does exist, but that we can fight cynicism, ignorance, and hatred. We must extol the greatness of our spiritual heritage and cultural tradition, and the magnificence of the human spirit that can transcend the horrors of an inferno and rise, like a phoenix from the ashes, with hope, fervor, and strength.[1]

Louis Lowy learned many of his professional values in childhood: a love of learning; a sense of responsibility for family and, more generally, for those weaker than himself; a respect for human worth and dignity; and a commitment to distributive social justice. He attributed his values to his family and to his Jewish heritage, although he did not believe in God.

Growing up in Central Europe in the 1920s and 1930s, he viewed the political turmoil that surrounded him as an ongoing struggle between rationality and irrationality. He thought that "the democratic way of life and the democratic process of doing things . . . provide the best means for meeting the problems of our complex society."[2] In the best of worlds, Louis believed, people would prepare for democracy by participating in their families and communities. Even when people had lost their families and communities, however, as in prisons and concentration camps, they retained a lifelong potential to hope, to learn, and to contribute to others through social participation.

A Jewish Home

Louis Lowy (originally Löwy) was born in Munich on June 14, 1920, the only child of a mixed Jewish and Catholic marriage. The Löwy family was scattered across the former Austro-Hungarian Empire from Budapest to Vienna to Prague. At the turn of the century, Louis's paternal grandfather, the son of a Bohemian village rabbi, found work in Vienna in the new industry of producing ready-made clothes. He eventually became branch manager of a garment factory in Prague and later in Munich. Louis's father, Max, grew up in Vienna with dreams of a medical career. Discouraged by the university quota system on Jews, however, he accepted a position in the garment factory where his father worked. When he moved to Munich, Max met Thekla Anna Bolz, who came from a German Catholic family. Thekla converted to Judaism so that she and Max could marry in a synagogue. Her family attended the wedding.

The Hapsburg monarchy broke apart in 1919, and the Löwys had the opportunity to choose citizenship either in Austria or in the new nation of Czechoslovakia. Louis's father and grandfather decided to become Czech citizens, and Louis's parents moved from Munich to Prague in 1920, when

Louis was a few months old. Like many Jews in Prague, the Löwys spoke German at home.

The great inflation of the early 1920s threw the Löwys and millions of others into hard times. Louis's father lost his job, and the family moved to a small tenement apartment, where Louis's mother earned a modest income by serving lunches to students. Hitler's first putsch in 1923 marked "a turning point" for the family, particularly for Louis's mother, when one of her brothers became an ardent member of the Nazi party.

The German economy began to improve in 1924 when the Dawes Plan eased the burden of reparations payments from the Great War. The Löwys moved back to Munich, and Louis's father found a job as an accountant in the Adler bed-feather factory. On Sunday afternoons, they visited Grandfather Löwy and his daughters, enjoying long conversations over coffee and cake. According to Holocaust researcher Maria Hirsch Rosenbloom, survivors often cherished "the positive value system that derived from early family and community experiences,"[3] and when Louis wrote about families as the basis for democracy, he drew from his memories of "a frugal, but pleasant family life":

> A democratic society, which makes heavy demands on an alert citizenry, cannot function properly if those who make up the citizenry are either ill-informed or apathetic to democratic participation. The world has grown small, and each day our interdependence is brought into sharper focus. An understanding of the issues involved, an intelligent discussion of problems, an active participation in a democratic society, and last but not least, a feeling of well-being, of being at peace with oneself and one's family, are the foundations upon which to build a democratic society that can face its challenges and survive not only for its own sake but for the sake of civilization.[4]

By the age of nine, Louis was aware of the crash of 1929 and the poverty all around him:

> It was a society of beggars. Beggars lined up in front of the churches. They came with baskets to the backyards of houses, and some would

play the fiddle or other instruments. I felt for them and so did my mother and father, and they would throw down money in a piece of paper. It was heartbreaking, because they seemed to me to be very talented.[5]

Louis learned, in his words, "to live on two levels": the level of often fearful political awareness and the level of everyday life. He passed beggars and street fights on the way to school, but he focused his attention on schoolwork and friends. Then Louis turned to literature, philosophy, and music to make sense of it all. It troubled him that critics reviled Bertolt Brecht and Kurt Weill's *Three Penny Opera,* which he found so true to life.

Louis did not experience "personal anti-Semitism" at school—one of his friends even invited him to join the Hitler Youth!—"but I knew that I was different, because I was raised in a Jewish home." The Löwys kept a Jewish household, observing the Sabbath and other religious holidays, and Louis accompanied his father to synagogue, impressed by the top hat that his father wore. "It was a much more religious life than I have ever led in my own life."

As he grew older, Louis prayed with his father out of respect for tradition and culture rather than religious belief. "As a child I always said my prayers at night, but it was without conviction. Where is God? Why do people have to go through all that? What have they done to deserve it?" He read the Bible as evidence of human nature, rather than divine law: "If they had to give commandments, there must be something in people that require the commandments, 'Thou shall not steal; thou shall not kill.'"

Often Louis felt like "an outsider" who did not know where he belonged. He was raised as a Jew in a family "that was mostly Catholic." He spoke German when he lived in Prague, but he was a Czech foreigner when he lived in Munich. "I had a lack of identity. Or put another way, I had so many identities that I didn't know which one I was! But I always knew that I was Jewish." Louis sensed that his mother also felt ambivalent about her identity. "She felt Catholic," although she lived as a Jew.

In his later writing, Louis considered social belonging, "the sense of being linked with the community," as "a universal human need."[6] He planned one of the first senior centers in the United States in order to provide older people "with a social institution that is rightfully theirs, as much as all other age groups can claim social institutions as their own."[7] In particular, Louis valued "cultural self-awareness" as an aspect of social belonging. In the early 1950s, he encouraged social workers in Jewish community centers to help people "express themselves as Jews in the American democracy and learn to derive satisfactions from contributing Jewish values to the American culture as a whole."[8] Educators, adult educators, and social workers motivate people "toward a genuine interest in their cultural heritage" because "awareness of the cultural values of ethnic groups contributes not only toward their own security and well-being as a group but also toward the cultural fabric of America."[9]

Louis's father suffered from bronchial asthma, a condition that incapacitated him in the early 1930s and periodically for the rest of his life. Louis's mother continued to help support the family by running a lunchtime table for students. "My mother was the will in the family. She held our small family together." In addition to his mother's small income, Louis's family relied on health insurance and his father's disability pension. Like their grandparents and great-grandparents before them, the Löwys benefited from a social welfare system that had been introduced by Bismarck in 1865 and expanded during the Weimar Republic: "To us, these benefits were not extraordinary. Not having them would have been extraordinary." As a social worker in the United States, Louis later advocated for a more generous social welfare policy. "Our objective is to deliver services to people in such a way that they consider them as their right and can accept them with dignity and utilize them to their maximum advantage."[10]

Louis remembered German Jewish families who could have emigrated in the early 1930s, but who were afraid, in the midst of the Depression, to lose their social security benefits. "In the United States, to be poor was a sin. In Europe, to be poor wasn't a sin, it was a misfortune. There was a greater sense of societal responsibility than individual responsibility." Ironically, for Jews, "Hitler did not dismantle the social security system; he improved it." A disability pension was sent to Louis's father at his Prague address until 1945, a year after his death at Auschwitz.

Hoping against hope that Hitler was "a temporary aberration in a democratic system," the Löwys were shocked when the elections of 1930

1. Europe, 1933. Map by Joseph Stoll, Syracuse University Cartographic Laboratory.

gave the Nazis more seats than any other party in the Reichstag. Louis's paternal grandfather, the only grandparent he knew, died in 1932, "oblivious of what was to come." In January 1933, Hitler became chancellor, and in March, although 56 percent of the electorate still opposed him, he and his cabinet assumed full legislative and economic power.[11] On April 1, Hitler called for a boycott of Jewish businesses and stores. Louis stayed indoors all day. His neighbors did not welcome the boycott, but they did not protest against it. Throughout his later career, Louis would call for "eternal vigilance" against all forms of prejudice and discrimination as the personal and professional obligation of social workers: "More and more we have to come forth without being invited."[12]

A Big Adventure

Louis was called to the Torah as a bar mitzvah on his thirteenth birthday, June 14, 1933, becoming a man in Jewish law. His father then revealed plans to send him to England, out of harm's way. With help from the Adlers, who owned the bed-feather factory where Louis's father worked, he arranged for Louis to live with the family of a business associate in London and to study in an English school. In September, Louis set out on a "big adventure," traveling by himself on the train to Hamburg and then by ship to "the white cliffs of Dover":

> I remember it was in September of 1933 and we went to the railroad sta-
> tion in Munich. I was given a sign with my name and I went by myself
> to Hamburg by train, a long trip, and from Hamburg by ship to Dover.
> I still remember the coast, "the white cliffs of Dover." And I landed on
> the dock in Dover, and then I was taken to the train—everything had
> been arranged for me—and I proceeded to Victoria Station in London,
> where I was picked up by the business friend of my father, a man by the
> name of King.

The Kings were "kind and decent people," Anglicans who were doing a good deed by giving refuge to a Jewish child. They spoke no German, however, and in contrast to Louis's affectionate family, they seemed unfeeling and cold. Even the house felt cold from the lack of central heating, and Louis felt abandoned in his little room:

> I felt totally bewildered, and I cried. The Kings asked me, "Why do
> you cry? You have nice things here. Go play; go to school." But I had a
> hunger for home, for parents, for the cities, the amenities, the language,
> the culture. England was more alien to me than America ever was after
> the war!
>
> But then I began to read the British newspapers, the *Daily Telegraph*
> in the morning and the *Times*. The press was a major revelation to me!
> There had been a free press before in the Weimar Republic, but I was
> too young to remember it. Here, I could follow letters to the editor. The
> *Times* in fact opened to the letters to the editor at the first page, rather
> than headlines. I read all the papers: the *Daily Mail,* the *Expert.* The
> *Manchester Guardian* was one of my favorites. It's called the *Guardian*
> now. In the British newspapers I read for the first time about the dangers
> of "Herr Hitler," particularly for the Jews.
>
> I went to school, but I was an outsider. You rarely became a friend in
> England. You became an acquaintance. I felt alien because I had a very
> different frame of reference. Most of my classmates were apolitical. They
> were more interested in sports than anybody I've seen anywhere. They

were interested in getting out of the miserable times and avoiding war at any cost. So I didn't belong there. I didn't belong there.

And when puberty reared its head, I was really an outsider! I spoke English with a German accent and with a non-upper-class British accent on top of it, so my chances of competing for a girlfriend were minimal!

Louis was surprised by the poverty in England and by the relative weakness of social welfare and health care protections, even for middle-class families like the Kings: "Everybody I met had awful teeth!" During his thirty months in England, he visited Manchester, Leeds, and Birmingham, where he was appalled by "slums," a word that he never could translate into any other language. He read all the works of Charles Dickens in an effort to understand British poverty.

At the same time, Louis came to appreciate the British sense of humor, courteous civil service, and democratic institutions, as in the peaceful demonstrations in Hyde Park:

What I liked about the English was their "stiff upper lip" and their determination and the humor, the Cockney humor, in which they could poke fun at themselves. I felt very comfortable with the democratic institutions in England, the freedom of speech and the free press and the Hyde Park corner. I went to political rallies, Hyde Park rallies. I was not used to the exuberance of freedom of speech where they yelled, "Down with the King!" and "Down with the Prime Minister!" and "We don't want war!"

And I went to the theater; there was a lot of theater. Some of it was in Cockney and I didn't understand. But I saw Shakespeare at the Globe Theatre and *Danton's Death* by Georg Büchner, a very powerful drama about the French Revolution that was translated [from the German] into English.

England was a class-ridden society, more than I was used to, and that's why the Labour Party was building up and getting stronger and stronger. I was attracted to the Fabians [the British socialist society], and George Bernard Shaw became a great hero of mine. I was very much taken with his play *The Chocolate Soldier* [an operetta based on Shaw's play *Arms and the Man*] about a soldier who doesn't want to go to war, and by *Pygmalion* and *Heartbreak House* and *Major Barbara*.

I began to read American literature. We read American literature at school, not just British literature, and I read *Main Street* and *Babbitt* by Sinclair Lewis. William Faulkner I couldn't read; I couldn't get into life in Mississippi! If I were to single out the two most influential American writers for me at that time they were Theodore Dreiser and Upton Sinclair.

All through his stay in England, Louis waited anxiously to hear from his family. Letters took four to six weeks to arrive by sea mail, and, invariably, the news went from bad to worse. When Louis's parents sent him to England, they had planned to move to Prague. Louis's father suffered a relapse of his asthma, however, and he was sent to a "spa" or clinic on the Austrian border. With the passage of the Nuremberg Laws, in September 1935, German Jews were stripped of their rights as citizens. "Looking back, there was still a vain hope that all this would be overturned. The other countries would not allow this to happen in the middle of Europe."

As Louis's mother's family began to distance themselves from "Jewish contacts," his mother found it increasingly difficult to cope on her own. The Löwys urgently sought an escape from Germany. Finally, Louis's mother wrote to Louis for help. Could he find a way for them to enter England? If not, he should return to Munich to assist the family in moving to Prague.

Louis would later define interdependence of children and parents as a familial goal:

There has been a mistaken notion that it is a parental responsibility to free children from parental ties toward a sort of "mythical" independence, rather than to help children become emancipated in order to be ready to help their own parents at a later stage in life and thereby learn how to be older themselves. In other words, we should help our children to learn greater interdependence rather than independence.[13]

The King family petitioned the Home Office on the Löwy family's behalf, but the requirements for immigration—one thousand pounds and, even more impossible, certificates of good health—were beyond their means. In January 1936, the Kings arranged for Louis's passage back to

Germany. "International travel had become more complicated" since Louis had left Munich, and the return journey took longer than Louis expected because the train did not go through France.

When Louis reached Munich, he found his mother distraught and his father "totally incapacitated." Louis immediately began planning the family's immigration to Prague. At the age of fifteen, he assumed responsibilities that he would later call "filial maturity," a developmental task of adulthood:

> This is a time when parents can no longer be looked upon as a rock of support and often do need comfort, support and affection from their offspring . . . when their offspring need to be depended upon in times of stress or trouble, or for advice, nurturance, or tangible assistance. In a "filial crisis" the adult son or daughter does not take on a *parental* role vis-à-vis his aging parent; rather he/she takes on a *filial* role. That indicates that he/she can be depended upon and therefore is dependable as far as the parent is concerned. The healthy resolution of this "filial crisis" leaves behind the rebellion against one's parents initiated during adolescence and often unresolved long after. One sees them now as mature adults would see them, as someone who has made peace with their foibles, strengths and weaknesses, needs, and rights, with a life before the child was even born.[14]

In February 1936, Louis made the eight-hour train ride to Prague to find an apartment. He was stunned by the beauty of the city: "I had never seen such a beautiful city before. I had been there as a child, but now I saw through the eyes of Kafka the many steeples and this glow and this ancientness." Louis visited the Jewish cemetery where his great-grandfather Rabbi Löwy was buried, feeling at home in the history of the city. An adult cousin who lived in Prague helped Louis rent an apartment, open a bank account, and negotiate with the Czech bureaucracy. "Everything had to be filled out in two languages, German and Czech."

As with the Löwys, many German Jews made "great hopeful moves" to Prague or to Vienna, turning to the Jewish community for help. The Jüdische Kultusgemeinde (Jewish Community Council) assisted the Löwys by helping them pack, recommending a forwarding agent who would move the furniture, and putting the family in touch with the Jewish welfare agency in Prague. Louis may have remembered the Jewish community organizations when, years later in the United States, he addressed the National Conference of Settlements and Neighborhood Centers on the issue of urban flight. At a time when affluent people were leaving the cities, he believed

> the settlement house or neighborhood house has a responsibility to serve those who stay behind. A settlement house should not say: 25 percent or 50 percent or 60 percent of the people will move. Now let's go with them. What about those who remain behind? And what about the people who move into this neighborhood? What about the newcomers? One definite responsibility is to help the newcomers adjust to their new situation, namely that they should feel at home.[15]

A Cultural Crossroad

On April 2, 1936, "a glorious April day," the Löwys boarded the train to Prague. They spent the night in a hotel, and the next morning moved into their newly rented three-room apartment near the Vltava River: "It was a typical, comfortable European apartment." Once the family was settled, Louis looked forward to a normal adolescent life. He found a part-time job as an English language typist for a glove factory, and he enrolled in the Mikulansku-Gymnasium, the German-speaking university-preparatory school.

After the poverty he had seen in the United Kingdom, Louis had high hopes for Czechoslovakia as a democratic state that afforded the best of both worlds, capitalism and socialism:

> I had read up to prepare myself for going to Czechoslovakia. Who were the people? Who are the political parties? I wanted to know what is this country like, and I found out that it was a relatively democratic country with a strong middle class, an industrial base, the wealthiest being 1 or 2 percent [of the population] and the poorest, 1 or 2 percent. Of all the successor states to the Hapsburg monarchy, Czechoslovakia probably had the soundest base. It was capitalistic, but it was mixed capitalism and socialism. It was close to what Sweden is today.

Louis found that the students in Prague were "highly politicized." In contrast to his classmates in England, nearly everyone in his preparatory school identified with a political group: "There were the Nazis, the non-Nazis, and the anti-Nazis, the Communists, the Social Democrats, and the Liberal Democrats." Jewish students formed political groups as liberals, conservatives, Zionists, and "Red Falcons, who were the Social Democrats." Louis enjoyed social outings with the Red Falcons, but it was the International Paneuropean Union that most captured his imagination:

> I was foremost a socialist and a humanitarian, but if you asked me, "Who are you?" I mean, that's an idea. I saw myself as a Jew, not a religious Jew, but a German-speaking Jew living in the central part of Europe. At one time, I called myself a Central European, *Mitteleuropäer* in German. If you had asked me at that time, "Who are you?" that would have been my response.
>
> In fact, I was a member of the Paneuropean Union, an organization that was founded by [Richard] Coudenhove-Kalergi. The Nazis killed him. He was an intellectual. He came from Austria originally, and he dreamed of a united Europe. That was always a big dream and many of us, the cosmopolitans, the socialists, were all members of Coudenhove-Kalergi's Paneuropa. It was a socialist ideal, not a communist unification, but a socialist, humanitarian ideal of building a better world.

Although Louis had an internationalist point of view, the political figure whom he most admired was Tomáš Garrigue Masaryk, the Czech nationalist who had served as president of the Czech Republic:

> We studied Czech nationalistic literature, and I found out that everything wasn't hunky dory in the Hapsburg monarchy! This was a country bent on its own destruction, eventually. I learned a great deal about that from a Czech point of view, and the most impressive figure to me in Prague was Tomáš Garrigue Masaryk.
>
> Many Jewish kids in Prague were called "Tomas," because Masaryk had defended a Jewish vagrant by the name of Leopold Hilsner, who was accused of ritual murder. That was in 1900, before the Czech Republic was founded. Hilsner was what you would call a bum, a good-for-nothing,

but Masaryk said, "That's not the issue," and he took it upon himself as a professor of the University of Prague and as a leader of the Czech delegation in parliament to publicly defend this guy, which earned him a lot of wrath among anti-Semites. He stood up for Hilsner, and at that time, in the context of the *Zeitgeist* [the spirit of the times], that was unheard of! And then Masaryk became president of the Czech Republic and he was a philosopher! And I had read Plato on the philosopher king, and to me, Masaryk was one of the most inspiring political figures.

If you want to say who impressed me most of anybody living, not a fictional character, but somebody living, it was Tomáš Garrigue Masaryk. He was the first encounter that I had of a humanitarian who stood for social justice and who could do something within the political arena, who could formulate social policy and have the stamp of power behind it.

And he was fair. He was considered a great friend of the Jews. He was a nationalistic Czech, but he respected all the "minorities." There were 22 percent Germans in Czechoslovakia, which was its downfall eventually, about a fourth of the country. There were Hungarians, Slovaks, and there were Jews. You could declare yourself a Czech, a German, or a Jew, and Jews were considered a national group and protected by the Geneva Treaty.

Masaryk was president of the Czech Republic from January 1920, when the Republic was born, until 1935, when he retired at age eighty. On his birthday on the 7th of March, there always was a big celebration, and I'll never forget when he died in 1937 [on September 14], we all cried, and from down near the Vltava River all the way up to the castle, people stood in a vigil all night long.

Louis's faith in politics was tested by the Spanish Civil War. On July 17, 1936, nationalist generals in the Spanish army rose up against the Second Spanish Republic. Through three years of devastating fighting, volunteers from other countries, including some classmates of Louis's, went to Spain to defend the republic. The nationalists were supported by the Axis powers, however, and on April 1, 1939, General Francisco Franco was installed as the dictator of Spain.

The young Louis briefly considered joining the International Brigade:

Spain was the banner, the flag around which we all rallied. We knew that Franco was a fascist and that Mussolini supported him and Hitler supported him. And that was when there was a solidarity movement of the youth, great pull to join the International Brigade. There was a big outcry from the leftists and the anti-Nazis, and whether they were Jews or non-Jews, there was a kind of unity among the socialists, the German-speaking, the Czech-speaking, the Yiddishers, the Bundists, and the Zionists, all of them were united.

I once voiced my opinion that I may join the volunteers in Spain. My mother said, "Oh, you won't join anything! You're crazy! You stay put, and we'll be sitting out the Nazis right here. You don't have to fight them!"

But these things had a tremendous influence on my thinking. Here is injustice really done to people. They have done nothing wrong, and they're in a civil war abetted by the Allies and the impotence of the League of Nations. It was a loss of faith in the ideal, in any ideals that they would do something about it. Masaryk and the Spanish Civil War were watersheds in my life.

Louis's passionate interest in politics did not distract him from studying: "As far as my life was concerned, I was interested in studying and learning; that was the important thing." Most of his time was devoted to preparing for the *Matura,* the rigorous university entrance examination. The curriculum required history, geography, mathematics, music, and literature read in Latin, Greek, German, French, English, and Czech. Louis once asked a professor how to prepare for the examination; "What do you have to know?" "Everything!" the professor replied. As Louis explained:

It was an enormous, demanding undertaking, but once you got into the system, you learned how to learn, how to read, how to consume. You knew about Montesquieu; you knew about the American Revolution. You read German everyday; there was quite an emphasis on German literature and music. You were drilled and you studied, and you wrote essay exams. It was a continuous grind, six days a week—not, in retrospect, a system that I would recommend!—but you couldn't help but learn.

At last Louis had found a place where he belonged. Prague, for Louis, was a center of learning, "a crossroad of German, Czech, and Jewish culture" and a meeting place of cultural and intellectual life. "It was an explosion of culture. When you turned on the radio, you had opera; you had music, Czech music, Russian music. Everybody hummed music." Louis went to the opera, the symphony, and the theater with his parents and friends. "Subscriptions cost next to nothing," he recalled. "I took in more theater and music in Prague than at any other time. The first time I heard Toscanini conduct was in Prague: very impressive!"

After performances, they sometimes went to café houses to ask for autographs from the actors and musicians. Usually, however, "It was over at eleven o'clock, and then you went home, back to your books, and you burned the midnight oil." In the winter, Louis also enjoyed going to hockey games with his family: "The Czechs were very good hockey players." He went to the movies on Sundays to see Soviet films, such as *The Battleship Potemkin,* and American musicals, such as *Broadway Melody* and *Alexander's Ragtime Band.*

It was on March 12, 1938, as he was leaving the opera house, that Louis had "an enormous shock." Newspaper vendors were yelling, "Swastika over Vienna!" Hitler had marched into Austria.

Louis passed the *Matura,* the university-entrance examination a few weeks later, "knowing more about the liberal arts world" at the age of eighteen than he would ever know again. The *Matura* entitled him to enroll in the university of his choice, and in April 1938 he entered the Faculty of Philosophy at Charles University, the German university in Prague and one of the oldest universities in Europe.

Charles University consisted of four faculties, those of law, medicine, theology, and philosophy, and each faculty was organized as a scholarly community, rather than as a bureaucratic school. Students prepared for their examinations without a prescribed curriculum. No courses were required. "You were on your own, and your life was in the library. Some professors, if they were kind enough, would give a reading list," and advanced students recommended readings and lectures in their fields. Each morning, Louis checked the bulletin board for the day's lectures, and he chose which lectures to attend and which seminar discussions to join. At the end of a lecture, the professor signed the small notebooks, "a kind of portable documentation," that students carried. In the evenings, Louis enjoyed the custom of strolling along the Vltava River, debating with other students and taking care to greet any professors who walked by.

The Faculty of Philosophy, where Louis enrolled, included the liberal arts, social sciences, and natural sciences. Initially Louis focused on philology and linguistics as a means to understanding different cultures. Gradually, however, he was drawn to the history of social, political, and economic thought. He wondered about the meaning of poverty, the origins of charity, and the effects of revolutionary movements on the poor. "I was interested in what had happened in the world, in the philosophical underpinnings of the social movements in various countries." Louis responded to the political ferment around him by trying to understand it, and many years later at Boston University, he found it "ironic that social work study has not accorded economic and political theory a foremost place among the disciplines that condition human existence and influence the social environment of man."[16] As part of his philosophical studies, Louis read sociological and psychological theorists whose works would later inform the social work curriculum in the United States:

> I studied history, I studied philosophy, I studied sociological principles. I read Max Weber, and for the first time, I heard about American sociologists. I studied Sigmund Freud as a philosopher, the philosophy of Freud, of Alfred Adler, of Carl Gustav Jung, and the French child psychiatrist Jean Piaget. I read all of Freud's general introductory lectures, *Civilization and Its Discontents, Moses and Monotheism.* They were new ideas! I learned some of the principles of psychiatry, the ego structure, the unconscious, the dream interpretation, the case of Dora. I wasn't too impressed with that, but with Freud's philosophical underpinnings, his understanding of man in a generic sense. That left a deep imprint on me because in most of what I had studied before I had learned of

rationality, and here comes somebody who understands the irrationality, the underworld of the mind.

Louis hated violence, which could lead only to "misery, destruction, and loss," and he avoided the student demonstrations that left "blood in the streets" every Sunday. Nonetheless, when Czechoslovakia mobilized in May 1938, Louis was drafted into the army:

> I started in the university on April 1, 1938, and in May there was a mobilization called by President Edvard Beneš, who was the successor to Masaryk. Beneš was a decent man, but he didn't have the charisma or the nucleus of what Masaryk stood for. He was a politician, a decent man who couldn't cope. Probably nobody else could have either. I don't blame him.
>
> And so we were called to the front! I had to learn to handle a gun. I didn't enjoy one minute of that!

The mobilization lasted only for two weeks. Under pressure from the Allies, Czechoslovakia demobilized, and Louis returned thankfully to his studies. During "an exceptionally beautiful June," Louis prepared for his preliminary examinations, oral and written examinations that were conducted in German, English, and Czech. Although concerned about his proficiency in Czech, Louis passed his examinations in July 1938 and began the four-month summer recess.

Louis's goal in life was to become a professor at the gymnasium or the university, but the long path to a professorship was expensive, and he wondered whether he would be able to afford it. As a backup plan, he enrolled in an intensive summer course at the Pedagogic Academy or teacher's college, where he earned his diploma as an elementary school teacher. Here Louis was introduced to social pedagogy, a method of engaging small groups of children in experiential learning. One day per week, Louis practiced social pedagogy in a public elementary school. Louis preferred teaching interactively with small groups to lecturing authoritatively before a large hall: "I enjoyed it very much!"

As he prepared to return to the university in October, Louis's prospects were darkened by world affairs. In hopes of avoiding a war with Germany, British prime minister Neville Chamberlin convened a meeting in Munich of the four powers—Great Britain, Germany, Italy, and France—and negotiated an agreement that broke apart Czechoslovakia. On October 1, 1938, Czechoslovakia ceded the industrial Sudetenland to Germany. "Munich became a word of infamy," Louis recalled, and "October 1 was a national day of mourning." When he returned to Charles University, Louis found "a stronghold of the Nazis," and he left for Christmas vacation, knowing that "there was no sense for a Jewish boy to go on":

> My studies were certainly not in the foreground anymore. What's the use of studying? Now it was a question of survival. The cost of living rose tremendously. The Sudetenland, which was one of the most productive parts of the country, was no longer available to the economy of Czechoslovakia, so there was scarcity and a prewar atmosphere.

As Louis turned to supporting his family, his fluency in English and his gift for teaching served him well. Throughout his university career, Louis had earned a small income as an English-language tutor. Now, with so many people trying to emigrate, English lessons were in greater demand than ever before, and Louis gave eight to ten lessons per day. A creative teacher, he engaged his adult students in practical conversations and his younger students in storytelling. Children in his classes enacted Englebert Humperdinck's children's opera *Hänsel and Gretel* in English. Louis's goal was to teach people "how to learn and to continue learning throughout their lifetime":

> Unexpected learning occurs as a result of creative processes at work. Such a learning outcome is not the result of predetermined objectives, but rather the result of a liberating force that comes into being through a good teaching-learning experience. It is the hallmark of a good teacher to get this kind of creative process going and to help students discover modes of attacking a problem in their own novel way.[17]

Louis's teaching was interrupted when, on March 14, 1939, Czech president Emil Hácha surrendered the government to Hitler. The Löwys were no longer citizens of Czechoslovakia; they were subjects of the Protectorate of Bohemia and Moravia—and of the German Reich:

And so it happened on March 15th, 1939, that the Nazis marched into Prague. It was a snowy day. I remember seeing people crying in Prague Square as the tanks came and the German soldiers. And the next morning, I was arrested by the Gestapo.

No Way Out

At four o'clock in the morning of March 16, 1939, two members of the SS, the feared Nazi stormtroopers, pounded on the door of the Löwys' apartment. "Louis Löwy, out!" they cried. "I saw these two big SS men in black uniforms. They didn't push me, they just guided me. They didn't need to push me."

Louis was marched through the city to the municipal prison, where "there were thousands and thousands of others." The prison was too small to hold them, and after three weeks, they were sent to the municipal prison in Pankcraz, which was the prison for criminal offenders on the outskirts of the city:

And so I was a prisoner. I couldn't really tell you how I felt: numb, scared numb. Scared about what will happen to me, cut off from home, from any communication. What will these Nazis do? We weren't afraid of the Czech guards. They hated the Nazis just as much as we did. They gave us cigarettes; they were scared themselves.

There were hundreds of people in a cell; they were just makeshift halls for us to be in. And eventually I began to talk to people. I tried Czech, I tried German. There was plenty of time to think and talk! There were intelligent people with us. It was an elite crowd, and I was one of the youngest and most insignificant from a status and value point of view for the Nazis.

I talked to a guy whose name was Arnold Marle, who was the stage manager of the German theater in Prague. It turned out that he was the son-in-law of Sigmund Freud. He was an Orthodox Jew. He never performed on *Shabbos* [Sabbath]; he never smoked on *Shabbos*. He was very religious. And we talked about the stage and about Freud, and he told me a little bit about Freud's household. We had a kind of proximity and friendship even though our situation was a total catastrophe.

Then the Gestapo came and interrogated us one by one. First, in a very businesslike fashion: "What is your name? What were you doing? What university, what organizations did you belong to? Give us names of others!"

We found very quickly that they were interested in names and denunciations. Then they let us go back to the cell, which was a relief, being out of the clutches of the Gestapo. We spent two or three days in the cell, and then they came for us again, always a different interrogator: "Do you have anything further to say?"

The Gestapo headquarters were in the Petschek bank building, an imposing structure that faced the German theater. In one interrogation, Louis mentioned that he often went to the theater:

"So you like Germans, you like Wagner?" he asked. I said, "Certain parts of Wagner I like very much." So we talked about opera, music. He began you might say a civil conversation with me. I didn't know how to figure out the psychology of these guys! And then I went back to my cell. It went on for weeks and weeks, and it became the wear and tear of the unknown. We had some soup and some bread.

Then the torture masters came, and they began to hit and knock out teeth. "Who was with you? Who was in this? All right, you go back to prison until you tell us!" After three or four days at two in the morning or eight in the evening—you could guess the time by the daylight—they came again.

Then one day, he gave me a piece of paper, and he said, "You can read German. Sign here!" It was a confession that I was an enemy of the state who had conspired against the state and therefore that I was liable for criminal prosecution. Don't ask me why, but I refused to sign! I felt that the German sense of legality was always undergirding this. They wanted this to be legal. He said, "You're not going to sign? I'll show you what we're going to do with you," and he gave me a slap. "Back to the cell!"

I told Marle, and he said, "You should have signed, you know. Everybody signs and maybe we can get it over with."

The next morning, I had a call: "Louis Löwy, present yourself! Here are your clothes; here are your suspenders, leave! And be out of the country by September! If not, we have a long hand, and wherever you hide, we will find you."

Well, I suspected that it got too crowded with so many prisoners, and they saw that I was such a small fry that I didn't matter. The Nazis weren't bent on extermination at that time; they had an occupation policy. They had no experience with a hostile population like the Czechs, and they were trying to prevent an uprising. The Austrians had been pliable, but with the Czechs, they didn't know. Maybe we had organized cells, maybe we had allies. So they were still proceeding in a manner that was logical from their point of view—not just, but logical. Not every Jew was arrested, but if you were from Germany or you were in the university, you were automatically suspect.

So I got out. It was a hot June day, and I was with my winter coat. I had been arrested in the snow, in March. From Pankraz, I knew Streetcar 23 went to the inner city, so I took it. I had no money, but the Czech conductor knew where I was coming from, and I went home.

My family was stunned. They said, "My God! What happened to you?" My mother had had a nervous breakdown by that time, and she was in the hospital. My father was very sick, and my uncle from Pilsen, who had been a cook, was running the household. He kept the house together.

I was afraid. I was far more afraid at that time then at any time in my life, even in the concentration camps. Whenever the doorbell rang, I was hiding somewhere because the Gestapo said that by September I had to be out of the country. I started furiously writing letters to America. I went to the British consulate, to the Cuban consulate, to the Dominican consulate, and everywhere there were lines and lines of people.

In June 1939, when Louis returned home, the Nuremburg laws began taking effect in the Protectorate. Classified as an alien race, Jews were purged from the universities, the civil service, private businesses, and the professions, and they were required to wear yellow badges printed with the Star of David whenever they left their homes. When food rationing took effect for the general population, additional restrictions applied to Jews.[18] In Louis's words:

The German laws were applied with more chicaneries, more restrictions. You had to register. You had to put on the yellow star. You couldn't go out after eight o'clock. You couldn't study. You couldn't have housekeepers. You couldn't sit on the park bench. You couldn't go to the movies. You couldn't go shopping. But we were still in the apartment! We were under the illusion that we would stay there, pursuing the same life, under very difficult, restricted conditions, not pleasant, but bearable.

Adolf Eichmann, director of the section of the Gestapo responsible for Jewish evacuations, initially sought to cleanse the Reich of its Jewish population by forced emigration. Few countries, however, were willing to receive Jewish immigrants, particularly those without funds. Louis's cellmate Arnold Marle and his wife, Lilly Freud-Marle, escaped to London, but out of 118,000 Jews who lived in occupied Bohemia and Moravia, only 26,000 found a way out.[19] The Löwys were not among them. On September 1, 1939, Louis's deadline for leaving the country, Germany invaded Poland. Britain and France declared war two days later.

Then it was war and the borders were shut. There was no more time for people to get out. I was scared, but eventually you recover, you recover, you recover. My life was teaching English, the same as before. We lived off the black market. Food was scarce, and it was good that I could make money, because things were expensive.

During the next seven months, from October 1939, to April 1940, there was an eerie calm in Western Europe that became known as the "phony war."

And so we waited and waited. We hoped that the English would invade, the French would invade. Instead, Hitler invaded Norway, Denmark, Belgium, Holland, France. On the 14th of June, 1940, Paris was taken. That was a big blow. There now was a possibility that Germany would win the war! Germany would invade England and England would buckle under. When Churchill became prime minister [on May 10, 1940], he inspired some hope, but we knew that England was not prepared to fight this machine, which was beyond anybody's expectation.

By the autumn of 1941, it had become clear to Eichmann that the policy of expelling Jews from Europe by forced emigration had failed. Changing tactics, the Nazis forbade further Jewish emigration.[20] Terrible rumors spread through Prague about the concentration camp in Dachau, reaching even Louis's mother in the mental hospital. "We will all end up in Dachau," she predicted.

In November, Prague's Jewish community was informed that a ghetto was being established in Terezín ("Theresienstadt" in German), a walled garrison town in the picturesque countryside just thirty miles north of Prague. Built in 1780 by Emperor Joseph II and named for his mother, Maria Theresa, Terezín had a population of seven thousand, including a small military base. Eichmann chose Terezín as the site of the ghetto for its surrounding wall, barracks housing, prison (the Small Fortress), and proximity to a railroad station. He feared, however, that Terezín would be too small for his purposes. Once the Czech residents and soldiers had left, the ghetto would hold as many as fifty thousand Jews at a time.

Jakob Edelstein, a leader of Prague's Zionist movement, agreed to serve as mayor or "Elder" of the ghetto in hopes of building a self-administered, self-sufficient city where Czech Jews would safely live out the war.[21] The Nazis, however, planned Terezín as a transit camp, not a refuge. Jews from the Protectorate and later, from other parts of Europe would be sent there temporarily before being deported to concentration camps and death camps in the East. Some elderly Jews from Austria and Germany were told that they would be protected in Terezín in deference to their international prominence or military service, and some of their lives were spared. Famously, the Nazis appreciated the potential of Terezín for propaganda to the outside world. When the Red Cross or other international visitors arrived, the ghetto would be disguised as a seemingly humane city for Jews.[22]

Louis and his family were given a week's notice to prepare for transport to Terezín. They were to report on December 7, 1941, to the Trade Palace in the north of the city. Louis's mother was released from the hospital; Louis, his father, and his uncle packed some food, some clothes, and some shoes—they were allowed fifty kilos per person—and shut up the apartment that had been their safe haven in Prague. As they walked to the Trade Palace, Louis saw the newspaper headlines from the street: "The Guns Speak in the Pacific!" The Japanese had bombed Pearl Harbor:

> On that day, despite the fact that we went to a much unknown fate, we felt a certain buoyancy: Now America was in the war! And so we marched off. And then began my career in Terezín as a social worker.

2

The Terezín Ghetto

THE TRADE PALACE IN PRAGUE was a cavernous hall where, in happier times, a trade fair had been held each spring and fall.[1] Louis, who was now twenty-one years old, observed the gathering crowd. A group of Bohemian artists, including the graphic artist Bedrich Fritta, were not carrying any luggage. "Maybe they thought it would be confiscated anyway." The guards were "Viennese Nazis" who were close to Louis's own age. It was only when he reached the registration table that Louis began to appreciate the seriousness of his situation:

> The first thing I remember was that you had to surrender your identity card. The identity card was a certificate issued in lieu of a passport because Jews no longer were allowed to have the Protectorate passport. They got instead a red certificate with a name, a picture, and a "J" inside. You had to carry it around. Everybody in the Reich, German and non-German, had to carry certification all the time. You could be stopped in the street. And I remember the feeling that if you give up a paper identification then maybe there's more to it than giving up a paper!

The Löwys waited for three days in the Trade Palace, until on December 10, 1941, they were marched to the train station, where "they put us into freight trains, those cattle trains":

> We were told that we would be going to Terezín to build up the ghetto, with the understanding that while the war lasted we would be staying there and do some work for the German war machine, building machinery. It would be a ghetto run by the Jews themselves, or a particular Jewish council under Nazi supervision, where Jews would continue to wear their own clothes with the yellow star.

We only surmised and rumored about what could happen. We had no inkling that this was not the plan that the Nazis had for the Jews. After all, many had emigrated already. There was the Warsaw ghetto, the Lodz ghetto, now many would be sent to the Terezín ghetto. Who could know? America just entered the war. Maybe it was a matter of six weeks and the war would be over.

The Löwys were among the first families to be deported to Terezín and they arrived before housing and sanitation facilities had been prepared or food and basic supplies, such as cooking pots, had been provided:

We arrived there and it was winter, and there was no heat and hardly any food, although we had taken some food along, which we were advised to do. Then they started a kitchen, and Jews were running a kitchen, cooking potatoes.

It was a plummeting of living standards. We lived together in these big barracks, which had been army barracks, about 1,000 people of all ages, men and women separated, with 150 people or 200 people in a room. My father was with me in one of those barracks. My mother was there. They put up a special camp hospital, and she was placed right in there.

As they tried to adapt to their surroundings, the men in Louis's barracks reminisced about their former interests and occupations. Some men had been prisoners of war during the last war, and as soldiers they had been protected by the Geneva Conventions. No such protections would help them now. Within a few days of their arrival, the commandant of the ghetto, SS Lieutenant Siegfried Seidl, ordered everyone to assemble in the town square:

He gave us our instructions. It would be up to us how we manage ourselves. We would get some food—some bread, some soup, some potatoes—and some wood, which we could burn in the belly stoves. There would be strict enforcement of the rules: Anybody found with a cigarette would be hanged. There would be no learning. Anybody found teaching or having any books would be hanged. Anybody found with a newspaper would be hanged. There will be more joining you from the Reich. That's it!

At that time smoking was a very common practice, not like today, and the ban on cigarettes was considered a very great deprivation. Everything to do with intellectual activity was forbidden, newspapers, books, and of course, the passing on of information [from the outside world]. You could always get information, especially through the Czech guards, and people got hold of cigarettes, but if you were found . . .

One day they marched us out to the town square. They had prepared a gallows, and they made us witness the stringing up of seven. Two allegedly had tried to escape. Others were found in possession of books and reading materials.

Every day more trains arrived from Prague, from Brno, and the other Czech cities, and we were faced with organizing the camp. It was literally a building up from nothing for survival, and that's when I got interested in community organization. What to do? There were kids— seven year olds, ten year olds—and people in their seventies, some sick, some healthy. And then I thought about helping this person walk, helping this person take his medicine which he had brought along. And seeing the kids, we couldn't teach anything, so we sang some of the songs we knew.

The Jewish administrators of the ghetto worked with limited resources under close Nazi supervision. From offices in the Madgeburg barracks, they allocated food and housing, assigned work, organized cultural activities, and developed special accommodations for children and the aged.[2] Louis became a youth leader in the Magdeburg barracks, where he cared for a room of thirty boys. He volunteered for the position in the spirit of "creative altruism," which combined creativity, "a necessary condition for effective service to other people," with altruism, "a regard for and devotion to the interests of others through service." Louis later described creative altruism as the historical justification for social work intervention.[3] Beyond altruism, however, Louis was motivated by the need for a social purpose: "I was going out of my mind with nothing to do!"

Transports to the East

Louis had scarcely begun his new job when, in January, he and his parents were ordered to assemble for transport. One thousand people were to be deported "to the East":

> That was the most shocking experience! The whole camp was aghast, because we had thought that we would be staying there, not in great conditions, but survivable. Now we heard that this was a transit camp, a collection camp, and from now on there would be more and more Jews brought from certain regions of Europe, and then these Jews would be shipped further "to the East." By that time the camp must have contained maybe fifteen thousand to twenty thousand people, and the Nazis said one thousand people had to be assembled: men women, children, they didn't care. The selection had to be done by the Jewish leadership, and they were caught in a terrible position of deciding who's to go and who's not to go. And I don't know on what basis, I was one of those selected.
>
> I was working there [in the Madgeburg barracks] so I had access to Edelstein, the Jewish Elder, who was like the mayor of the camp. He said, "Well, you have a chance to get out of this transport because your mother is not Jewish, so I'll see what we can do. But meanwhile you're to report."
>
> So we went to the railroad siding and were loaded onto the train, and then at the last minute they pulled us out, my father, my mother, and me. It was a kind of reprieve. So we came back and picked up where we had left off.

On January 20, 1942, about the time of the first transports from Terezín, Nazi officials met in Berlin to plan logistics for the "Final Solution," the mass killing of Europe's Jews. The Wannsee Conference, as it became known, organized the transportation of Jews to six death camps that had been constructed in November and December for the purpose of "mass killing by asphyxiation."[4] It is uncertain today what Terezín's Jewish leadership knew about the destinations of transports "to the East."[5] Louis imagined long, perilous journeys to harsh labor camps or concentration camps that few people would survive:

We heard rumors that they were sent to much more sinister camps, and therefore to stay in Terezín became almost a life prerequisite. The Nazis had set up the total demolition machinery in Auschwitz, in Treblinka, in Sobibór, but that was in place, unbeknownst to us.

Hunger, malnutrition, and overcrowding left ghetto residents vulnerable to dysentery, encephalitis, hepatitis, typhus, malaria, scarlet fever, and other infectious diseases. Louis suffered from three relapses of infectious hepatitis. With 150 to 200 people dying in Terezín each day, Louis "went out on the burial grounds and volunteered. There were no coffins. There were only rags and bags." Louis's mother died in August 1942, and he buried her with his own hands.

By October, there was no more room in the cemetery. A crematorium was built with a capacity of 190 corpses per day.[6]

Hope for a Future

Trains continued to bring the Jews of Western Europe to Terezín, and the garrison town that had been built for seven thousand soldiers now held as many as fifty thousand people at a time:

> Meanwhile, the camp grew bigger and bigger. Eventually, the trains from Germany stopped, because there were hardly any Jews left in Germany, and Jews arrived from Austria, France, Denmark, from the rest of Europe, except from Poland. Apparently, in retrospect, the magic number was forty-five thousand to fifty thousand. When that number was reached, new transports were organized to the East.

Each new train to Terezín brought hundreds of children, some who came with families and others who came alone. Louis joined with other young adults in caring for them. In September 1942, under the direction of Fredy Hirsch, the youth leaders established a separate children's barracks or *Jugendheim* [youth home] in building L414.[7]

The youth in L414, where Louis worked, were predominantly German-speaking, but a second home for Czech-speaking children was later established nearby. Children and youth in L414 lived in rooms with twenty to thirty children of their own age under the care of one or two

1. Terezín today. Photographer unknown. Postcard. Building on far left served as barracks L414. Courtesy of Edith Lowy.

youth leaders. Boys and girls were housed on separate floors. Louis was responsible for a room of about thirty boys who ranged in age from ten to fourteen years:

> So I picked up my activities organizing youth groups. What should all these kids do? They can't write, they have no pencils, they have no books, and so we tell them stories. I told them about my trip to England, about the English worlds that I had experienced. I told them about Marxism, Leninism, and socialism—the things that I knew. I taught them English. I taught them French. The day was occupied by teaching, by doing all these things that were forbidden, by reliving the world that that those of us who were older could still remember: the music, the art, the literature. We set up a kind of informal schedule, but meanwhile all these transports were always going on.

According to Ursula Pawel, a youth leader for girls, Louis was "a compassionate, intelligent, able young teacher" who was loved by the children in his care.[8] As a father figure, he understood that "love and affection are prime forces in the parent-child relationship" and that love is no less important to the parent than to the child.[9] Louis later taught that institutional settings can never replace families, whether for children or for older adults:

> For those who lack families nearby, we must think of developing surrogates, people who volunteer or are trained to give the same kind of comfort, and show the same kind of concern, as family members; who can provide the individualized and personal attention for which there is no substitute.[10]

The youth leaders in L414 comforted their charges, but they could not protect them from incessant hunger or from the epidemics and transports that carried nearly all of Terezín's children to their deaths. Nonetheless, the youth leaders resisted the Nazis in the most radical way possible, by preparing Jewish children for a future.

Many of the youth leaders were Zionists, and they sang songs and told stories that looked forward to a new life in Palestine. Louis was not a Zionist, but a Social Democrat who believed in democratic participation as the means to a socially just world. Group activities, in Louis's view, could prepare children for democracy by respecting "the worth and dignity of the individual" and by assuring each member that "his contribution to the total group is worthwhile."[11] More fundamentally, "the group can provide what the ego needs—hope and a sense of the future."[12] Louis later described the youth leaders in Terezín, whatever their political orientations, as sharing the basic assumptions of social work: that people can grow and change throughout life in response to their environment, and that the environment "can be adapted for beneficial activity."[13]

Louis was particularly concerned with education as the source of personal and social fulfillment and as the means of instilling hope for a future. Throughout his own life, Louis had dealt with suffering by trying to understand it. He had turned to literature, history, philosophy, and the arts to find the reasons for "beggars everywhere" and "blood in the streets" of Prague. Now as a youth leader, he used education to nurture and to encourage others. Although the Nazis prohibited formal classes, Louis drew from his prewar experiences at the Pedagogical Academy, where he had taught small groups of children through experiential learn-ing. Traveling from room to room in L414, he taught English, French, his-tory, philosophy, and literature through games, stories, and plays.

Edith "Ditta" Jedlinsky was fifteen years old when she and her mother, Hilda, arrived in Terezín from Vienna in October 1942, and she met Louis when she moved into L414. Louis and Ditta would be married in the Deggendorf Displaced Persons Center after the war. As Ditta recalled:

> Louis was always very active, and he began teaching, which was for-bidden, absolutely forbidden. He formed informal little classes and he taught us English and he taught us history. The first time I met him he came to our room with the twenty-five girls, and he gave an English lesson about the time, about the clock and the watch. I noticed that he had beautiful hands that he used when he explained things. . . . Louis taught us history—I learned about Napoleon—and we learned English, mainly. We had no books, and we had no paper, no pencils. It was all oral instruction. We took it very seriously.[14]

Changing the Rules

The strange history of Terezín took a decisive turn when, in November 1942, about a year after the establishment of the ghetto, the International Red Cross requested permission to visit. The Red Cross was put off until June 1944, but the initial request sparked Adolf Eichmann's interest in using Terezín for propaganda purposes. With its many musicians, actors, artists, and intellectuals, Terezín could become known for its flourishing cultural life, demonstrating to the world the Nazis' humane treatment of Jews. With such purposes in mind, the Nazis changed the rules of ghetto life. Residents now could borrow books from a lending library or shop in a store with merchandise that had been confiscated from new arriv-als. Musicians could reclaim their instruments. Artists could work on approved projects, such as designing ghetto currency.

Terezín became a tourist attraction for Nazi dignitaries and SS offi-cials, with some benefits to the Jews. When the ophthalmologist Rich-ard Stein was deported to the ghetto to operate on an SS official, he was allowed to treat Jews, including Louis, who had contracted a severe eye infection that blinded him for several months. Dr. Stein operated on Louis and saved his sight.

As always, however, forbidden activities were punishable by death. Bedrich Fritta, the Bohemian artist whom Louis had seen arriving at the Trade Palace, was among the many artists who secretly documented ghetto conditions in paintings and drawings. They smuggled their art works out of Terezín or hid them in the barracks walls. In June 1944, Fritta was arrested and tortured in the Little Fortress before being deported to Auschwitz, where he was killed. Some of his hidden works were recovered after the war.[15]

The Dance of Death

At the age of fifteen, Ditta Jedlinsky experienced the dizzying contradictions of Terezín as "the dance of death":

> Terezín was a very strange place. I used to call it "the dance of death." We had all our teenage flings and crushes and activities, but then reality came into the picture, and transports took place, and people disappeared. And when there were no transports, there were epidemics. There was typhoid, there was hepatitis, there was scarlet fever, there was dysentery. It came in waves, and people died in enormously large numbers when these epidemics were on. Louis's mother died of dysentery in Terezín.
>
> So it was really a strange place, because for teenagers, while there was no illness or no transports, we could pretend that life was normal. We didn't have much to eat, in fact we were hungry, but we didn't talk about that; that wasn't to be talked about. I recall one day somebody brought in some potato skins and then somebody else came into the room. We shoved the potato skins under the bed. We were so ashamed to eat potato skins! Today this is an "in" thing that you pay five dollars for a serving of potato skins. But at that time, it was because there was nothing else. I don't even know how we got the potato skins, because we didn't get the potatoes!
>
> So it was a very strange place. It was like a dance of death that ultimately ended in disaster for most of us. But while we were there, we decorated the ceiling of the room; we did all kinds of things to make it

more normal. And Louis certainly did his part by teaching, by studying the plays with us, and all.

There was free time and we went out and I visited my mother. There were concerts, there was theater, and they were on a high level, because there were an awful lot of artists and professional people there as prisoners. And the Nazis evidently condoned that. They opened shops, and the shops were stocked with merchandise that they had confiscated when the people came in. So one day, we had paper money—I think I still have some upstairs—and one day I went and bought a blouse. And then I came out and a girl saw me and said, "That's my blouse!" And I said, "No, I just bought it in the store." It obviously was her blouse, but now it was mine, because I had bought it. So it's kind of crazy, the whole thing. There was a café house without food, but with an orchestra.

It's terribly hard, even for me who was there, it's hard to comprehend that all this could converge. You had all the amenities of cultural life, and all the shortages of prison life, and the impending danger of deportation and ultimate death, and all at the same time. It was totally schizophrenic! But when you were a teenager, and participating in all the experiences, you could easily not see the other side. Until it came to you, when you, too, fell sick or were deported.

Ditta remembered when fourteen-year-old Werner "Vern" Drehmel bounded into Terezín with a soccer ball under his arm. Vern arrived in March 1943 from Hamburg, where his father had died and his mother had been hospitalized. She was killed in May of that year. As Vern recalled:

I met Louis, who was in charge of a room in L414 to which I had been assigned. There were about thirty guys living there. I suspect that I was the last fellow to be placed there because I found myself sleeping next to Louis. So who was Louis? He was friendly; he was welcoming. I looked at him very admiringly. He seemed very knowledgeable, very calm, interested in learning about me as I guess he did the same with the other guys in the group.

Eventually we developed some routines, routines imposed upon us by the ghetto administration. Those who were able-bodied would have to report to a work assignment station in the mornings, and then would be delegated to go to the various places where our work might be some use. I was doing various kinds of work, such as sorting potatoes in the commandant's home cellar. It provided an opportunity to steal potatoes. I would wear two pairs of pants, one with the bottoms tied at the ankles, and another pair of pants over the tied down ones. And interestingly that's about the only job I remember doing, because there was great deal of anxiety attached to that!

Whatever happened during the days, at night we would sit on chairs around Louis, and frequently we read dramas, specifically German authors, such as [Friedrich von] Schiller, who was a very romantic, freedom-loving dramatist, and [Johann Wolfgang von] Goethe. It didn't matter, really, whom we were reading, because it was illegal and somewhat dangerous when I first arrived there. We would all take different roles and read those parts. It would be like a sit-down play. That was the formal learning that I specifically remember Louis providing for us. But there really was so much more that I learned, and I cannot quite tell you how. We learned about Louis's experiences in England. Louis told us that there was a place in London, the Speakers' Corner in Hyde Park, where you could say anything you want as long as it was truthful. You could parade against the regime of the prime minister, use ballots not bullets.

Louis told us about the United States Constitution, and we learned the Preamble and the Bill of Rights. This was without formal texts; we didn't have the United States Constitution to read in Terezín! It was all oral sharing of information and knowledge. And there was no question in my mind that I wanted to go to the United States and to live as a free person.

The superiority of Germans and German armor and fighter pilots was all I ever saw or heard of until I arrived at Terezín, which was my salvation in becoming a person. Louis was my friend; he was my teacher. He was the most important person in my personal development. He helped me develop political philosophy, social philosophy. Certainly he affected in a primary way my view of trying to be an honest person living an honest life. And I suspect that he affected many other kids in a similar manner who were not lucky enough to survive.

Louis instilled in us a sense of defiance, yet it was always tempered with a sense of fairness to the other. For instance, Louis wrote out quotations from Schiller's poems, big paper banners that we posted on the bunks to give us a sense of defiance and spirit:

Der Mensch ist frei geschaffen, ist frei / Und wurd' er in Ketten geboren (Man is created free, and is free / Even though born in chains).[16]

Dem Verdienste seine Kronen / Untergang der Luegenbrut (Give the crowns to those who earn them / Defeat to the pack of liars)![17]

We were taking our chances sometimes! The SS would come by and inspect. We never knew when they might come. Luckily, they never realized that the banners applied to them. They felt flattered that we liked Schiller!

The Nazis had all this power. They looked like demigods to us, with their boots like mirrors, their uniforms, their polished buttons. Louis let us know that these people were not superior to us, and thanks to Louis, I was idealistic enough to believe that evil could not survive. So I knew that life was worth living! I knew that the Germans would lose the war, and consequently, I wanted to be there when it happened.[18]

Of all his activities in Terezín, Louis was best known for his production of children's plays. At first, the children and youth in Louis's drama groups had spoken their parts in secret, but by the spring of 1943, they were allowed to perform in public, and Louis's theatrical productions attracted standing-room-only crowds in the attic of L414. Drawing from his memory of opera, children's literature, and German theater, Louis prepared and directed scripts based on Puccini's opera *Turandot;* Schiller's play *Maria Stuart,* and Erich Kästner's children's story *Emil and the Detectives.* More than sixty years later, survivors with whom I met vividly remembered their parts in these productions. Ditta, who played Kennedy in *Maria Stuart,* recalled:

We studied plays, classical plays that we performed, and I was in the cast! We did *Maria Stuart* by Schiller, and other plays, and it was a phenomenal thing to undertake under the circumstances. Eventually we performed those plays in the attic of the home. One of the boys did the electrical work, and he went around stealing light-bulbs somewhere.

Everybody from the camp could come and listen to it and watch it. It was terribly exciting!

Vern Drehmel, who also performed in *Maria Stuart,* was moved by the prologue that Louis wrote for the occasion:

Louis wrote a beautiful prologue for the play that made it suitable for our circumstances, the injustices, etc. I played Mortimer, who was a romantic, a would-be lover of Maria Stuart. Ditta was also in that play. She played a lady-in-waiting. When I remember the play, I still remember my performance! When we went to the [Deggendorf] reunion in 1978, there were people older than I am and they remembered the play, particularly my death scene! The whole thing was well-attended, and we all thought that we were really great. Louis really had us believing in what we were doing.

2. Poster to theater performance of F. Schiller, *Maria Stuart* (PT 4019). Artist unknown. September 1943. By permission of Památník Terezín (Terezín Memorial), Hermann's Collection, copyright Zuzana Dvořáková. Cast members included director Louis Löwy, Werner (Vern) Drehmel, and Ditta Jedlinsky (misspelled on poster).

Reinhard Frank was fourteen years old when he arrived in Terezín in June 1943. Reinhard first met Louis when he joined the cast of *Emil and the Detectives:*

> My first conscious contact with Louis was for the production of a play which was based on *Emil and the Detectives* by Erich Kästner. It was a very popular book for kids. This whole play takes place in Berlin, and somehow I got involved in it, because I came from Berlin. I was given the name of a character who does not exist in the book called "the Bull."[19]

Shortly after the war, when the author Erich Kästner learned that his stories had been performed in Terezín, he sought out members of the cast. His resulting essay, *Wert und Unwert des Menshen* (The worth and worthlessness of men), was published in the newspaper *Neue Zeitung,* in February 1946: "Somebody recently wrote to me that in Thereisenstadt, thirty children performed in my play *Emil and the Detectives.* Of these thirty children, only three are still alive."[20]

Over time, Louis expanded his teaching to include adult education programs, including lessons in English, French, and history.[21] A schedule of cultural activities for June 1944 listed three lectures by Louis.[22] His remarks on coeducation in Terezín, delivered on June 13, have not survived; however, his lecture "Erziehungsfragen in Theresienstadt" (Issues concerning education in Terezín), delivered on June 18, 1944, presented what was, under the circumstances, a radical philosophy of education. Young people would not be imprisoned in mind or in character so long as they gained "an intimate acquaintance with world culture," the very culture that National Socialism sought to destroy:

> The problem of education is difficult; the problem of education in Terezín is more than just complicated. The environment of Terezín has an immense effect on the development of young people, and educational work here requires a still higher emphasis on all relevant factors. The goal, here and elsewhere, is to educate an unbiased person, of strong character, who can recognize his life task and integrate himself into society. The situation here is a tremendous hindrance to reaching this goal, but the educator should never lose sight of it. . . .

The youth here are healthy and full of life energy. We as educators should exploit this energy and prepare the young people for further creative activities and advances. A prerequisite for that is intimate acquaintance with world culture. If we cannot reach perfection, we must make every effort to approach it as closely as possible. I have tried to approach this hard task and also contribute something to its implementation. Let the spirit of this work bring its fruits in future days![23]

In his next lecture, on June 22, "Educational Work in Terezín," Louis reviewed the "systematic cultural program" that he had offered during the previous year, June 1943 to June 1944.[24] The curriculum had centered on six areas: literature, music, history, languages, educational problems, and self-employment of youth. Louis had engaged the active participation of his students in "Literary Evenings" with readings of the poetry of Goethe, Schiller, and Shakespeare; "Selections from World Literature" with readings from the works of Ben Spanier, Claire Arnstein, Marianne Offer, and Ernst Raden; and "Readings from Dramas," including Schiller's *Maria Stuart* and *Wallenstein,* Shakespeare's *Hamlet* and *Othello,* and Goethe's *Faust* and *Egmont.* Louis may have called upon the talents of artists and of other educators when he arranged "Musical Evenings" on the works of Bach, Handel, Haydn, Beethoven, Mozart, and Mendelsson-Bartholdy. In exploring "Themes from World and Cultural History," he had encouraged youth to enter "live discussions with sociological observations." Language study had included "geographical observations in the format of 'Travels around the World.'" Youth had taken charge of discussions on "Educational Problems," and they gave presentations related to the "Self-Employment of Youth" on such themes as "Knowledge Is Power," "Ask Me 500 Times," and "Reading Books."

The Terezín audience understood that few of Louis's students were allowed to pursue this "cultural program" from start to finish. Even so, Louis had succeeded in his primary goal of sustaining, for at least some young people, a belief in the future. As Klaus Scheurenberg, a survivor of Terezín, remembered in his autobiography:

We organized a group of eight fellows who had a motto: "One for all and all for one." We drank our *Ersatzkaffee* together, our breakfast was a ritual. We could discuss our problems together. A feeling that you have friends who understand you and will help you, that you are not alone, gave us courage.

We decided to do something in the evenings, too. We wanted not to get tired and studied English. . . . We would crawl into a garret and have somebody on guard, so that we were not taken unawares. A young man whose name was Louis Löwy gave us English lessons. From that time, I have a small notebook in which I put down my exercises, which Louis later rewrote in a larger book. It fits conveniently into my trouser pocket. I don't know where and when I stole it. Today it has for me of unimaginable value. I have also entered names of inmates and, on a dotted line, fates of some people I have met. When I am looking at the roommate lists today, I get dizzy. Of eighty young people, only six are alive today.

I also read in this little book: "Here are the English Books. Here is the answer you will send them. Damn, I have written it all wrong; Louis will put it straight." Louis had convinced us that we could survive and then we'd definitely need English. We studied with fiery zeal. When we could, we spoke with each other only in English. When the war was over and an American car took our chief rabbi, Leo Baeck, I greeted the driver, an American soldier, with a passionate [English] "Good-bye."[25]

On June 23, 1944, the day after Louis's lecture "Educational Work in Terezín," a delegation from the International Red Cross was at last allowed to visit the ghetto. Meticulous preparations marked the culmination of the Nazi propaganda campaign.[26] In the weeks before the visit, in order to reduce the appearance of overcrowding, SS Colonel Karl Rahm, who was now commandant of the ghetto, ordered the deportation of seventy-five hundred ghetto residents. Ditta and her mother were selected for transport in May. Louis and Ditta had formed a friendship, "more than a friendship," in Ditta's words: "We promised to find each other after the war, but we really wondered whether we would ever see each other again."

Louis cancelled his children's production of Moliére's *Le Malade Imaginaire* when half the cast were deported. Rahm had prepared a different kind of theater for the delegation from the International Red Cross, which included commissioners of the International Red Cross, the Danish

Red Cross, and the German Red Cross.[27] Following an elaborately staged route, the delegates viewed streets with names rather than numbers, buildings with curtains in the windows and grass and flowers planted outside, and residents playing carefully scripted roles. The ruse was so successful, from Rahm's point of view, that he ordered Kurt Gerron, a prominent actor in the ghetto, to make a film, *Der Führer Schenkt den Juden Eine Stadt* (The Führer presents a city to the Jews). Gerron was deported and killed at Auschwitz shortly after completing the film, which was distributed in the neutral countries.

The propaganda value of Terezín reached as far as Auschwitz-Birkenau, where, in September 1943, Eichmann ordered that a special "Family Camp" be established for Terezín Jews. In contrast to other inmates of Auschwitz-Birkenau, those in the Family Camp were spared the terror of daily selections, and they were encouraged to send postcards back to the ghetto reporting that they were well. On March 7, one day after prisoners had written reassuring postcards, thousands of Family Camp inmates were sent to the gas chambers.[28]

The Red Cross visit to Terezín was to be the death knell for the Family Camp. Accepting Rahm's false promise that there would be no further deportations from the ghetto, delegates from the Danish Red Cross issued a favorable report on living conditions of Danish Jews in Terezín. As a result, the Danish Red Cross declined the opportunity to visit the Terezín Family Camp at Auschwitz-Birkenau. No longer needed for propaganda, the Family Camp was destroyed at the end of June 1944. Of 18,000 inmates, 15,000 were killed, including all of the children.[29]

Louis could never believe that anyone was deceived by the Terezín propaganda campaign:

> The Nazis somehow felt constrained to put up the show. They set up such a showplace to counteract what was by then common knowledge about what they were really doing. I imagined that the [Red Cross] delegation was not fooled.

In the end, the mortality statistics from Terezín spoke for themselves. Of 140,000 Jews who passed through the ghetto, 33,000 died there. Of

87,000 who were deported from the ghetto, 83,000 were killed. Of 15,000 children who lived in Terezín, those in other words who were younger than 15 years, approximately 10 percent survived.[30]

Louis continued teaching in Terezín until Yom Kippur (Day of Atonement), September 27, 1944, when he was deported to Auschwitz. Vern Drehmel and Reinhard Frank soon followed. Louis's father died on the final transport from Terezín to Auschwitz on October 28, 1944.

Many years later, on the occasion of Louis's seventieth birthday, Vern remembered what Louis had meant to the youth of L414:

> I was on the verge of adolescence, parentless, confused, lacking perspective. Louis was in his early manhood. He was the adult, in charge of thirty or so kids with whom I was making my home in one room upon arrival in Terezín. Each fellow had recently been either separated from his parents or orphaned; each had been torn from his home, extended family, school, playmates, community.
>
> We had arrived in a ghetto, not knowing for how long or what our destination would be. People were dying of malnutrition or typhus. The conditions were extreme. Was there any future? Would we, indeed, survive?
>
> It was in these circumstances that Louis must have performed his very best piece of social group work. He helped us to develop a sense of cohesiveness, identity, mutual caring; under threat of death for teaching, he shared with us his extensive knowledge of literature, drama and poetry, helping us to transcend our surroundings, to dream about and taste the very liberty, freedom and dignity denied us. He helped us to feel important, proud. Unlike those who had the guns, we were gaining knowledge, and all of us had begun to believe the Schiller quotation that "knowledge is power." We were developing a sense of self.
>
> I attribute my survival as a human being—and hopefully a *Mensch* (an honorable man)—to Louis. I was fortunate enough to meet him and stay connected with him until the very days of our deliverance.[31]

Escape from Auschwitz

LOUIS LOWY NEVER FELT that he could put his memories of Auschwitz into words: "I can tell about it, I can narrate about it, but I have never been able to digest what happened." All through his life, he had sought comfort in learning. He had faith, if not in God, then in the potential of human progress as expressed in history, philosophy, literature, and the arts. When the doors of the boxcar opened at Auschwitz-Birkenau, nothing that Louis had studied, not even Dante, prepared him for what he found:

> And then we were in those trains, and the gates opened up in Auschwitz, and that is the most horrendous thought left in my mind: That day! The vision, the smell, the stench, the chimneys, the yelling and the arrival box and the beast let loose! It was hell breaking loose. It was Dante's Inferno: "Those who entered here," but Dante could not have written what hell could be like. [Josef] Mengele was standing there; I still see his face.
>
> We were thrown out of those cattle cars and then lined up, and they yelled, "Left! Right! Left! Right!" and nobody had any idea what that really meant. So some went left and some went right. I wasn't separated from anybody because I didn't come with anybody. Some people came with wives, husbands.
>
> It was a total shock. We were so totally dumbfounded that we lost our sense of time, our sense of place, our orientation, our intelligence. You lost any sense of control over who you were and what you were and how you were. You completely lost a sense of self. It's very hard to describe, because what is a sense of self? You didn't know anymore who you were, or who the next person was that was thrown out of the car, or who were these beasts that were standing at the ramp? They had

uniforms, and they yelled, and they had whips and guns. They destroyed any sense of being.

And then we were herded into the barracks. It was fall already and very cold, muddy, miserable Polish weather. And then there is a blank. If you ask me what happens next, I couldn't tell you.

Loss of Self

The enormity of Auschwitz was impossible to comprehend, even for the prisoners who lived and died there. From 1942 to 1944, 1.1 million Jews from all over Nazi-occupied Europe were deported to Auschwitz, where 1 million were killed. Of 200,000 non-Jewish prisoners, 110,000 were killed, the largest of these populations being Poles, Roma, and Soviet prisoners of war.[1]

After June 1944, when the Theresienstadt Family Camp was destroyed, the transports from Terezín were destined for Auschwitz-Birkenau, one of three main camps in the Auschwitz concentration camp complex. Louis and other new arrivals were thrown from the trains into a bewildering "selection" process. Most prisoners were sent "to the right," to four large gas chambers and crematoria, facilities that had been designed for systematic mass asphyxiation by Zyklon B gas. Those prisoners whom the SS guards selected for forced labor were sent "to the left," to a seemingly endless expanse of wooden barracks surrounded by electrified barbed wire.

Auschwitz-Birkenau had been planned as a camp for the "Untermensch" or subhumans in the Nazi scheme of racial classification. Originally built by and for Soviet prisoners of war, the barracks were designed with less living space per inmate than "standard concentration camps" in Germany.[2] Huge wooden huts housed 744 inmates on three tiers of wooden shelves, 4 inmates per shelf, or 11 square feet per person. Once on their bunks, the inmates did not have space to move, and when someone died, as often happened, his bunkmates could not remove the body.[3] Latrines were "little more than open sewers enclosed by a shed," and one latrine was built per 7,000 inmates, nearly all of whom suffered from dysentery or diarrhea.[4]

Shock and despair left Louis with sketchy memories of his first days in Auschwitz-Birkenau:

Once a week or three times a week or five times a week, there would be a selection. People were lined up, and they [the SS guards] picked every third or every fifth person—who knows what system they had?—to go into the chimneys. So you waited from selection to selection and you tried to survive. Some people worked in details outside. They marched out in columns, and the rest were left in those barracks all day long with nothing to do.

It was a life of hunger, and survival was a full-time occupation. Survival meant to eat your soup, maybe to get a little bit more soup or a little bit more bread through bartering. Sometimes the dead were still getting their rations of bread and the people were like vultures.

Vern Drehmel was deported from Terezín to Auschwitz-Birkenau shortly after Louis, in late September 1944, accompanied by two young children who were his orphaned cousins:

Two cousins of mine were on the same transport as I was to Auschwitz. They were six and eight years old. And when we got to Auschwitz, I was sent to the left, and they were both sent to the right. There were about sixteen hundred people from Terezín on the transport. Thirty or so were sent to the left and all the others sent to the right. I protested. I said, "Pardon, I would like to go there [to the right] with my charges!" There was safety in numbers, and I felt deprived of my little cousins. They were killed that night.

I've always had a way of getting people to pay attention to me, and sports were a great avenue. I was a soccer fan. When you have something in common with a guard, like soccer, you are no longer just a "God damn Jewish pig." So I started talking to a guard about soccer, and then I asked, "Where are all those people going? My little cousins are just six and eight years old." And he said, "They're going to the bakery. You'll find out tonight." What he meant was I'd see the smoke.

A few days later, when Vern caught sight of Louis, he was alarmed by the change in his teacher and friend:

I learned that Louis was in a certain barracks, and I somehow finagled permission from the *Kapo* [the inmate foreman], who was in charge of the barracks, to go over there to visit my friend. There I found Louis, sitting on the ground, catatonic, breathing but dead.

Reinhard Frank, another youth from Terezín, arrived at Auschwitz-Birkenau at about the same time as Vern. Reinhard also was amazed by Louis's appearance:

> On my first or second day in Auschwitz, I saw Louis and Vern standing in this muddy road outside the hut where we were housed. All I remember is Louis and Vern standing there, holding each other, embracing each other, both of them crying. I had never seen Louis like this, so different, so wrecked, so totally disturbed.

Louis had never been in greater danger. If Vern had not found him, he might have become what was known in the camp as a *Muselmann,* a prisoner who had lost the strength or the will to live. Such prisoners made prime targets for selection by the SS.[5] Fortunately, Vern gained permission to move into Louis's barracks, and Louis, with his young friend to care for, returned to his former self.

In later years, many death camp survivors testified that they had persevered for the sake of a loved one, and so it was for Louis and Vern.[6] As Vern recalled:

> Louis needed me, as much as I needed him, and from that time on, Louis again assumed his appropriate role towards me. That's really how Louis lived. He had to provide for others, he had to give to others. He relied on teaching, which was his mission in life. From then on, we were together at every roll call, standing next to each other.

Louis and Vern were standing together when they were registered and tattooed for assignment in a satellite labor camp, and for the rest of their lives they would bear consecutive identification numbers on their arms: Louis, B12743, and Vern, B12744. As Louis recovered his sense of purpose, he once again sought reasons to hope:

> You wanted to be tattooed because tattooing meant you were not selected immediately for the gas chamber. That didn't guarantee the

future, but for the moment you were registered as a number and therefore you could be called for labor.

Louis and Vern also took heart from the sounds of Allied planes flying overhead:

> We heard the Allied planes. They were so high up in the sky that you could hardly see them, but we knew the difference by the sounds of the motor. You could hardly hear any German Messerschmitts anymore. The airspace was totally controlled by the Americans, the British, and the Russians. And we were hoping that they would drop bombs on us.

The US War Department rejected proposals from European and American Jewish leaders to bomb the gas chambers and railway lines at Auschwitz-Birkenau. In the summer and fall of 1944, however, the US Air Force mounted massive bombing campaigns against armaments factories in the surrounding region of Upper Silesia.[7]

Destruction Through Work

In mid- to late October, Louis, Vern, and Reinhard were among those assigned to leave Auchwitz-Birkenau to work on the reconstruction of the Gleiwitzer Hütte munitions factory. They marched with the work detail for about thirty miles to Gleiwitz III, a satellite labor camp that was located outside the industrial town of Gliwice (Gleiwitz, in German). A former warehouse served as the barracks, where six hundred prisoners slept on the ground on straw sacks in wooden frames. The inmates each received a blanket, a true luxury to them, but as Louis learned in the morning, the guards had "an obsession," about making beds. As Reinhard explained, "The beds had to be made perfectly every morning. Somebody would come by with a piece of wood and make sure that they were absolutely flat. Try to do that with a sack stuffed with hay!" According to Louis, "If there was a little wrinkle, you got lashes."

Gleiwitz III was run in accordance with SS policy of *Vernichtung durch Arbeit* (destruction through work), a policy more effective in killing prisoners than in spurring industrial production.[8] Like most prisoners, Louis, Vern, and Reinhard dug ditches and leveled terrain, working outdoors in subzero temperatures without adequate nourishment, clothing, or tools.[9] Reinhard, who was in a different work detail from Louis and Vern, remembered beatings from the guards:

> There were various forms of punishments for stealing a towel, which I had done, because it was cold. You had to walk on all fours over heaps of sand and they would beat you up or send dogs.

Despite the brutal conditions at Gleiwitz III, Louis, Vern, and Reinhard felt fortunate to be there. In Reinhard's words, "It was salvation as far as we were concerned. Once we were out of Auschwitz, we were not subject to daily selections." Now their greatest fears were injury or illness because any prisoner who fell behind in his work would be sent back to Auschwitz-Birkenau to be killed.

For Vern and Reinhard, surviving Gleiwitz meant learning to be wary of everyone, even fellow prisoners. In their earlier lives in Germany and Terezín, they had never experienced what emerged as a hazard of the Gleiwitz barracks, the animosity between German and Polish Jews. In Vern's words, "The Polish Jews had it in for us! They called us *Jeckes* [jackets] because we always wore jackets before the war." Louis, with his gift for languages, related more easily to inmates from various backgrounds. He picked up enough Yiddish to communicate with Eastern European Jews, and his sense of humor helped bridge differences in culture and class.

As a general rule however, Louis kept his head down. As he advised, "Keep the lowest, lowest, profile that you can. Stand in the middle, never on the side, never in front. Try to find a place where no one will notice you, and above all, never volunteer!" It was a measure of his desperation, therefore, that Louis raised his hand one morning at roll call when the guards asked if anyone was a technical designer: "I didn't even know what a technical designer was! I only knew instinctively that I wouldn't survive that winter outdoors and this was a chance to get out of the cold."

As luck would have it, Louis was assigned to assist a civilian engineer who knew little more than Louis about technical design:

> They picked three or four of us young people, and I was chosen to be a technical designer. I didn't think of the consequences. What will

happen? I don't know how to design. Yes, I had learned mathematics and geometry in the Gymnasium, but to ask me to design something . . .

I went there into the office, and I still see him in front of me, Engineer Vittma, blond, in this thirties, in civilian clothes, and I was thinking, "He should be in the *Wehrmacht!* He must have had some deals to stay out of it!" He had an inside job away from the front through some connections.

He spoke to me in German. "Mensch," he said; that was a typical north German way of speaking, "I need this and this done," and when I answered him in German, he was just stunned! "How can you speak such flawless German?" He was used to foreign Polish workers and Russian laborers, and I don't think he had ever seen a Jew.

He began chatting with me because he had somebody who spoke his language. He talked about the war, how terrible it was for his family who were bombed out. He asked me quite extensively how I ended up there, and I told him a little bit about my life. And I must say, without any equivocation, that he didn't know that there were Jews who had lived in Germany since the Romans or that the Jews were not all devils as they were portrayed. Here I was, a person who grew up in the German traditional culture, and he just couldn't fathom it!

We met every morning, and he brought the newspaper, and we read about the Battle of the Bulge [December 16, 1944, to January 25, 1945]. Occasionally he left a newspaper or a piece of bread in the wastebasket.

And what did I do there? All kinds of busy work on a desk. Even I could tell that this guy didn't know his ass from his elbow! He probably knew as much about engineering as I did! He showed me blueprints of screws and all that. What could I read in a blueprint? He said, "We need a new calendar for the new year." He couldn't get a calendar, so I designed one. Big deal! That I could do! He kept me busy, because he wanted to seem busy. He was afraid that if he didn't have this sinecure, that they might now draft him with the Russians at the door.

On Christmas of 1944, all too aware of the "Russians at the door," the Glewitzer Hütte factory gave a party for their slave laborers. For Vern, it was a day beyond belief:

All of a sudden on Christmas day, we were given hot showers! Hot
showers! Are you kidding? This cannot be true! And then we were all
ushered into the mess hall, where there were big banners that said in
German: "Merry Christmas! Gleiwitz III, for the Christmas celebration, salutes the guests!" We were guests? And then we had a special
meal. By then they must have known that the war was ending, and they
were buttering us up.

Upon Louis's recommendation, Vern also was requisitioned for work
inside the factory, where he was even less prepared than Louis for his
responsibilities:

I was put to work in the storeroom where they kept the tools. I heard
that this was one of the best jobs they had, but I didn't know this tool
from that tool. I proved myself deficient in my knowledge of tools! So
then they sent me onto the factory floor. Now I had to produce. I had to
operate a steel-cutting lathe. We were making contacts for sea mines for
the German Navy. You had to know what you were doing, and I didn't!

Then sometime in January, panic time was coming, because German navy officers were coming to inspect our product, and there was no
way that they could possibly accept what I had done! And lo and behold,
we heard the big guns of the Russian army. The Russians were about to
start their winter offensive toward Krakow. So for us, and certainly for
me, it could not possibly come at a more fortuitous time, because it kept
the navy inspectors from rejecting our work.

Auschwitz ultimately supplied forty thousand forced laborers to private factories in Upper Silesia in 1944, yielding defective products but
millions of marks in profits for the SS, the private industrialists, and the
state.[10] The scheme came crashing to an end on January 17, 1945, when,
in a chaotic flight from the advancing Red Army, the SS destroyed the
gas chambers and crematoria, the camp books and records, and, to the
extent possible, all human evidence of what they had done at Auschwitz.
Upon orders from Reichsfuehrer SS Heinrich Himmler, all inmates of the
concentration camp complex were to be evacuated or killed. Those able
to walk were to be marched westward toward concentration camps in

Austria and Germany. Those who were too weak to be evacuated were to be shot.

Death March

The prisoners of Gleiwitz III set out on the "death march" before dawn with little food and no water in the subzero cold. Prisoners who slowed the pace by falling or bending down were shot, and hundreds of corpses lined the road. As Louis recalled:

> We marched for days and days, hearing aerial bombardment and machine gunfire and seeing the German troops retreating like Napoleon from Moscow. Some of the Nazis threw away their arms. Some threw away their uniforms. Some of the SS guards who were marching us were afraid to be caught, and they ran away. Others were fanatical, and they shot everybody who could not continue to march. At night, they locked us up in various camps or they sent us into the open air.

Reinhard Frank was vividly aware of the advancing Soviet army:

> It was one of the coldest winters of the Second World War, and sound carries much better and further in the extreme cold. We could clearly hear major artillery, so we knew the Russian front must be very close to us.
>
> Every night we were locked up somewhere else. The area where we were, in Upper Silesia, was full with all sorts of camps: concentration camps like Auschwitz-Birkenau, labor camps that were subsidiary camps of Auchswitz-Birkenau [such as Gleiwitz III], work camps for foreign workers, prisoner of war camps, and Stalag camps, which were camps for prisoners of war from foreign air forces. The whole area was full, one camp after another. And every night we would be locked up in another camp.
>
> Then after a week or so, we came to a village called Blechhammer, which was a major center of various camps. It had been bombarded by the US Air Force at various times, because there were chemical factories there. We were locked in a camp with wooden barracks, not a concentration camp, but a camp that had been for foreign laborers.

Louis and Vern marched with Kurt Kohorn, a young man from Pilsen whom Louis had first met in Terezín. Supporting each other physically and emotionally, the three struggled to keep pace. It seemed to Louis that they were marching in circles because they had crossed the Oder River several times. Finally, on the night when they reached Blechhammer, Louis decided that he could not continue any further. As Louis remembered:

> When we arrived at Blechhammer, still under Nazi guard, I remember saying to Vern and to Kurt, "I cannot go on. I cannot go on physically. I'd rather stay here, be shot or lie out in the snow and freeze to death." And Vern and Kurt were not in much better shape. And the next day, when they ordered us to line up for the march, we stayed behind. We did not assemble again.
>
> So what would they do to us? Shoot us? There comes a point when you don't give a damn. Even if your survival drive is strong, there comes a point when your survival drive stops, or when another drive, a drive for relief from suffering, takes over. And that is what took over at that time. We had heard that the best way to escape is to lie down in the snow and freeze to death. It's a very merciful death, and we tried it.
>
> But the Nazis now felt, "Let's escape with our lives!" They were trying to get out as quickly as possible, and therefore their thoroughness was less. They left us behind. It was our liberation.

On the same morning, Reinhard also decided to hide:

> The morning when we were supposed to have roll call and leave this camp, every one of us, totally independently, Louis, Vern, myself, and a few other guys decided not to appear for roll call. We knew that the Russians could only be a few kilometers away. Lots of people had the same idea at the same point of time: "It's now or never," so to speak. I hid underneath a building. Eventually the Germans tried to grab whoever they could. They realized from the roll call that there were quite a few people missing, but they set fire to a few of the buildings and left.
>
> And then I walked around. I ran into Louis and I ran into Vern. We just decided to stay in one of these many wooden barracks which were in this camp. In the end, we were a group of seven: There was Louis, there

was Vern, there was Kurt Kohorn, and then there were three other guys: two brothers by the name of Georg and Heinz Schindler, and another guy called Gerhard Steinhagen. They were Berliners who had met each other in the camps. Somehow or other, Louis knew these other guys who joined our group.

As Vern remembered, the group escaped from the death march just in time:

I tell you, everything I've experienced has been primarily good luck! We learned later that our camp members from Gleiwitz were all shot and killed at the Oder River, which was about a day's march away, on the night that we had left. They couldn't keep up, couldn't walk any more without food. So they shot the whole group. There were always some survivors of these mass killings, and they reported what had happened. We made it just in time.

Freed from the death march, the seven young men were caught in the "no-man's land" between the German and Russian lines. They heard artillery fire all around the camp, and, just when all seemed quiet, a grenade would explode in front of them. From January 20 to 27, SS units combed the area with orders to shoot any surviving prisoners.[11] Louis remembered the return of the SS patrols: "We heard shooting again, and then we ducked instinctively and they shot at us." Everyone lay still in the snow as if they had been left for dead. Vern curiously looked up, and Louis pushed his head down and held him under a towel.

The SS patrols came back several times, as Vern recalled:

In January of 1945 it was my birthday. I had my sixteenth birthday in the forest in Blechhammer. There was a storeroom where we suspected there was food. It hadn't been broken into yet, and we were eager for it. People stormed it en masse, other people who had been in the concentration camps. And Louis said, "We better not go there, because people are going to kill each other trying to get in." So we waited. And the Nazis came back and burned the building, and people were burned to death there. And when we came out of hiding, we saw people were cooking food next to the burning corpses.

As Reinhard remembered the incident, the SS set up machine guns and shot people as they ran from the burning building. They then loaded the bodies onto trucks and drove away.

Liberation

On January 27, when the Soviet army finally liberated Auschwitz, the last of the SS patrols had left an estimated eight thousand prisoners alive in the concentration camp complex and the surrounding area.[12] The gunfire ceased, and Louis and his group cautiously emerged from the camp where they had been hiding:

> We ventured out of the camp, and we looked around, and we saw a lot of corpses, Germans, Jews, Poles, Russians. We were like scavengers in a lost world. Soon we stumbled upon this place that had been, as we found out, a former POW camp for British prisoners of war. There were barracks, but in better shape than at the other camps, with bunk beds. The Nazis had observed the Geneva Conventions with the British and American prisoners of war, although not with the Russians or the Poles.
>
> There were Red Cross parcels with jam and cigarettes. There were cans of condensed milk and tins of food. There were British army-issue blankets and outfits of British battle dress, those Montgomery style uniforms with epaulettes. They were like the battle dress that most of the Allies wore, not the Americans, but the British, the Dutch, the French Legion, the Czech Legion, the Polish all wore these kinds of uniforms, except they had different insignias on the left shoulder. So we took off our prison garb, and we put on the British uniforms, and we put on the boots that we found.
>
> The camp was deserted, deserted like Robinson Crusoe, and we stayed there, silent in the woods of Poland. And as we took over that place and settled in, I, in a sense, took over leadership of the group. We organized: Who would take care of getting water? Who would forage for food? We melted snow—snow is black when it is melted—and we found an enormous amount of grapes from Bulgaria. We ate grapes and looked out and there was emptiness.

Vern, the soccer player, was delighted to find a pair of soccer shoes:

I found a pair of soccer shoes, my first luxury item! I played soccer in those rescued boots; I wore them all through Europe. They entered the [United] States with me. How fond I was of those shoes!

Reinhard assumed responsibility for cooking, as he recalled:

I became the cook for this whole group. I nearly poisoned everybody! I found a dead cow in the field. I sliced it open and cooked it, and we all got very sick. Together with Vern I found a storage place with hundreds of bottles of mineral water. It was wonderful to use it for cooking because you could cook frozen potatoes, which were really inedible, but we cooked anything we could find. I also used water from a storage tank in the neighborhood. It was frozen over. I used to hack a hole everyday and take a bucket. And one day I came, and Russian soldiers were there, and they wanted to know what I was doing. In my few words of Russian, I told them, "I am taking water." So they showed me where the ice had melted. There were three or four dead bodies floating around. I couldn't help it! Our feeding habits were not overly hygienic!

Freedom was fragile, as Louis well knew, and the Soviet Army posed a new threat to his small group. As Louis recalled:

For days nothing happened except the fear that the Germans would come back. And then one day, when we were just sitting around, we saw a Russian patrol coming up the road. I spoke Czech and Russian and made myself understood. They said that they were looking for Nazi bands. We showed him our tattoos, and one of the Russian officers was Jewish. He said in Russian, "They are Jews?" And then he said to me, "Stay still and wait. We will provide for you," and they left us alone and marched off.

Louis learned that the Russians had taken over a former Nazi labor camp and turned it into a refugee camp in nearby Katowitz:

And that's when I said, "We're not going to any camp, Russian or otherwise. We are going our own way." So we cleared out of Blechhamer. We escaped on foot. We were already in better shape, and eventually we walked to Katowitz, a Polish city with a railway station, which wasn't that far. But when we got to Katowitz, there were Russians, and they rounded us up and put us into a camp for refugees. There was food, but the camp was guarded. And I said, "We're not going to stay."

Literature, as always, was Louis's frame of reference, and he planned an escape worthy of *Der Hauptmann von Köpenick* (The captain of Köpenick), a popular play by the German Jewish writer Carl Zuckmayer.[13] The hero of the play was a poor cobbler who became the captain of Köpenick when he purchased a secondhand military uniform. He put on the uniform, ordered a troop of guardsman to take over the town hall, and then made away with the town funds:

> So one night, it was Vern and my turn to stand guard. We [inmates] had to take turns standing guards at night, because there weren't enough Russians. They gave us rifles, which we didn't know how to shoot, for standing guard. And I said, "Let's play *Der Hauptmann von Köpenick*. Let's organize as a disciplined group of soldiers and march out of the camp!" So the seven us of lined up in our British battle dress and we marched down to the main gate, and I saluted. I said to the guard in Czech, "We're marching over to the next camp by order of the commandant!" And he saluted us and let us go!
>
> As soon as we were out of the campgrounds, we laughed! We found our way to the Katowitz railroad station, and we climbed into a train that was parked there. It was nighttime, and we couldn't see very well. As it turned out, we were in a coal train! We were making ourselves comfortable in the coal, until the next morning we saw each other, and everybody looked like a miner! And eventually the train moved and we went with it, to where, we didn't know. And we decided that we will stay together, the seven of us: Vern, Kurt, Reinhardt, myself, and the three others from Germany.

The small band of survivors trusted in Louis and in his ability to lead them to safety. With his fluency in four languages, Louis had become the spokesperson for the group. As Louis explained, "Everyone was dependent especially on Kurt and me because we spoke Czech and they only spoke German, and speaking German was a death sentence in those days." At twenty-four years of age, Louis was the oldest of the group, the others ranging in age from Kurt Kohorn, who was twenty, to Vern Drehmel and

2. Central Europe, 1945: Louis Löwy leads young men in a journey across Europe, January to May 1945. Map by Joseph Stoll, Syracuse University Cartographic Laboratory.

Reinhard Frank who were now sixteen. Louis was also the best educated and the most widely traveled, having lived in England and having led his own family in their move from Munich to Prague before the war. More than knowledge or experience, however, Louis understood his preparation for leadership as a state of mind:

> I probably was stronger in mindset than any of us, not physically, but in terms of determination. Once I had that sense of freedom, that sense of abandon, I took what I knew were foolish risks. The Russians were certainly not harmless, but I thought, "What can happen to you after you have survived Auschwitz? Nothing!"

The coal train carried the group deeper into Poland, and as they rode, Louis proposed a plan. They would continue to travel eastward, away from the Western front, and they would make their way to Budapest, to Bucharest, and on to Constanța on the Black Sea.[14] From there, if the war was not yet over, they would try to reach Palestine. They would use the helpful disguise of their British uniforms to assume whatever national identities would assure their safe passage. When they disembarked in a small town in Poland, for example, they became Czech partisans, as Vern recalled:

> When we got to Poland, first of all, we decided not to be Jewish. Thanks to our British uniforms, we became Czech university students who had been imprisoned by the Germans. We traveled as Czech Catholics. That meant the church soup kitchens were open to us! And we received many blessings as Czechs on our way back to Czechoslovakia. Only Louis and Kurt were fluent in Czech. The rest of us had to be quiet. We knew some phrases, enough to get along, but we certainly could not carry on a conversation in Czech.

Reinhard remembered the difficulties of maintaining their false identities:

> Our first stop in Poland was to get some documentation. We went to the Polish Red Cross—I cannot remember in which town. The very first document we got was a slip of paper with some Russian words that said, "Refugee." All of us except Louis and Kurt were German Jews, and we decided—I assume the ideas for this must have come from Louis—that it would be dangerous for us in Poland to have names which are too Germanic. Also you really didn't feel comfortable to be Jews. So in my document, I changed my name from Reinhard to Reiner, and I was a Czech partisan on my way back home.
>
> We were at times billeted with Polish families. We split up. Louis decided who went with whom, and usually it was just overnight. I remember I was with Kurt Kohorn, and Kurt knew exactly how many words in Czech and Polish I had learned. We were put up with a family with children, and we were given something to eat and a bed for the night. Kurt helped the kids with their schoolwork and obviously I couldn't be totally silent, so I would say a few things in bad Czech, and Kurt constantly interrupted me, because he knew I couldn't say anymore. These people constantly looked at Kurt, thinking, "How rude he is!"

The group traveled through Poland by train and by foot, and they accumulated more and more possessions: blankets, tins of food, and even books that they had found. As Vern recalled:

In February 1945, it was so icy and windy that people were falling in the streets. We had all this junk by now. We were schlepping all this stuff. And after several days of traveling we saw a house with a pushcart outside. A pushcart! It was like finding a Rolls Royce! You pile everything on there and pull and shove and it would be hardly any work at all! We approached it with great joy. And out comes this elderly lady with a kerchief around her head and an apron raised to her face, crying, crying, "How can you take that away? We need it to bring in the harvest!"

We just looked at each other. And Louis said we could not take that. We could not do that to her. As I think back, this was wartime. These people had been our enemies. And still, we could not take the pushcart. I attribute this to Louis. He had this sense of fairness, of treating people with respect.

Vagabonds Through Europe

As the war raged on in the west, a "sea of refugees" made their way through Eastern Europe, as Vern remembered:

Eastern Europe was a sea of refugees of all varieties and all kinds. They all had to stay somewhere, so former army barracks or former factories were all occupied by people on the move. We traveled by freight train. All the big transit stations had people going in every direction possible. The trains were rolling to the west full of armaments and troops, and then the empty cars would go east. We would hop those, ever hopeful that they went our way. People always would talk to you, tell you where you could find this, where you could find that, where did people sleep, where did people find food. We never had any money.

We actually were arrested four or five different times! We had papers, but not always the right papers. The Russians were in charge. If they saw something that had a stamp on it, then it was official. Most of the Russian soldiers were illiterate. They couldn't read, but it didn't matter if the paper had a stamp on it. But sometimes misfortune would befall us, and somebody could read, and our papers had nothing to do with what they were looking for! One day we were masquerading as Americans, and one of the Russians said to us that he had a cousin in

Chicago. Did we know his cousin in Chicago? "No," Louis said, "We're not from Chicago. We're from New York!"

Although the group had no money, the farmers were willing to trade bread and cheese for news about the war, particularly good news, as Reinhard recalled:

> Louis had this great idea that people liked to hear good news. So Louis would go to farmers and tell them that if they gave us some bread and milk, we would tell them some good news. He would tell them that in our estimation, the war would be over in the next four weeks. And they would give us bread and cheese, and we would lie in the fields.

Everyone gained weight, growing taller and stronger on farmers' food. As Louis recalled:

> We were roaming around as vagabonds through Eastern Europe. The trains were not going by timetable, but they were just going and going, and we went wherever the trains went. Everything was in flux. We told tall stories to the farmers, and they gave us food. The farmers always had food. We grew up very quickly. I've never looked so good!

Many strangers offered hospitality. In Slovakia, they stayed with the Roma in a gypsy camp. In Debrecen, Hungary, an opera diva invited Louis to her home. In Budapest, Jewish families took them in. As Louis remembered:

> Budapest was totally destroyed but there were Jewish communities, and there we identified ourselves as Jews. From Budapest, we sat on a train that ended in Seghet, and when we arrived, there were Russian soldiers everywhere. We were not unaware of the danger that they could pose for us! But they had only one goal: "To Berlin!" So we told them: "Yes! To Berlin!" And they were very pleased that other antifascists were cheering them on!

Their next stop was Oradea-Mare, on the Romanian border, a city that seemed miraculously untouched by war. As Vern recalled:

> We made it to Oradea-Mare, which was known as the little Paris of the Balkans. We were the first survivors to make it back to this town. The

Socialist party got wind of us. One of the leaders came to see us, and he invited us to the Socialist Club. We entered by a big foyer with a grand piano and a piano player playing Glenn Miller's, "In the Mood." That was my first exposure to American swing. Fantastic! It's hard to imagine what it was like, hearing this upbeat American music on a piano! The guy was great, I thought. They fed us a meal, and gave us an apartment with a maid. And this was the Socialist Club!

The next day we went to find the Socialist Club at lunchtime. We had breakfast in the apartment. Maybe this lady cooked for us, I don't remember. But we were walking back to the apartment, taking in the sights, and we see this patisserie, a big rich store with big windows filled with goodies and whipped cream and butter. We hadn't seen cream or butter in a long time, and here they seemed to have it! We must have some! And there was a glass plate between us and the goodies, and no money in our pockets. We were standing there in utter awe that such things still existed.

And someone came by and recognized us and invited us in. We consumed fifty-six pieces of patisserie! The follow up to that was we became addicted to these goodies. Every day we passed by the store. And then Kurt or some other guy would say, "I smell the arrival of a beneficiary!" We were *Schnorrers* [spongers] par excellence!

Louis felt as though "a dark cloud" passed over the group when, on April 12, they learned that President Roosevelt had died. Seeing the black-draped newspaper photograph, Louis wondered whether the new American president, Harry Truman, would make a separate peace.

It was time, Louis decided, to resume their journey eastward, as far from the war as possible, to Bucharest and then on to the port of Constanţa. If the war had not ended by the time they reached Constanţa, then they would seek passage to Palestine. Travel to Bucharest posed a challenge, however. The only train was reserved for diplomats and military officers.

According to Reinhard, it was Gerhard Steinhagen, the most dashing member of their group, who saved the day by befriending the stationmaster's daughter. As Reinhard recalled:

The train came from somewhere else. Somehow the stationmaster's daughter persuaded her father to arrange for a compartment to be reserved. And when the train came through the station, he put the signal on red for the train to stop. We got in and we were settled in a compartment that had room for eight people on two benches. It was a beautiful train ride over the Carpathian Mountains. And halfway through the trip, some high-ranking Russian military guy—or was he Romanian?—anyhow, some high-ranking officer knocked at our compartment door, and asked whether we would permit him to take the one remaining seat!

The group reached Bucharest on April 28, a Friday night, and Louis was impressed by the prosperity of the city and of the Jewish community that had survived there: "It was a revelation!" Although they were welcomed by Jewish families, the group immediately aroused the suspicion of the British authorities, as Vern explained:

Bucharest was an impressive modern city with wide boulevards, street cars, fairly active commerce, it seemed. On our first day, as we walked about in our British battle dress, a British troop car stopped, and we were invited for coffee at the British legation. Louis with his proper, charming English, said, "Isn't this a laugh? We survive Auschwitz and we get arrested by our British allies!" They corrected us. "We're not arresting you; we're just inviting you for coffee." There was nothing else we could do but to agree to accept their invitation!

They took us to the legation. There was a big staircase and a British officer came down the steps, and he cried, "*Chaverim!*"—that's Hebrew for "comrades." He was from the Jewish Brigade of the British Army! And this officer took us to the commander of the legation, who told us that he was sorry that we had to wear uniforms when we were civilians. Of course, for us to wear a uniform was a boon; it was our ticket for free passage everywhere!

As it turned out, we had been picked up because the legation's basement had been broken into the night before, and uniforms had been stolen. And so they thought maybe we had some connection with that.

The commander wrote out a form to take to the Joint [American Jewish Joint Distribution Committee] to have us issued civilian clothes, but it was *Shabbos* [the Jewish Sabbath] and they were not open. We acquired civilian clothes the following day.

We had brought suitcases with us, actually. They were mostly filled with German literature that we had acquired somewhere along the way—Schiller, Goethe, Heine. So we put our uniforms in the suitcases. Of course, we did not throw away the uniforms, because they might still come in handy.

Louis found the Czech Consulate in Bucharest, and he and Kurt, the two Czech citizens in the group, registered there, giving official notice to the world that they were still alive. When they learned of Hitler's suicide on April 30, Louis and the group still intended to continue on to the port of Constanța:

> But then came the eighth of May, and we heard King George and Truman and Stalin and Churchill on the radio. It was V-E Day [Victory in Europe Day]. It was the liberation. And we said, "Now, we're not going to Palestine. We're going home to Prague!"

Retrieving their British uniforms, the group played *The Captain of Köpenick* once again. As Vern recalled:

> It was V-E Day, so now we would go back to see who among our families and friends had survived. But how do you get from Bucharest to Budapest? By diplomatic train! We went to the train station in Bucharest. We

3. Louis Löwy in British uniform, Bucharest, April 1945. Photographer unknown. Courtesy of Edith Lowy.

4. Reinhard Frank in British uniform, Bucharest, April 1945. Photographer unknown. Courtesy of Edith Lowy.

lined up in two rows of three with Louis ahead. There was an array of windows and steel bars in front of us. And when the ticket agent saw us, Louis gave loud commands that "We are in the British army and we have to get back to Budapest!" So we had our tickets to Budapest charged to the British legation!

We made it to Budapest, and from there, there were no more private cars or anything but the freight trains. So we took our suitcases and hopped on a freight train moving west.

We rode along the Danube River. We had a lot of luggage by now, which we wanted to protect, so one of us would have to stand guard at night while the others slept. It was Kurt's duty this particular time. The train rumbled to a halt along the Danube on a beautiful moonlit night. It could have been something magical.

But instead, it was some Russian soldiers who stopped the train with their Tommy guns. They were looking for goods. They came to our suitcases, and they picked up the two heaviest suitcases we had, but those are the ones with books! They thought it would be liquor or something good. We were unhappy that they took them, but we were glad that that was all they took.

Of course, we had learned much earlier what the Russian soldiers did with books, and we thought that this was wrong. They had this coarse Russian tobacco, and they would go to some houses, take books, rip out the pages, and use them for cigarette paper. We called those cigarettes "hand grenades." That was the only use they had for books.

So eventually we made it to Prague. Louis was very attached to Prague. His eyes filled. He sang a song about "Prague, you are so beautiful!" But none of the people we had hoped for were alive.

Louis, Vern, and Reinhard attributed their surviving Auschwitz to good luck. As Vern liked to say, "I am the luckiest man alive." Louis had prepared to die as a prisoner, but once he had escaped the death march, he found the determination to lead his small group across Europe, from Blechhammer to Budapest, from Budapest to Bucharest, and from Bucharest all the way back to Prague. Louis would later teach "active endurance" as a part of social work:

We endure this world of increasing paradoxes and yet we carry out our daily activities and perform our professional functions. We should, however, not merely endure passively, but also learn to endure actively, to hold out amidst adversity and difficulties, to prevail amidst a sea of troubles, to be a hammer rather than anvil, to bear up under such frustrating contradictions and not to be intimidated by the enormity of the problems and crises. Active endurance means substituting hope for despair, persevering rather than giving up, persisting rather than surrendering in the face of difficult odds, and helping to sustain our clients, our group members, our constituents, and ourselves through mutual support.[15]

The Social Statesman

"RETURNING" WAS THE TITLE of Louis Lowy's first publication after the war. Writing for the inaugural issue of *Deggendorf Center Revue,* the newspaper of Deggendorf Displaced Persons Center, Louis defined "the problem of the Jews" who could never return to their homes:

> The terrific war is over. Hitler's fascism has been defeated. Mankind has been liberated from the yoke of slavery. The idea and the victims of the fight have been justified, but many problems remain for those who were saved. . . . One of the greatest problems is the problem of the Jews.
>
> Nazi rule drove the Jews to the verge of ruin. A small remnant of Jews was saved. Now this small remnant must face earthshaking facts: Not only have we lost families and dear friends who can never be replaced, not only does reflection cause continuous mourning in our hearts, but also our views of the present and future are unclear as never before.[1]

Louis wrote from personal experience. When he reached Prague in May 1945, Louis found that Czech nationalism had overshadowed the tolerant, cosmopolitan culture that he remembered. Prague citizens had expelled ethnic Germans from the city, and with the approval of the Allies, Czechoslovakia was now forcing nearly three million ethnic Germans from the Sudetenland. Ironically, the climate was no less hostile to German-speaking Jews than to the *Volksdeutsche,*[2] and if any of Louis's family or friends had made it back to Prague, he did not find them:

> As soon as we heard the war was over, I wanted to go back to Prague, and the others in the group, where should they go? They followed. Prague was in a state of revolution. Because it was a Czech city, there was Czech nationalism, anthems. I looked for people, and none of

them were left. Prague was a living cemetery to me. I went to the Jüdische Kultusgemeinde (Jewish Community Council) and registered, and I found that everybody that I had known was gone. Vern and I looked at my old apartment, and meanwhile it had been taken over, formerly by Nazis and now by Czech families. I went to the cemetery to visit my great grandfather's grave, and then we said, "What are we going to do? Where shall we go?" And we went back to Terezín. We took the train, and I remember thinking, "it's a sad thing: our only home is Terezín now."

Everybody Was Gone

It was less than a year and seemingly a lifetime ago when Louis had been deported from Terezín, and he hoped against hope to find relatives and friends whom he had left behind: "I looked for my father, and I knew I wouldn't find him. Everybody looked, and we knew it was a fool's errand, but we thought there were still some people there who never were deported from Terezín."

Few prisoners in Terezín, only 17,000 out of 140,000, had survived. Some older German Jews who had been prominent before the war were spared; Eichmann had held them in reserve as possible assets in his propaganda campaigns. In addition, in a reversal of the dreaded "transports to the East," 13,000 prisoners had entered the ghetto in forced death marches and transports from Auschwitz, Ravensbrück, and other concentration camps during the last weeks of the war.[3] They were "walking skeletons," in Ruth Bondy's words, and on May 10, when the Soviet Army liberated Terezín, a typhus epidemic was devastating the population.[4]

Louis and his group were "smuggled in" to the still-quarantined ghetto:

So we went back to Terezín, and thank God, we had decent food by now, Red Cross parcels, and we were installed in houses and barracks. The city was better administered than before the war, but basically not too different, except that there were no Nazis around and the Russians were a very benevolent administration. The Russian commandant, who was Jewish, by the way, was a very nice commander. He was very concerned about what would happen to the Jewish population.

The Soviet commandant, M. A. Kuzmin, feared for the future of the Jews in Terezín, who, like most surviving Jews, had lost not only their families and homes but also their countries.[5] Central European Jews had been stripped of their citizenship by the Nuremberg Laws, and those who visited their hometowns and cities often used the same words as Louis in describing "living cemeteries," where they would never again feel welcome, safe, or secure. Eastern European Jews were met with sometimes violent anti-Semitism when they tried to go home. After forty-two Jews were killed in a pogrom in Kielce, Poland, in July 1946, thousands who had been repatriated in Poland and the Soviet Union fled to the Western-occupied zones of Germany, Austria, and Italy.[6]

The Allied military forces had been planning for the anticipated refugee crisis since 1943, when the US Army coined the term "displaced persons" (or DPs) to categorize those refugees who would be entitled to Allied protection.[7] The American, British, French, and Soviet armies agreed to assume responsibility for the relief and repatriation of displaced persons in the sectors of Germany and Austria that they controlled, and the United Nations Relief and Rehabilitation Administration (UNRRA), the first United Nations agency to come into being, was founded in 1943 to assist the military in providing relief.[8] As Louis explained:

> There were millions of refugees. They were not just Jews. They were Russians, Poles, Hungarians, you name them, from all over Europe. When you were registered as a displaced person, you had an identity, a legal status that was in place of any citizenship that you might have had. You were under the auspices of UNRRA. You were entitled to rations, and you were entitled, above all, to live in the DP camps.

It was SHAEF (Supreme Headquarters Allied Expeditionary Force), under the command of General Dwight D. Eisenhower, that had primary responsibility for the protection of displaced persons in the US-occupied zones of Germany and Austria, including the provision of "transportation, housing, fuel, food, medical care, and security."[9] Presidential envoy Earl G. Harrison credited SHAEF with a "phenomenal performance" in repatriating four million out of six million displaced persons in the three months after V-E Day.[10]

In years of planning for war refugees, however, the Allies had failed to prepare for a displaced Jewish population that was homeless, stateless, and with nowhere to go. Out of 6 million displaced persons in the summer of 1945, only 100,000 were Jews, with an additional 150,000 Polish and Eastern European Jews arriving in Germany and Austria by the end of the year.[11] Jewish refugees continued to flee Eastern Europe even though there were few countries willing to receive them, and the proportion of Jewish displaced persons in UNRRA camps increased from 6 percent in 1945 to 25 percent in 1947.[12]

During the first summer after liberation in 1945, many Jews who had been imprisoned in concentration camps remained in the same camps, now displaced persons camps, behind barbed wire. Jewish army chaplains were among their only visitors, and, appalled by the conditions, they alerted American war correspondents and Jewish American leaders back home.[13] President Harry S. Truman responded to the negative press. On June 22, he appointed Harrison as his special envoy "to inquire into the conditions and needs of those among the displaced persons . . . in the SHAEF area of Germany—with particular reference to the Jewish refugees who may possibly be stateless and non-repatriable."[14]

Harrison was an impeccable choice. Dean of the University of Pennsylvania School of Law and American representative to the Intergovernmental Committee of Refugees, he enjoyed the respect of the US State Department and the wider diplomatic community. After inspecting displaced persons camps in July and August 1945, Harrison issued a report that "threw a bombshell into American government circles at home and American and Allied military circles in Europe."[15] In Harrison's words:

> Generally speaking, three months after V-E day and even longer after the liberation of individual groups, many Jewish displaced persons . . . are living under guard behind barbed-wire fences, in camps of several descriptions (built by the Germans for slave-laborers or for Jews) including some of the most notorious of the concentration camps, amidst crowded, frequently unsanitary and generally grim conditions,

in complete idleness, with no opportunity, except surreptitiously, to communicate with the outside world, waiting, hoping for some word of encouragement and action in their behalf. . . .

At many of the camps and centers, including those where serious starvation cases are, there is a marked and serious lack of needed medical supplies. . . . Many of the Jewish displaced persons, late in July, had no clothing other than their concentration camp garb, a rather hideous striped pajama effect—while others, to their chagrin, were obliged to wear German SS uniforms. It is questionable which clothing they hate the more.[16]

As the "first and plainest need" of Jewish displaced populations, Harrison called for recognizing "the actual status of Jews" as a national group rather than categorizing them by former nationality.[17] Those Jews who had been moved from former concentration camps to different UNRRA facilities were often placed with hostile non-Jewish populations who had sympathized with the Nazis. It was the view of the British, French, and some US military commanders, such as General George Patton, that Jewish displaced persons should be treated as part of their national groups and repatriated accordingly—German Jews returned to Germany, Polish Jews to Poland—notwithstanding their loss of citizenship in those countries or the persecution that they had suffered.[18] Harrison's conclusion was widely quoted in the American press:

As matters now stand, we appear to be treating the Jews as the Nazis treated them except that we do not exterminate them. They are in concentration camps in large numbers under our military guard instead of SS troops. One is led to wonder whether the German people, seeing this, are not supposing that we are following or at least condoning Nazi policy.[19]

President Truman cabled Eisenhower "urging a rapid improvement in the situation," and Eisenhower replied that "all matters in Harrison's report are being remedied with utmost speed consistent with the difficulties of the situation."[20] Eisenhower specified that "persons of Jewish faith . . . who are without nationality or who do not desire to return to their country of origin, except Russians, are being assembled in separate centers" and "teams experienced in care of Jews are being installed" (it was Soviet policy to repatriate all Soviet citizens, including Jews). In addition, military commanders were being directed to requisition adequate accommodation, to remove armed guards from the camps, and to give Jewish displaced persons the freedom to come and go. A Central Tracing Bureau was expediting the search for families, and plans were being made "to have UNRRA assume maximum operating responsibility" for the displaced persons camps by October 1945.[21]

Eisenhower further assured Truman that Jewish displaced persons were being relocated from former concentration camps as soon as they were out of quarantine and well enough to travel. In a directive to his subordinate commanders, Eisenhower concluded: "Everything should be done to encourage displaced persons to understand that they have been freed from tyranny."[22] When Patton refused to abide by these directives, he was reassigned from his command of the Third Army.

The ultimate fate of the Jewish displaced persons, as Eisenhower realized, was beyond military control. It was the politicians of the world who would decide whether to open immigration to Palestine and to the United States, Great Britain, and other countries. The Harrison report particularly urged Great Britain to increase immigration certificates to Palestine.[23] Nonetheless, Eisenhower was determined to improve the performance of the US Army in regard to the treatment of Jewish displaced persons.[24] Reversing an earlier policy decision, he appointed a special advisor on Jewish affairs, choosing the senior Jewish army chaplain in Europe, Rabbi Judah Nadich, for the position.[25] Nadich was followed by a civilian advisor, Judge Simon Hirsch Rifkind, in October 1945. As Nadich remembered: "I was constantly engaged in visiting Jewish survivors in the DP camps . . . learning their situation and what they themselves desired. . . . Eisenhower would, soon afterward, issue orders based on my recommendations. I cannot recall any such recommendation on which he did not act favorably."[26]

It was into this volatile political context that Louis Lowy led a community of Jews from Terezín, which was under Soviet occupation, into the American zone. The Jewish residents of Terezín had formed a committee to plan for dissolution of the ghetto, and Louis presented himself to Rabbi Leo Baeck, the head of the Dissolution Committee, as a volunteer.

According to Reinhard Frank and Vern Drehmel, Louis assumed responsibility for making contact with the Third Army. Louis did not mention this incident in his own oral narrative, and Reinhard and Vern offered somewhat different accounts. As Reinhard Frank remembered, Louis communicated with the US military by means of Radio Prague:

> We decided early on that we had to get out of the Russian zone of influence. We knew that General Patton had advanced as far as Pilsen, and I remember traveling with Louis to Prague. For some reason, I was often the one who was traveling with Louis somewhere. And he went to the transmitter of Radio Prague, and he broadcast an appeal that was supposed to reach General Patton, saying that there were a lot of Jewish people in Terezín who had relatives in the West and who wanted to get out from the Russian zone to the American zone. I cannot remember how he did it. Anyhow, General Patton did send one of his officers to Terezín, and it was then decided—it was under Louis's guidance that this took place—that whoever had relatives in the Western world would be transported out of Terezín to the American zone of occupation.

In Vern's recollection, Louis went to Munich to contact the US Army:

> We were in Russian territory, but most of the survivors in Terezín wanted to go to the West. The US Army was in Bavaria, which was abutting the Czech border. Louis went off and managed to get in touch with the US military authorities, apprising them of the fact there was a pocket of several hundred Jewish survivors who desired to immigrate eventually to the United States and Britain.
>
> Louis was a little guy—dripping wet, I don't think he ever exceeded a hundred pounds—and here's this little guy, and he goes off into the wilderness. He knew where Munich was; he knew what Munich was like, since he had spent a lot of time living there in his early years. Having such a wonderful command of the English language enabled him to establish a sense of authority, the authority of representing the point of view of people. He was purposeful in his behavior, as he always was.

Whatever part Louis had played in summoning assistance, an UNRRA relief team reached Terezín shortly after the quarantine was lifted in June

1945. The UNRRA personnel included American, British, and French civilians, none of whom spoke German, the language of most of the Jewish population. As Louis recalled:

> The UNRRA people were in uniform, olive drab, like a military uniform without the buttons. The Allies were organizing for people to get back to their home communities, and UNRRA was setting up displaced persons camps in the American and British occupied zones, for example in Berlin. And I said, "Look, I am ready to work. I speak German, Czech, English, and French." And they said, "Yes, we need somebody who can help." So Kurt [Kohorn], Vern, and I volunteered. We interviewed about five hundred people who didn't have a place to go. And then we volunteered to be leaders of the transports to the mysterious displaced persons camp.

Vern remembered the journey to the American zone as a "first ride into freedom":

> We ended up with a whole series of trucks, driven by UNRRA personnel, which came down to Terezín and drove us into the American zone of occupation. This was a huge leap into freedom because it was extremely difficult to negotiate with the Russian authorities. They did not live by a series of laws. It came down to individual decisions: well, the captain said this, or the commandant said that. It was capricious. So Louis arranged that we move into the American zone, and hundreds of people clamored onto these trucks on our first ride into freedom. The US was the land of the free.

As they drove through the Bavarian forest, Louis observed his fellow passengers:

> UNRRA organized trucks, which were driven by the British, and so we rode in British trucks down the beautiful landscape. As we drove, we saw mostly GIs and the defeated German population. They looked hungry. And it was interesting: none of us had any desire to harm them or to hurt them or to yell at them. Nobody did. Nobody! We felt a satisfaction that they were now defeated, but nobody showed any visible signs of

revenge. Besides, I don't think anybody was that interested. We wanted to get out of this and start a new life.

At last, the convoy reached Winzer, where a camp had been established in an old German barracks. Louis recalled:

> When we reached Winzer, we could see that there was some food ready, but the camp was not well prepared. The camp was run by the French, a French colonel. He was an anti-Semite, and I do not use that term lightly! He would call people, "Jew," instead of by name. "You, Jew!" he would call me, "*Assemblez les Juifs!*" [Assemble the Jews!] And I would say, "I don't understand, '*Assemblez les Juifs*.'" He saw that I wasn't a coward. You needed to show some daring. After all, who was this colonel to me after the Nazis?

As was still common in the summer of 1945, the Jews from Terezín were placed in a camp where most of the residents were non-Jews. Eventually, the predominant population in Camp Winzer would be Ukrainians who had been forced laborers for the Nazis.[27] The new arrivals from Terezín were troubled not only by physical hardships in the camp, but also by the mutual distrust of the Jewish and non-Jewish populations. As Vern remembered:

> We ended up in an UNRRA displaced persons camp in Winzer with a primarily Eastern European, non-Jewish population. There were Poles, Russians, Czechs, Serbs, Ukrainians—people who were not well-disposed to the Jews. They were thinking that any Jew who had survived was one who slipped away and should have been dead had the Germans been more efficient! We felt very acutely uncomfortable there.
>
> I can't tell you how many days we spent there, but they were not many, thanks to negotiations carried on by Louis. Louis was able to get in contact with a rabbi who was attached to Eisenhower's staff, some very well-connected rabbi [possibly Rabbi Judah Nadich], who was actually responsible for getting us out of that predicament to our own site at Deggendorf, to which we were transferred.

Louis's leadership in Winzer was later commended in a tribute in the *Deggendorf Center Revue:*

Beginning with the time of our arrival in Winzer and Deggendorf, you already demonstrated your ability as our "foreign minister," . . . and it was your achievement, that with the summoning of the MMLA Team [French Mission Militaire Liaison Administrative Welfare Team] and the arrival of UNRRA, that tolerable living and residential conditions were created.[28]

After a week or two in Camp Winzer, Louis welcomed the opportunity to move to Deggendorf, where a displaced persons camp was being established specifically for Jews. As Louis recalled:

A short time later, there was an internal reorganization of UNRRA. The Americans and the British took over the leadership of UNRRA, and the Americans said, "There will be a transport to Deggendorf." We always shivered when we heard the word "transport," but I said, "These are not Nazi transports anymore; these are American and British transports. These are our friends." The Americans showed us some maps, and I saw that Deggendorf was on the Danube about one hundred kilometers north of Munich. That already was reassuring to me because the Danube River led somewhere.

Louis described the town of Deggendorf as "a small garrison town with a colorful medieval history," but it was a history best known for the persecution of Jews. A woodcut in the Nuremberg Chronicle famously depicts "The Burning of the Jews of Deggendorf during the Black Death, 1348–1350," when townspeople blamed Jews for causing the plague.[29] Under the Nazi regime, the Deggendorf barracks had housed both a military school for the *Unteroffiziere* (non-commissioned officers) of the Wehrmacht and a concentration camp.[30]

To the Jews from Camp Winzer, however, the Deggendorf barracks, now requisitioned by UNRRA, were a welcome sight. Reinhard remembered "big, solid concrete brick buildings in a park-like setting. We even had a swimming pool there! We shared rooms. There wasn't enough space for all of us." As Louis recalled:

We were the first five hundred to arrive, all survivors from Terezín, and we went in and we took over the old barracks, and those barracks were convenient. The Danube River was nearby. There was no rail track to get around; travel was all done by truck, American and British trucks. Then the first UNRRA director came, an American named Carl Atkin. He was Jewish. He said, "Who's in charge here?"

I said, "I am. I led the transport down from Winzer."

He said, "*Du bis a Yid? Gey gezunt!*" [In Yiddish: "Are you Jewish? Go in good health!"]. And he embraced me.

Carl Atkin later told me that he was Jewish, and that he came from Hollywood, California. He had been in the shoe business. When he got out of the army he volunteered for UNRRA. He spoke no German, and of course that was a big disadvantage. By the way, I found out that the United States Army was totally at the mercy of German interpreters, while the Russian officers spoke German probably as fluently as anybody can learn it. The Americans had to rely on the Germans. They were babes in the woods!

So Carl Atkin was pleased that I spoke German. I could communicate. And he said, "Look, Louis, we have to set up this whole thing. You will be the *macher*" [big shot].

I said, "What does that mean?"

"You will be in charge of the camp. You know these people; you know their language, their customs, their idiosyncrasies. I give you all the authority short of the ultimate authority for security of the camp, all the support you need within the limits of UNRRA regulations and Army regulations."

And I said, "I'll see what I can do." And so I got to set up the camp! It was a self-administration: "Let these people run their own show." I had three UNRRA people in the welfare office: two Americans, a secretary and an assistant bookkeeper, and one social welfare officer, Miss Powers, who was British.

And that's where I got my experience in community organization. The UNRRA provided food, and they put beds into the barracks according to army style. But there was an empty existence basically. What would people do all day? There were five hundred people of all ages. And then UNRRA brought in three hundred more people from Terezín.

The Jews in the Deggendorf Center felt a kinship based on their common history in Terezín, as Vern recalled:

We had the experience of Terezín in common. An additional experience was that many people had returned to Terezín in the same manner as we had after the war to see who were left of those we loved. Terezín had been a natural place to go back to. It was a place where we were still, to some extent, individuals, human beings who had escaped from the terror mills. There were eight hundred people; that would be the population that Louis moved to the promised land of Deggendorf.

In August 1945, a new population arrived in the Deggendorf Center: three hundred Polish Jews with a different language, culture, and historical experience from that of the Jews from Terezín. As Carl Atkin had predicted, Louis drew upon his knowledge of people, "their language, their customs, and their idiosyncrasies" to help the newcomers feel at home:

There was a transport of Polish Jews. They had gone back to Poland, the pogroms in Poland, and when they left again, they came to Deggendorf and they were accommodated in the camp. And for many people, it was

5. Vern Drehmel and Louis Löwy, Deggendorf Displaced Persons Center, ca. 1945. Photographer unknown. Courtesy of Edith Lowy.

a first relationship between the Central European Jews and the Eastern European Jews. There hadn't always been a harmonious relationship in the past, but I was able to bridge a great deal. There were still hardened positions, but many of the Eastern European Jews somehow trusted me. I spoke a little Yiddish, not fluently, but much more than the German group, who thought it was beneath their dignity to speak Yiddish.

I was young, and they said, "You're so young to be the leader!" I remember the representative of the Eastern European community [possibly Szymon Gutman], and he said, "You're a good Yid. You're a good Yid despite the fact that you come from the *Jeckes!*" [literally, "jackets," slang for German Jews]. And there was one Schlomo Sztejndel who was a Zionist. He had been to Palestine and had organized there, and I said, "Go ahead! We're free to organize now."

It was interesting, when we had weddings, the representative of the Eastern European community would bring a fish, a carp, and that was a rarity in those days. It was imported. It was a traditional gift at weddings in Eastern Europe.

Our Will to Live Has Made Us Strong

When Rabbi Judah Nadich, Eisenhower's advisor on Jewish affairs, visited the Deggendorf Center in August 1945, he found a Jewish community that was demographically unique.[31] After briefly accommodating 300 Yugoslavian former prisoners of war, the Deggendorf Center by then had an entirely Jewish population, including the 800 German or German-speaking Jews who had been liberated from Terezín and the 300 Yiddish-speaking Jews who had fled from Poland. In contrast, the Jewish displaced populations of other UNRRA camps were predominantly Polish and Eastern European.[32] The proportion of Eastern European to Central European Jews in Deggendorf would eventually grow, however. The roster of the Deggendorf Center for January 1, 1946, listed 1,305 residents, an increase of approximately 200 Eastern Europeans from the time of Nadich's August visit.[33]

In other camps that Nadich had visited, most Jews hoped to immigrate to Palestine. In the Deggendorf Center, however, the United States was the more popular destination. Of those who expressed a preference,

209 chose the United States; 177 chose Palestine; 117, England; 82, Switzerland; 21, various South American countries; 18, Australia; 14, Sweden, and "the rest, scattered."[34]

Most surprising of all, the Jewish population in Deggendorf was disproportionately and even miraculously old, with an average age of fifty years. Eichmann had spared the lives of some internationally renowned older prisoners in Terezín, and as a result, more than 30 percent of the 1,100 Jews in the Deggendorf Center, 350 people, were aged sixty or above. In stark contrast, an UNRRA census of all Jewish displaced persons in Europe found that only 3.6 percent of women and 4.8 percent of men were older than forty-five years.[35]

Louis's lifelong interest in gerontology and, particularly, in the interdependence of generations may have begun with his leadership of the Deggendorf Center. Having lost his own parents, the twenty-five-year-old Louis sought advisors from among his parents' generation, an opportunity that he did not take for granted. He looked to his elders for administrative talent, knowledge, and experience even as they entrusted their safety and their futures to his care:[36]

So I said, "Who are these people?" and I looked through the list, and I got together with a number of people who had various skills. Some of them were in their forties and fifties. In their lives before the Nazis, they were people of skill in administration, in business, in the professions, in health. Some were once ministers in Berlin. I tapped people who knew what to do.

Erna Sonnenberger [aged 53] had been the executive secretary to Konrad Adenauer, the mayor of Cologne [Adenauer would later become the first chancellor of the Federal Republic of Germany]. She had administered the city for him. She was a real savvy administrator. And she said, "Well, you have to set up departments." So we set up a chart with departments for work, for housing, for food, for education, for culture. We set up a court system. There were lawyers with us who had survived. Heinrich Liebrecht [aged 48], who was half-Jewish, was a lawyer who spoke German and English. He said, "I'd be glad to help you." Adolf Blau [aged 51] had been a civil servant in Vienna. He was an Orthodox Jew.

I put Louis Jakobowitz [aged 48] in charge of the Emigration Department. I still remember him. He had been in charge of the forced emigration of Jews from Berlin under the Nazis. He had survived in Terezín. I asked him, "Would you mind?" And he said, "Oh, I would be delighted!" All these people put their skills at my disposal.

Some of Louis's advisors were reluctant to deal directly with uniformed UNRRA or military personnel. They remembered their experiences in Terezín, which they had originally planned as a self-administered Jewish city under Nazi control—ultimately, of course, disastrous Nazi control. Louis, however, was far from being intimidated by people in uniform. He had spent the last months of the war impersonating people in uniform! His challenge in mediating with Carl Atkin and other UNRRA staff was in adapting to the informal American style: "I mediated with Carl Atkin, and very soon he started to use first names: 'You call me Carl, and I'll call you Louis.' I found it very difficult in the beginning!"

For all their suffering in Terezín, Louis and his advisors had gained the invaluable experience of building a city from its very beginning—Louis had reached Terezín before the cooking pots did—and in so far as the ghetto population had organized its own social, educational, and cultural life, Terezín offered a model for *Jüdische Selbstverwaltung* (Jewish self-government) in the Deggendorf Center. As Louis explained:

I was the head, you might say, the mayor of the Deggendorf Center, and there was no competition for leadership. There were others who knew much more than I did, but they didn't come forth. They were too old, or they didn't speak English, or they were tired out, worn out by the whole thing. They were still squeamish about people in uniform; even when it was a friend in a uniform, they were afraid of authority. So they were glad that a youngster—literally, a youngster!—with energy and drive was putting things together. But they were willing to help, and we put our heads together every day. I was working fifteen, sixteen hours a day.

I knew people, and I brought them in, and I said, "You be in charge of this; you be in charge of that." There was a cook from Terezín who survived, and I put him in charge of the kitchen. He was a Czech and he cooked reasonably decent food. The old people were in pretty bad shape; many of them were sick; they couldn't move around, so I set up a separate home for the aged, a special wing of the barracks where the older people could live, such as we had had in Terezín, and I put up a special kitchen for the older people. I arranged with Atkin for the older people to have extra food. Those experiences were my first brush with gerontology.

There were people who could give lectures, people who could give recitals, theatrical performances. So I went back to that. I followed some of the patterns that were developed in Terezín. I set up a kindergarten. I negotiated with German schoolteachers in the town for a school. I said, "I want our young people to go to school." We had twenty, maybe twenty-five young people, and the German teachers set up courses. They were glad that we trusted them; they felt this would be in their favor if there were ever charges against them for sympathizing with the Nazis.

The development of Jewish self-government in the Deggendorf Center and in other Jewish displaced persons camps was part of a larger political and cultural movement in which surviving European Jews were organizing to represent themselves to the Allied authorities and to the outside world. On July 1, 1945, shortly after his arrival in Deggendorf, Louis traveled to the nearby Feldafing camp, where he met with Jewish leaders of forty other displaced persons camps in Bavaria. The inaugural meeting of what would become the Central Committee of Liberated Jews in the United States Occupied Zone of Germany had been planned by the head of the displaced persons camp at St. Ottilien hospital, Zalman Grinberg, whose son Louis had taught in Terezín, and by Rabbi Abraham J. Klausner, a US Army chaplain.[37] Louis traveled to St. Ottilien for a second larger meeting of ninety-four Jewish leaders a few weeks later, and subcommittees began meeting in Deggendorf and other camps.[38] During the next year, the Central Committee of Liberated Jews established headquarters in Munich, and convened a congress that elected leaders Zalman Grinberg and Samuel Gringauz, and in September 1946 gained the recognition of SHAEF as "the legal and democratic representation of the liberated Jews in the American zone."[39]

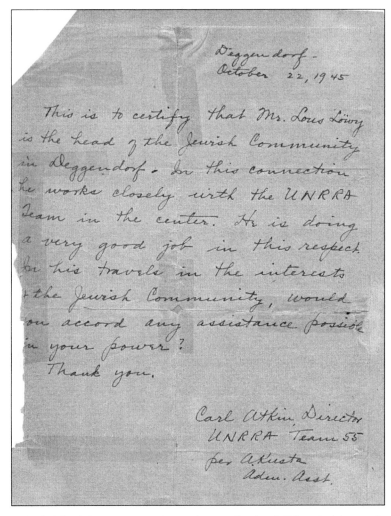

6. Carl Atkin's letter requesting assistance for Louis Löwy in his travels "in the interests of the Jewish community," October 22, 1945. Courtesy of Edith Lowy.

Louis's own hopes for the future were sustained by his participation in the larger Jewish community. As Louis later reflected in the *Deggendorf Center Revue:*

The problems that had to be met and the expectations under which we came were so different from the reality that awaited us. Only after information from Munich, when we made connection to the world, did we learn that we weren't alone in a foreign country, that we were only part of a larger Jewish community and that we weren't the only liberated Jews. This recognition gave us courage, hope, and strength, and with this basis we could overcome what seemed impossible. It began a time of struggle in Deggendorf.[40]

What Kind of Liberators Are These?

During the "time of struggle" that was the summer of 1945, the Third Army issued instructions that fundamentally threatened the emerging Jewish community in the Deggendorf Center. Carl Atkin received orders to prepare for the arrival of five hundred additional displaced persons in Deggendorf. The new arrivals would not be Jews from Poland, as in the last transport, but *Volksdeutsche* from Czechoslovakia.

The term *Volksdeutsche,* as used by the Nazis, referred not only to ethnicity, language, and cultural heritage, but also to the political affiliation of Germans in Nazi-occupied countries. Ethnic Germans who registered as *Volksdeutsche* were rewarded with privileges that included generous rations and property that had been confiscated from Jews.[41] Louis was appalled by the ignorance behind the American plan:

The UNRRA director, Carl Atkin, called me into his office, and he said, "Louis, I have to talk to you. I just got orders from the American Army that five hundred additional people will be coming into the camp."

I said, "But we are at capacity. There is no more room. Who are these people?"

And he said, "They're the *Volksdeutsche.*" These were the exiled Nazis from Czechoslovakia. And I said, "They want to bring those in here? With a thousand Jews? They don't know what they're doing!"

He said, "Being Jewish, I can understand, but these are the orders from General Patton!"

I said, "Look, Carl, there's going to be unrest! I don't think they can arrive here safely with these other people." Not that I was so concerned about the *Volksdeutsche,* but I was concerned about inciting riots. "So far, the Jewish population has behaved. You would expect that after what they had been through they would go out and kill the German population next door. But they have done absolutely nothing in revenge. But if these *Volksdeutsche* should come in, then I predict revenge."

Then Atkin sent me to Munich. He said, "Why don't you go to Munich? I cannot do this. It's better if you go."

So I went to the Third Army headquarters. I was running literally alongside a truck to catch a ride because there were no trains to Munich. And I went to the headquarters of the Third Army, which was Patton's Army, and I spoke and I yelled.

They said, "It was a miracle that *you* were liberated. And now these *Volksdeutsche* are refugees. They are in the same boat as you are!"

And that's when I began to doubt the sanity of American policy making. I thought, "My God! What kind of liberators are these? What do they understand?" I was very angry at the Americans because I thought they were naïve.

In his determination to stand up to the military authorities, Louis began to realize his responsibilities for "leadership, adamant leadership" of the Deggendorf Center. With support from leaders of the Central Committee of Liberated Jews, possibly Zalman Grinberg and Abraham Klausner, the US Army chaplain, and with help from Rabbi Judah Nadich, Eisenhower's special advisor on Jewish affairs, Louis advocated for protecting the status of the Deggendorf Center as a "special center for Jews," a position consistent with Eisenhower's new policy on Jewish displaced persons. In the end, the *Volksdeutsche* were sent to a different camp.

Louis's next encounter with the US Army came in the person of General Eisenhower himself. Louis would treasure his memory of meeting Eisenhower, who was "more like a friendly father talking than the supreme Allied commander."

In the summer of 1945, when the Deggendorf Center faced acute shortages of food and other necessities, UNRRA was entirely dependent upon the US military for provisions. Private philanthropies, such as the American Jewish Joint Distribution Committee, did not yet have access to the displaced persons camps in Bavaria, and surplus Red Cross parcels, originally intended for prisoners of war, were stockpiled in warehouses beyond UNRRA's reach. When Rabbi Nadich toured Jewish displaced persons camps on behalf of General Eisenhower, he found that the Deggendorf Center, like other camps, was in dire need of food, medical supplies, coal, clothing, shoes, and materials for educational, cultural, and vocational pursuits.[42]

It was an accident of scheduling that Nadich was accompanied on his tour of the Deggendorf Center by Byron Price, who was on special assignment for President Truman.[43] Price would soon become the assistant secretary general to the United Nations. Price planned to hand-deliver to Truman copies of Nadich's reports, and it may have been the interest of Price—and therefore of President Truman—that explains how the relatively small Deggendorf Center came to the attention of General Eisenhower. At any rate, when Eisenhower planned to inspect five Jewish displaced persons camps on September 17, 1945, the Deggendorf Center was included on the itinerary.[44] As Louis recalled:

I said to Atkin, "The food supply is very meager. These people are hungry! We need Red Cross supplies." And he said, "Well, there's nothing I can do about it, but I understand that Eisenhower is going on an inspection tour of these camps because it has come to his attention through Rabbi Nadich that there are problems."

Eisenhower was still the supreme commander. And sure enough, it was announced that Eisenhower would do an inspection of Deggendorf. On what day? On Yom Kippur, 1945! Eisenhower is coming on Yom Kippur! Can you imagine? [Yom Kippur is the Day of Atonement, a holiest day of the Jewish Year].

So I went to the camp, and they said, "But we will be having [religious] services. The Orthodox Jews will be in *shul* [synagogue] all day."

And I said, "We'll have services, but we'll prepare for the visit." And I must say, I was overawed by the very thought! Whatever should we do? I had the idea to have a little girl give flowers. She would come and present flowers to Eisenhower.

And sure enough, on Yom Kippur, a big entourage arrived. I'll never forget it. Eisenhower came, and Byron Price and General McNarny and Judge Rifkind. He would become the civilian advisor on Jewish affairs.

All these people came. There must have been forty or fifty army people around. Oh my gosh! It was a big, big event!

And then Eisenhower gets out of the jeep, and here comes Eisenhower, and he takes off his hat! Imagine that! After what we were used to, he takes off his hat! And we shook hands. He gave a typical Eisenhower grin, and "Hello! How do you do?"

I said, "I'm charged by UNRRA to administer the camp."

And he said, "Nice meeting you!" And he was like a friendly father talking, not like the supreme Allied commander! The little girl came and gave him flowers. Some people took pictures. And I was flabbergasted. And they said, "Let's go to the office," and we went to the office that I had. I had a big office in the barracks.

The UNRRA director, Carl Atkin, was there, and everybody saluted. We introduced people, and they introduced Byron Price and Judge Rifkind, and so on, but I didn't give a damn who the other people were.

Then Eisenhower sat himself on the edge of the table. I will never forget the moment. And he said, "Now, will you tell me what you people need?" Just like that! He said, "I'm on inspection tour and I want to straighten out the situation of horror. I was in Bergen-Belsen, and I've seen what went on, and it was very moving, very moving. What do you people need?"

I said, "Well, the first thing we needed was freedom!"

And he said, "Never mind. What do you need?"

And Rifkind yells, "Tell him what you need!"

I understood, and I had prepared, I must say, so I said, "Well, sir, here is a list. We need food; some people need kosher food. We need more beds; we need more hospital equipment; we need more children's equipment; we need clothes." I gave him a whole laundry list, and he had his staff writing and writing and writing and writing. And then he said, "It's done!"

And he wanted to look around, and we took him up to the synagogue where they were still *davening* [praying], and he put on his hat [it is customary to cover one's head in synagogue]. I was very, very impressed to have Eisenhower there, more impressed by Eisenhower than by any soldier I have met in my life, and I could see why he could evoke the image that he did.

They were there for an hour and a half, maybe two hours, and then they departed. And Eisenhower said, "All the best, and I hope all of you come to the USA!"

Well, within two days, it was like an invasion. The place was jumping with goods that arrived: beds, hospital equipment, penicillin that had just been discovered. Doctors got supplies. A hospital was built. Schoolbooks came, magazines came. A movie projector, films, and radios came. Boxing gloves, soccer balls, volleyballs, footballs, you name it! And the Red Cross parcels arrived. The daily diet was to be four thousand calories a day! You know what that is? We need about two

7. General Dwight D. Eisenhower, in the company of General McNarny and Carl Atkin, visits a kindergarten in either the Deggendorf or Neu Freimann displaced persons camp, September 1945. Photographer unknown. Photograph #38131. By permission of USHMM.

thousand calories. So many people began to call it Thickendorf, no longer Deggendorf, but Thickendorf, because everyone was gaining weight.
It was unbelievable! And Atkin said, "I told you what the supreme commander can do!" So then after that things went on, and life in Deggendorf was good, by and large.

The relationship between the Jewish community and its American liberators would never be an easy one, and Louis persevered through "contin-
ual bouts and battles" to build a working alliance that was based in mutual
cooperation and trust. As he later reflected in the *Deggendorf Center Revue:*

> Today many things seem self-evident which only weeks ago were objects
> of heavy contention. They had to be battled step by step. Months ago
> attitudes against us were very skeptical, even hostile. We were regarded
> as something uncomfortable, even destructive. This was due in the first
> place to the need for a foundation of confidence in the American author-
> ities as well as the UNRRA. But from opposition developed a shared
> basis of cooperation. Continual bouts and battles were required in order
> for confidence to grow into friendship and from there to develop into a
> working alliance which would be able to tackle our countless problems
> and, in some measure, to solve them.[45]

A Democratic Self-Government

A milestone in the development of the Deggendorf Center was the first
election of the Jewish Committee on October 15, 1945.[46] Although Carl
Atkin, the UNRRA director of the Deggendorf Center, had charged Louis
with establishing a Jewish self-government, the time had come, Louis
believed, for residents to choose their own leaders. The fundamental purpose of self-government was the restoration of democracy and the rule of
law, and for those who had been imprisoned in the Terezín ghetto, where
Jewish administrators had been appointed by the Nazis, an election would
affirm the freedom and self-determination of the Jewish community.

In planning the first election in the Deggendorf Center, Louis may
have conferred with leaders of the neighboring Landsberg Camp, which
followed a similar election process and timetable.[47] All residents of the
Deggendorf Center who were over the age of eighteen would be eligible to

vote and to nominate candidates for the five-member "Jewish Committee," the executive body of the Jewish self-government. The chairman of the Jewish Committee would be the candidate who received the most votes, and the next four most popular candidates would serve as the additional committee members. Polling stations "arranged for alphabetical groups" would distribute printed lists of the candidates.[48] In addition, a ballot box would be taken into the hospital so that the bedridden could vote.

During the week leading up to the election, twelve candidates entered into a spirited election campaign, and on the Monday morning of election day, residents were already gathered outside the polling stations when they opened at 8:00 A.M. The polls closed at 7:00 P.M., and as the ballot boxes were delivered to the UNRRA director's office, a crowd waited "with great excitement" for results to be posted on the camp bulletin board.[49]

Out of 880 eligible voters, 692 votes were cast, with two ballots found to be invalid. Louis Lowy was elected chairman of the Jewish Committee, with 576 votes. Other members of the Jewish Committee were Szymon Gutman (with 521 votes), Martin Heilbrunn (366 votes), Dr. Heinrich Liebrecht (339 votes), and Adolf Blau (316 votes). The *Deggendorf Center Revue* congratulated the winning candidates: "We are glad to greet these gentlemen, some of whom have demonstrated their ability in the past."[50]

In leading the formation of the Jewish self-government, Louis had demonstrated his abilities as an advocate, a mediator, and a "social statesman" who could realize a vision for social change. He would later describe social statesmanship as "an objective on the continuum of a social work career."[51] In his own long career as social worker, educator, and social statesman, the stakes would never be higher than when he led the Deggendorf Center, where a grieving people needed more than even General Eisenhower could provide. As chairman of the Jewish Committee, Louis would affirm the guiding principle of his life's work: that it is possible "to create conditions for people that allow them to fulfill themselves optimally, find their place in tomorrow's world, and participate constructively and actively in the society as part of a larger world order."[52] It would be through social participation and learning, Louis believed, that the transitory Jewish community would find its place in tomorrow's world.

Louis and Ditta

NEARLY ALL THE RESIDENTS of the Deggendorf Center were hoping to find others who had survived—family, friends, acquaintances from their hometowns—and some would continue hoping and searching for the rest of their lives.[1] Success or failure in finding a loved one depended less on formal tracing services than on gossip, rumor, chance, and luck, and so it was for Louis Lowy and Ditta Jedlinsky, who had promised to find each other after the war.

Louis and Ditta had parted in May 1944, when Ditta and her mother, Hilda Jedlinsky, were deported from Terezín to Auschwitz. The last Louis had heard of Ditta had been during the final months of the war, when he and his small band were making their way toward the Black Sea. As Vern Drehmel remembered, "Early in our travels, Louis had been told by someone that he had carried Ditta's corpse into a burial pit. Many people told stories like that," but often the stories were false. In October 1945, possibly on the day of the election in the Deggendorf Center, Louis learned that Ditta was alive. As Louis recalled:

There was a time when somebody in Deggendorf told me that he just came from Vienna. Of course, there was no traffic, but people did go back and forth. There were only army trucks and lorries, and the Americans took you around, and the British took you around, and the Russians took you around. There was no mail, except for the military government. The military had mail, and you could get something through the army. It was a society without a future.

But there were young guys from Deggendorf who went and tried [to find people] and eventually some reached Vienna. Vienna had already established a Jüdische Kultusgemeinde [Jewish Community Council] where people could meet. And so one of these guys came into the office, and he said, "Look, Louis, I have news for you!"

And I said, "What's the news?"

And he said, "I have just seen Ditta!"

"My God! Where did you see her?" I mean it was almost impossible to hear about anybody. The likelihood was so remote.

And he said, "Well, I met her in Vienna. She was at the Kultusgemeinde with her mother to find out who's around. But they are not living in Vienna. They are living in Slovakia, in Bratislava. There was nothing for them in Vienna anymore, so they wanted to see whether they could get into any of the displaced persons camps."

So I said, "Well, I'll go to Bratislava and see what's what."

Now that was easier said than done. First of all there was no transportation. So I negotiated with UNRRA, and they gave me space on a truck that went back and forth. The American troops were occupying Czechoslovakia. They were in Pilsen, about twenty miles from Prague. But from Pilsen, you had to go into the Russian occupation zone, which I wasn't particularly keen on doing! On top of that, there was another problem. I was a Czech citizen, and all Czech citizens were liable for the draft. The Czech government had immediately reintroduced the draft at the end of the war, and I had no desire to join the Czech Army! So I had to avoid being identified as a Czech, and I had to get myself through the Russian zone, which wasn't allowed, but anyhow, what wouldn't you do for love? And so I did it!

I managed to get to Pilsen, and from Pilsen, I went on a Russian train going with the troops. Again, the language helped a great deal. I got through and ended in Bratislava. I knew the address. I went to see Ditta and her mother, and by golly, they were there! And we stayed a few days, and then I said, "I'll take both of you to Deggendorf to the DP camp."

Finally I made the arrangements. I took others, too, by the way. I organized about twelve or fourteen people to take back with me. We went by train to Pilsen and from Pilsen, I managed to get a lift to the Bavarian border. But there was a curfew. You couldn't go out at night. So we stayed outside. It was in November 1945.

3. Central Europe, 1945: Louis finds Ditta, October to November 1945. Map by Joseph Stoll, Syracuse University Cartographic Laboratory.

And then the next morning, I went over to the American field station. There was an American GI, and he was just lounging around and chewing gum. "How are you?" I said. "I would like to get use of the field telephone." He was so lackadaisical. Thank God, he didn't give a damn! So I called the Americans, and the next day they sent a truck with several people from Deggendorf on it, including Vern.

Everybody was so pleased that they [Ditta and her mother] had come back with us, and they were registered as DPs. And a month later we got married.

As with Louis and Ditta, most adult survivors of the Holocaust would marry other survivors who could understand and empathize with their experiences. "Other survivors are our family," a resident of the Deggendorf Center would explain, and in a survey of survivors in the United States, William B. Helmreich found that 80 percent were married to other survivors.[2]

When Louis and Ditta found each other again, they discovered that during their separation from May 1944 to October 1945, Ditta's experiences had in many respects paralleled Louis's own. They each had suffered Auschwitz, forced labor, and a death march, and they each had come close to death. The most striking similarity in their experiences, however, was that they did not endure them alone. Just as Louis and Vern had depended upon one another for survival, so Ditta and her mother had cared for each other through their ordeal. In Ditta's words:

> With my mother, there was someone I could totally and completely trust. Without that, I would not have survived, and without me, she would not have survived, either. How valiantly she fought through that war! It is only possible in hindsight to see that there was no hope. So we kept on.[3]

Ditta's Story

Edith (Ditta) Jedlinsky was born on February 9, 1926, in Vienna, the only child of Hilda, a dressmaker and couturier, and Joseph, who worked as a sales representative for a leather-goods company. Joseph was deported with the first transport from Vienna, a transport of men only. Ditta remembered the last time she saw her father, when she and her mother accompanied him to the railway station on October 20, 1939. A few months later, they received a letter from Joseph with a photograph enclosed. He had escaped across the Soviet border and was working as a bookkeeper in a grain office. Thanks to his fluency in Russian, which he had learned as a prisoner of war during World War I, Joseph had found a relatively safe job, and Ditta and her mother always wondered whether he had survived the war.[4]

A few months after receiving Joseph's letter, Ditta and her mother were ordered to join him. Women were to assemble for a transport that supposedly would reunite them with their husbands. Suspecting a ruse, Ditta's mother refused to go. By October 1942, however, refusal was not an option, and Ditta, her mother, her aunt, Margarete Melzer, and her maternal grandmother were deported to the Terezín ghetto. Ditta, now fifteen years old, moved into the youth home in L414, where she met Louis Lowy. In May 1944, she and her mother were deported to Auschwitz.

It was fifty years later, in 1994, when Ditta narrated her wartime experiences for the Fortunoff Video Archive for Holocaust Testimonies.[5] Words failed Ditta, as they had failed Louis in his own oral narrative, when she tried to express her memories of Auschwitz. In contrast to her usual vivid storytelling, she gave this part of her testimony flatly, as if reading from a list, with few details and little emotion.

Holocaust scholar Lawrence Langer attributes the loss of fluency in many Holocaust testimonies to the disassociation of traumatic memories that have no place in everyday life: "Witnesses struggle with the impossible task of making their recollections of the camp experience coalesce with the rest of their lives."[6] As Ditta said, "I was there, and I went through it. I know it was me, but it's not the person I am now."

In her Holocaust testimony, Ditta remembered the sealed cattle car that she and her mother rode to Auschwitz, the people dying in the boxcar, the doors opening to "long lines and yelling," the Theresienstadt Family Camp, the hunger, and the *Frauenlager* (women's camp), where their clothes were confiscated, and where Ditta's mother made them underwear out of a dress. At the women's camp, they were selected to carry bricks. "It was a hot summer," as Ditta recalled:

> We were in Auschwitz from May to July 1944. We were there when we heard about D-Day [June 6, 1944]. Somehow we heard of it in Auschwitz. And then in July, we were selected and we were sent in cattle cars to a camp in Stutthof, far away to the north. We were glad to get out of Auschwitz.
>
> After a few weeks in the Stutthof camp, we were sent to work on a farm in Western Prussia. There were four women who were sent there from Stutthof. At night we were locked in a cellar with straw on the ground, but the food was adequate on the farm. There were also English POWs there and Russian peasant women, who were civilian prisoners.
>
> We helped with the potato harvest, cleaned the chicken coops and the pig sties, moved bundles. The farmer paid the camp by the head for workers, but we could not do as much as the Russian peasant women. If we could carry one bundle at a time, they could carry four or five!
>
> Speaking German was an asset—it had never occurred to them [the farmer's family] that Jews could speak German—and my mother let it be known that she was a dressmaker. As the weather turned colder, my mother was sent upstairs to a heated room with a sewing machine. We were fed more carefully, and the English POWs built a bed for us. We

were there on that farm from August to November 1944, when the Russians were approaching, and the farmer sent us back to Stutthof.

Now we were sent out to dig trenches. It sounds antediluvian when you consider that this was the Second World War! We were housed in little round huts, forty women to each hut, with a little stove and a chimney that went up through the roof. We had very little to eat. It was freezing cold, and we had wooden-soled shoes that made it difficult to walk.

Just as the Russians approached, we were shipped back to Stutthof. It was January of 1945, and they were dissolving the camp. There was a selection for either the death march or for the crematorium. By that time, my mother and I were in pretty bad shape, and they wanted us to go to the wrong side. So we snuck back in and they selected us again to go to the wrong side. It wasn't very well organized anymore. Then we looked at each other, and we said, "Well, we have nothing to lose!" Either we would die now or maybe have a chance. And by the time we tried through the third time, a different person was there to make the selection, and that is how I have come to tell you about it.

But that was only the beginning of the horror. We went on the death march. There were many people with us, and we didn't look like men and women anymore. We didn't know where we were going. We were walking through snow on the ground and corpses. The SS made us carry their guns and helmets. One night we stayed overnight in a barn, and when I woke up, my blanket was gone. There was no food, just dehydrated potatoes or beets put in water. We couldn't eat it, and when we found some beets in storage, we ate them raw.

When we couldn't continue anymore, my mother and I made the decision to stay behind, to go to sleep in the snow and die. That's what you do. But they wouldn't let us stay behind. They made us go on. We dragged on to another farm, and this time we refused to go on. We stayed behind there with about fifteen, twenty other people, until the farmer called the authorities and said, "I've got fifteen Jews here!"

So they came with a truck, loaded us up on the truck, and shipped us to another camp, but that was also in dissolution. I don't know whether it was a regular concentration camp or a prisoner of war camp. It was a desolate place, a little tiny place called, in German, Burggraben, not far from Danzig, Dansk, and that is where my mother and I got typhoid. Someone saved us by giving us pills.

Everything was in disarray by now. There was fighting, and suddenly the Germans left. The Germans didn't want to be taken prisoners, so they left. The camp was on its own, and a lot of people walked out and got killed in the crossfire. We stayed put, and a few days later, the Russians came in.

In this place, my mother and I were liberated by the Russians, on March 21, 1945. I call this my renaissance birthday. The day we were liberated by them, we were sitting in an old bunker to escape the shooting. A young Russian soldier spoke English to me. He gave me his bread ration.

The Russians said we had to stay there until they had taken Danzig, and then they shipped us to Danzig, where we were housed in a former villa that had been vandalized and destroyed. It was being used as a hospital. Some of the Russians were wild-looking, and they were raping everybody! We saved ourselves by saying that we had typhoid. It was a strange journey. It was not as simple as I'm telling you.

Through all the camps and all the working places, my mother and I were always together. The first time that there was a threat of our being separated was after we were liberated. The Russians wanted to send my mother to some hospital in Russia because she was very ill. And I said, "Well, I'll go with her."

They said, "Oh no! You can't go."

So I said, "Well, then she isn't going."

I had to fight with the Russians, because if they had taken my mother to that hospital, I would have never ever seen her again.

We were in Danzig until May 8, when the war ended. And then the Russians said, "Go home!" I didn't know how to go home! Nobody knew how to go home. They gave us a little slip of paper in lieu of some identification or passport. And they gave this one piece of paper to my mother and me and six Hungarian girls, one piece of paper, and they sent us packing. And the Hungarian girls, I think they were friends or related, but they were very hysterical.

We spent quite a bit of time trying to get back home from way up there. We were trying to get back home to Vienna. We got on trains, and the trains ran without reservation, without tickets, without payment. They just ran all over Europe to get all the displaced people of Europe back home or as close to home as they could get. There were Greeks here, and Frenchmen there, and Russians there, and Hungarians all over the place, and so the trains went, and some were cattle cars and some were passenger trains. It was not by timetable but by rumor. "The train on that track over there is going south, so let's get on that train." Or "That one is going west."

On one of those trains, I met a Polish engineer who spoke German. And he told me, from here you must come to this town, to this town, to this town, to this town, and when you come to that town, finally you get off the train and take a train west. So that was very helpful because nobody else told me that, and we did that. And when it came to the point of departure, the Hungarian girls went east, and we were going west to Vienna. And the Hungarian girls wanted my little slip of paper. And I threw it at them, and said, "Good riddance!"

My mother was so upset. "Oh, how can you do that?" my mother said, "Now we have nothing!"

But I said, "Really, it's meaningless. They wanted it."

We landed in Bratislava in Slovakia, and I asked people at the train station, "Where are the trains to Vienna?" And they said, "There are no trains because the railroad bridges have all been bombed!" So we decided to stay in Bratislava.

Then one day, I saw a woman on the street wearing my grandmother's dress. My mother had made it for her, and so I knew that it was her dress. My grandmother had been in Terezín, and we thought maybe we could find her. So we went on the train to Prague and then to Terezín to see if she was still there. We went with somebody who spoke Czech because it was dangerous to speak German. And when we were in Terezín, we found out that my grandmother had died a month before we came there. She had been waiting for us since liberation. She had never been deported. We found out that my mother's sister had been deported to Auschwitz and killed. And we found out that Louis had come back, but that he had left already for Deggendorf. So we went back to Bratislava.

I once went to Vienna with my mother on a Russian truck. It was totally illegal. They were not supposed to take civilians. And I went once more to Vienna by myself because I really thought maybe we could live there, but my mother and I found out that we couldn't live there. We just couldn't live there anymore. I'm sure that things would have been provided for us because at that time, everybody wanted to prove they hadn't been Nazis, but we felt it was really impossible for us to take root there again. I went to the place where we lived before, and the woman who took care of the building said, "We were good to you, weren't we?" You know, this whole falseness, we just couldn't take it.

But while we were in Vienna, I went to the Jüdische Kultusgemeinde, and I left word there and we registered there because that's what everybody did. Wherever you went, you registered. Should anybody come back alive, they would see that you had been there, that you are alive. I asked them in Vienna, "How can one get to Deggendorf?" because Louis was there.

They said, "Only by transport."

I said, "I'm not going on any more transports."

"But," they said, "there is somebody here visiting from Deggendorf." And I knew him! I had known that boy in Terezín! His name was Heinz Berger.

And I asked him, "Can you take a note from me to Louis?"

And he said, "Sure!"

So Heinz Berger came back to Deggendorf, and he wanted to talk to Louis. "I have an important message for you!" he said.

But it was the day of the election, and Louis said, "I'm very busy right now. You've got to wait."

So Heinz sat there and waited for hours, and finally Louis came out in the evening. They had just elected him the chairman of the Deggendorf Center. You know, Louis was very democratic. And Louis asked, "So what's the important message?"

And he said, "I saw Ditta in Vienna."

Louis had heard that I was dead. And here was somebody who had seen me alive! So Louis said, "My God! Ditta is alive! Why didn't you tell me?"

"Well, you said you were busy!"

Then I found out that Louis was coming. I don't know how I found out. I don't know how the communication happened. There was no mail service yet in Europe. There was no telephone. It was all by rumor. Even books you read say, "So and so happened to see so and so run into that one and conveyed the message to that one." It's hard today to comprehend this informal communication network.

And when Louis came, I was very nervous. I was at the movies in the afternoon. My mother said, "Louis was here already."

I said, "What does he look like?"

"Oh, he looks very nice. He was all dressed up in a suit and tie."

I had never seen him in a suit and tie, so I was very nervous. Also, I might add, after we were liberated, the Russians had cut off our hair, all the way shaved our hair off, because we had lice. So that was not a good thing!

But I remember, I had said at one time before we were liberated, "If I knew we would survive the war, I would voluntarily have my hair cut off." Because during the war the Nazis did this often, but our hair had not been cut. So the Russians cut off our hair for hygienic reasons. But anyway my hair grew very fast. It was cut off in May and by the end of the year, I had a permanent.

We had to wait a few days before we returned to Deggendorf because my mother was having a coat fixed by a tailor. So we waited a few days,

8. Ditta Jedlinsky in Bratislava, 1945. Photographer unknown. Courtesy of Edith Lowy.

and then we went. Louis had also picked up about twelve or fourteen other people to bring back. And the journey from Bratislava to Deggendorf was quite adventurous because we had to cross two demarcation lines, one from the Russian sector to the American sector and one from Czechoslovakia into Germany, which at that point was in the American zone. For Louis, this was a dangerous thing to do because he was a Czech citizen, and if they had caught him or insisted on it, he would have had to serve in the Czech army.

But we got through these demarcations, got off the train, and by then it was the night of November 1. It was cold. We had stayed

9. Wedding of Ditta Jedlinsky and Louis Löwy, Deggendorf Displaced Persons Center, December 2, 1945. Photographer unknown. Courtesy of Edith Lowy.

overnight in Prague, and when we left to cross the border into Germany, nobody would let us in their houses because they had curfew. So we twelve or fourteen people had to spend the night of November 2 in the woods. And the next morning, Louis called up and asked for a truck from Deggendorf to bring all these people there. That was the journey. And a month later, on December 2, we were married.

The Enchanting Bride

Louis and Ditta were actually married three times: first, by a rabbi in the Deggendorf Center; next, by the German mayor of the town of Deggendorf who was a justice of the peace; and finally, by the American military government. As Ditta explained, "Everybody who changed their status had to go to the American military government, so they had a kind of civil ceremony."

But it was the ceremony in the Deggendorf Center that mattered most to them.[7] Ditta's mother made a wedding gown with a long white slip out of white tulle that someone had found for her. Dr. Liebrecht, one of Louis's associates on the Jewish Committee, gave Ditta a bouquet of orchids that she carried down the aisle. Ditta saved many of her wedding gifts to this day, including a poem in calligraphy from the old-age home. Louis had chosen the date, December 2, in order that Carl Atkin, whose term with UNRRA was ending, could serve as best man, and the wedding reception was combined with Atkin's farewell party, as described in the *Deggendorf Center Revue:*

> On the 2nd of December, the marriage of our first committee chairman, Louis Löwy, to Ditta Jedlinsky took place in the fully packed theater hall in the context of the afternoon worship service. The enchanting bride came down the aisle to the strains of Mendelssohn's "Wedding March," led by her mother and her "aunt" Klara Abrahamsohn [an older woman who was an honorary member of the wedding party]. The train was carried by two little girls and two bridesmaids. After celebratory songs by Frau Aronson-Lind and Herr Luel, the bridegroom entered the *huppah* [wedding canopy], and the rites of betrothal were performed by Rabbi Levi. The marriage witnesses were Herr Carl Atkin and Herr Morris Henshal.

After the ceremony, the couple repaired to an adjoining room to receive the good wishes of their friends and acquaintances. Afterwards, the wedding guests returned to the theater hall, which had been transformed into a dining room, and enjoyed a delightful time.

Frau Aronson-Lind, Herr Kirschberg, Frau Bechmann, along with Herr Berlinski, Herr Henshal, and, last but not least, Louis Löwy himself brought the party to great success by a number of artistic presentations.

The wedding celebration was combined with a leaving party for Herr Atkin.[8]

Among the many speeches and tributes to Carl Atkin, Louis offered a solemn reflection. "Our gaze belongs to the future," he began:

The time which we have to share here must in the end be only a time of preparation, a transitional period to a new life in a new, free world. We should not think, however, that this new life will be a paradise for the young. Alongside all of the optimism that we should always retain, we must also be conscious that others will expect the same from us as we do from the rest of humanity. We may never ask for pity. Pity is dishonorable. We must put the man who is struggling for life into the wider world in order that he may successfully survive in the competitive arena. We will only succeed if we are inwardly taut, physically and psychically fit to go out and engage with relationships in another environment, that is, a new community.

Let us never forget that what the future looks like depends largely on us. Let us learn from the past what can be helpful for us in the future, and apply all our strength and energy to the problems that face us, so that, in the final analysis, our future and our children's future will have been meaningful.[9]

The wedding had more speeches and dignitaries than Ditta would have liked, but Louis was a public figure who never entirely went off duty. Only the discovery that Ditta was alive could have drawn him away from his responsibilities in the Deggendorf Center, and even then, he had combined his search for Ditta with his rescue of twelve to fourteen other displaced persons. As Louis was described by Joseph Königer in the

Deggendorf Center Revue: "We all know that you always place your entire working energy at the disposal of the committee and, thus, the camp, without consideration of your health or your family."[10]

Through forty-six years of marriage, Louis and Ditta were never separated again, and Ditta, perhaps more than anyone, appreciated his lifelong dedication to his work:

> He had this immense knowledge. You can say he was driven or you can say he was dedicated. He was a very dedicated person to his whole profession, to whatever he undertook, he did to the best of his ability, and his ability was outstanding.
>
> I said to him once, toward the end of his life, "You know, you are very fortunate."
>
> "Oh, why?"
>
> "Because," I said, "You are one of the few people who has truly reached his potential."

6

Deggendorf Displaced Persons Center

EVEN BEFORE THE WAR HAD ENDED, those Jews who had survived began to refer to themselves by a biblical name, the *She'erit Hapeletah,* meaning "the surviving remnant" or "the rest who remained." Legal names that had been imposed on the Jewish population, such as "stateless persons" or "non-repatriable Jews" did not begin to express their historical consciousness, their identity as a people, or the unfathomable dimensions of their loss.[1]

Leaders of the *She'erit Hapeletah* felt responsible for the Jewish people, although they understood their responsibilities in different ways. In Jewish displaced persons camps, the *She'erit Hapeletah* was symbolized by the drawing of "a tree stump from which a tiny leafed branch was sprouting," with each leaf representing the revival of Jewish cultural life.[2] The Central Committee of Liberated Jews expected the surviving remnant "to demonstrate to all Jews everywhere their involvement in a common fate": the establishment of a Jewish state in Palestine.[3]

Although Louis Lowy had no quarrel with Zionism, he understood the historical purpose of Judaism from a universal rather than a national point of view. In his article "Returning," for the *Deggendorf Center Revue,* he urged the "small remnant" to join in building the Jewish community in the Deggendorf Center and beyond. The Jews had represented humanitarian ideas for thousands of years, and now they were returning, if not to their families and homes, then to their struggle for "the rights of all the people in the world":

> The history of mankind is a continuous fight for progress and for the creation of humanity, the creation of a human community. All through history, despots have arisen who wanted to delay and hinder the way,

but in the end, even their actions have prepared the way forward. Now we are again facing a break of time. The economic and social structure of the past is broken, and the world is looking for new equivalents. . . .

The Jews have represented the ideas of a real humanity for thousands of years, and our prophets have expressed these thoughts in solemn words. We are at the eve of a new epoch which will fulfill the vision of the prophet Isaiah: "And He shall judge among the nations, and shall rebuke many people. And they shall beat their swords into plowshares. Nation shall not lift up sword against nation. Neither shall they learn war any more." We Jews are involved in this struggle. In this world which again recognizes the commandments of tolerance and human esteem, the Jews again have the obligation to assist in realizing these great ideas.

In the fight for the rights of all the people in the world, in the fight for progress and a new social world order, the Jews have been struggling and suffering. Suffering causes strength. We have learned suffering and have become strong, at least psychologically. Our belief in the victory of justice and our will to live have made us strong. . . .

We are willing to create. We are willing to work. We want to join in the great reconstruction. All we need is a base from where we can enter life again. . . . We want to become human beings again who contribute our shares in work and deeds, who are no longer objects but subjects deciding for ourselves and our fate.

Our small community here is in the midst of a hard struggle in finding the way back to life. The youth, especially, is trying to find the way. It is up to us to prepare our way into the future, conscious of the fact that we are Jews and willing to realize the idea of Judaism. In this way, we can contribute our share in reconstructing a new moral ethic and social world.[4]

The Jewish Self-Government

As chairman of the Jewish Committee of the Deggendorf Center, Louis guided the development of an increasingly complex administration, as illustrated in an organizational chart in the *Deggendorf Center Revue.*[5]

The Home Economics Department met specialized nutritional needs with a main kitchen, a kosher kitchen, a children's kitchen, an infants'

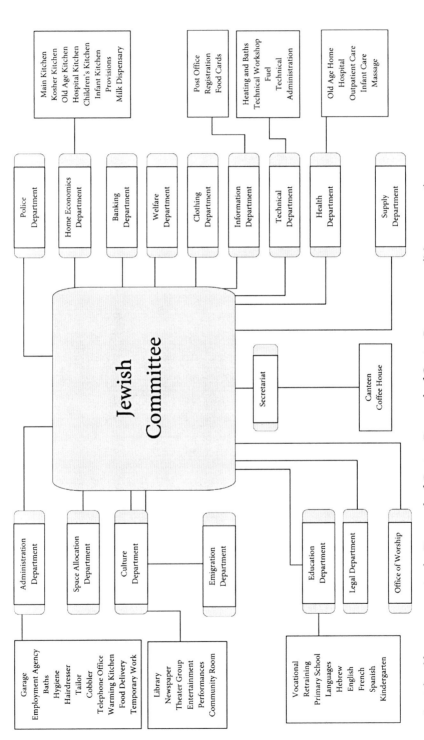

1. Jewish self-government in the Deggendorf Center, *Deggendorf Center Revue*, no. 10 (Mar. 30, 1946): 4.

kitchen, an old-age home kitchen, a hospital kitchen, and a milk dispensary. The Health Department ran the old-age home and a hundred-bed hospital that was staffed by one UNRRA doctor, Dr. Tauber, and seven physicians from the Jewish population.[6] Other health services included outpatient care, infant care, and massage. An employment agency offered a variety of jobs, essentially voluntary positions, with compensation in Deggendorf Dollars. As Louis remembered, "We had a bank, and we printed money for internal use: DP Camp Deggendorf Dollars. I signed those." Louis based the camp currency on US dollars, in consideration of most residents' destination of choice, the United States.

Visitors to the Deggendorf Center were particularly impressed by the Education Department, which served people of all ages, from young children in the kindergarten to adults seeking vocational training or language study.[7] The Culture Department administered a library that eventually held seventeen hundred books, a theater troupe, "entertainment programs," a community room, and two newspapers, initially the German and English language *Deggendorf Center Revue,* and later the Yiddish *Cum Ojfboj.*[8] The Office of Worship managed a synagogue and a *mikvah* (ritual bath). The vibrancy of cultural life was profiled by Kurt Buchenholz in an article for the *Deggendorf Center Revue:*

> During the last years of oppression, our cultural life was abruptly stopped and about to break down completely. Especially for the Jewish youth there was great danger to grow up without any culture. Regarding

10. The Deggendorf Dollar. Courtesy of Edith Lowy.

this fact, we thought it a primary duty to correct things immediately after our liberation. The members of the Culture Department devoted themselves to this task.

First of all, compulsory schooling for children from six to fourteen years was started. Qualified teachers out of our own ranks were doing this job, so that, with assistance of the UNRRA, we now are able to teach the children in a special house, being at our disposal; besides, all the pupils have their meals over there prepared in an extra children's kitchen. Special care had to be taken in the educational development of youngsters from fourteen to twenty years. The problem was solved by arranging special study teams to increase general knowledge.

Parallel to school instruction, courses in foreign languages were set up, e. g. English, French, Spanish, and Iwrith [modern Hebrew] for beginners as well as for advanced. People more advanced in English are given a chance to deepen their knowledge in an English club, much frequented and highly appreciated by a great number of camp inmates.

Friday and *Shabbos* services running from the beginning of our stay here always found a numerous congregation. Especially on the High Holidays [Rosh Hashanah and Yom Kippur], Orthodox and Liberal services could be celebrated in a dignified way.

Every night, part of our camp inmates are listening to broadcasting news from all parts of the world, enjoying besides musical entertainment such as concerts, operas, and so on by the loudspeaker. Not only by loudspeaker but also from our stage, we arranged all kinds of performances, e. g. concerts, literary evenings, plays, and Varieté [variety shows], and performances of the Zionist organized youth.[9]

Unique to the Deggendorf Center was one of Louis's proudest initiatives, the Emigration Department. As he recalled:

I had the idea to set up an Emigration Department and to register all the people. We asked people whether they had relatives in any other countries or in other UNRRA facilities, and we tried to help them find them. We printed up various files and registered all these people, everybody from A to Z, with name, date of birth, birthplace, last place of residence before deportation. We had this list printed,[10] and we mailed it through

UNRRA channels to the United States, to Britain, to France, to Palestine, and to the Jewish organizations: the HIAS [Hebrew Immigrant Aid Society] and the Joint [American Jewish Joint Distribution Committee]. We had a listing of all the residents of the Deggendorf Center as of January 1, 1946, which was distributed as far into the world as we had contacts. So that people would know that they survived; they are alive.

In addition to helping residents search for families, the Emigration Department assisted them in seeking or preparing documentation that they would need when emigration became possible. Louis created identity papers for people with no other means of documentation, as Reinhard Frank recalled:

I think I had an influence on the fact that Louis decided early on that we had to produce our own documents, homemade documents. The reason was I wanted to go to Switzerland, where my mother was. She was a Swiss citizen but had died, which I didn't know when I had arrived in Deggendorf. The Swiss refused to give me a visa unless this visa could

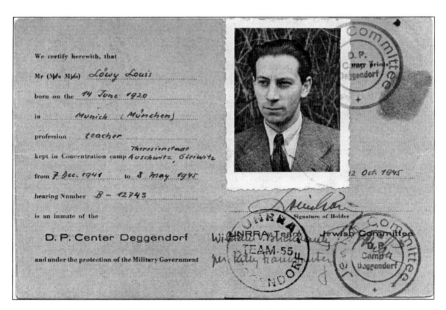

11. Identification card for Louis Löwy, Deggendorf Displaced Persons Center, May 8, 1945. Courtesy of Edith Lowy.

be stamped or attached to an official-looking document. We had zero, nothing. I remember talking with Louis, and I said, "Look, how can we do this?" And very shortly afterwards, I had a document signed by Louis, as director of the camp. We put fingerprints in it; we put photographs in it; we put the number from our arms in it. We used a nice big stamp. And I remember, I went with this thing to Munich to the Swiss Consulate and they said, "Ok, we can attach your visa to it."

I don't know whether other displaced person camps had similar documents or not. But I used this like a passport. This was the only document I had, even when I came to England [from Switzerland], for immigration to England. This was all I had.

Community Spirit

In registering with the Emigration Department, people gained some self-determination in a process that was beyond anyone's control. As Louis remembered, "When we went from Terezín to Winzer and from there to Deggendorf most of us believed that the intermittent stay would last only a few weeks, and in a short time all of us would be with our relatives in other countries."[11] It would, however, be nine months before the first group, approximately two hundred Jews, were able to emigrate from the Deggendorf Center, and many people waited for years.

In the meantime, Louis believed, people would hope for the future by preparing for the future, and Jewish self-government could contribute to the *Gemeinshaftsgeist,* the community spirit, by offering opportunities for social participation and learning. Cultural, educational, and civic pursuits would restore the values and traditions that families had cherished before the war. Taking an English class, reading a newspaper, attending a concert or a play, learning to use dollars with the new camp currency, turning to the new legal system to resolve a dispute, all these activities would give residents a sense of belonging and social purpose, the prerequisites for starting a new life.

The Deggendorf Center did not provide mental health care in the ways that we understand mental health care today, such as through psychotherapy or medications. As Louis explained:

We had survivors in our group who were psychiatrists, and they saw some people privately, but as for mental health, no efforts were made. I knew some people were depressed and in bad shape, and I sometimes raised these questions with the UNRRA welfare workers, and they said, "Well, we have no facilities for that." The physical we could attend to, but not the emotional. I didn't know enough. If I were to look at it today, it would be a different picture. I would have attended greatly to the emotional needs. But for people then, having survived and finding a way to emigrate, being reconnected with family members, that was to them mental health.

In the Deggendorf Center, as in other Jewish displaced persons camps, mental health was addressed through cultural means, and particularly through the revival of educational, religious, and political activities. As described by Holocaust researchers Michael Berenbaum and Abraham Peck: "In each of the DP camps there were theatrical activities, news-papers of diverse sorts, and educational programs at all levels . . . these diverse activities should be seen as a time line to link both the individuals and the group to a common past, logical present, and probable future. Educational and cultural activities played an important part in helping survivors construct their lives."[12]

In addition to reviving culture, Louis was concerned with restoring respect for the rule of law, particularly among the youth. Ever since Terezín, Louis had stood in loco parentis for young people who had never lived under a legal system that they could believe in. More often than not, they had survived the Nazi regime by breaking, evading, and resisting the law.[13] As Vern Drehmel remembered, "We used to have to lie a lot in order to get what we wanted. We could not deal with the people who were in authority openly and honestly."

In order to rehabilitate themselves for "normal life," the Deggendorf Center community needed to realize the possibility of a legal system that was fair and just, and in the Deggendorf Center, as in other displaced persons camps, the Jewish self-government established its own legal system and court of law.[14] As Louis explained in his article "Rehabilitation," in the *Deggendorf Center Revue,* the new law court in the Deggendorf Center would affirm "the absolute value of any human being":

12. *Deggendorf Center Revue*, no. 2 (mid-Nov. 1945): 1. Courtesy of Edith Lowy.

Our community here faces several problems which are more or less difficult to solve. But in spite of that we must never forget the principal problem that exists for us: Our self-rehabilitation. What does rehabilitation mean? . . . It is the reestablishment of the greatest values we possess, our soul, our heart, our humanity, our self-esteem. It is our return to becoming men with self-respect, conscious of the responsibility we are bearing for ourselves and for those who follow. . . .

The first step to regaining our self-respect is to acknowledge the absolute value of any human being. In the days of slavery gone by we ourselves had been victims to the policy of intolerance, of destruction of the human individuality. Man had become worthless. This fact caused our discrimination and the disaster all over the world. When we strive to achieve our rehabilitation as human beings, we must start with us and find our way back to ourselves.

The second step is to recognize again the principles of civilized life. Civilization is a standard of living which the citizen has approved. The human being is a social creature that is bound to live in contact with fellow-men. The simplest structure of a common way of living is a family; the more complicated structure is a community or state. Life within a community is normal. But life in a community obliges us to consider two points: The individual mode of living and the contact with the other fellow-men of the community.

Our community here is somewhat different from other communities in the so-called normal life. But one fact it has in common with all other communities: Here are human beings with their faults and imperfections as well as everywhere. But they are men and because of this fact, everybody deserves to be respected in the same way and when he makes a mistake, when he is on a wrong path, he is to be shown the right way. He is to be taken back to the path of righteousness, for his own sake and for the sake of the whole community. Everybody must realize that he is not only responsible for his actions towards himself, but also towards the others. . . .

And this is the very sense of our new established law court. . . . The first moment when we acknowledge that law and discipline are prevailing . . . then we comprehend the sense of a community and its value and need not be afraid of the future; then a great advance towards rehabilitation has been made.[15]

As it turned out, there was little or no crime in the Deggendorf Center, with the inevitable exception of trading in the *Schwarzmarkt* (black market). Throughout the American zone, displaced persons, occupying troops, and the general German population engaged in the illegal bartering that was a practical, if risky, response to hyperinflation and shortages of food, clothing, and other goods. Although residents of the Deggendorf Center had no "regular money"—Deggendorf Dollars were valueless outside the camp—they did have cigarettes, a currency more valuable than cash, as Louis recalled:

No money was exchanged, no regular money, but some people did all right in the black market. What you needed were goods: cigarettes, cigarettes, cigarettes! The biggest black-market currency was cigarettes, and each of the Red Cross packages had these big cartons of two hundred cigarettes, so they were worth a fortune! If you wanted to get money, you traded this with the German population or with the Hungarians who were living outside the camp. They paid a fortune for cigarettes. And a number of people [in the Deggendorf Center] were from Germany originally, and they still had contacts with the population from the former places they had come from—from Berlin, from Hamburg. So they contacted them when they had something to trade.

But the black market was also one of the biggest administrative headaches! Once some people brought a cow into the camp and slaughtered it in the back and auctioned off the parts to the German population!

Transactions such as these could attract the attention of US Military Police, who were generally suspicious of displaced persons.[16] The US Army typically employed translators from the local German population rather than from the displaced persons camps, and it was not surprising that American MPs favored the well-groomed, orderly German population, with their playful children and attractive women, over the strangely rag-tag Jewish refugees.[17] On the rare occasions when residents of the Deggendorf Center were arrested by the military police, Louis intervened by having their cases transferred from local or military courts to the self-administered law court in the Deggendorf Center.

Always Running

Whether he was mediating between the Jewish population and the military authorities, seeking philanthropic assistance from the American Joint Distribution Committee, or trying to raise community morale, Louis was "always running," as Vern Drehmel observed:

Once he had assumed this huge responsibility for all these people, Louis operated quite on his own. He was really snowed under with responsibilities, working ceaselessly to maintain high camp morale, which depended, of course, to a great extent, upon what would happen tomorrow.

Louis was really always running. He wasn't sitting working with his mind at a slow, leisurely pace. He was always harried. Once Ditta came back into his life, they were married, and he obviously had his own personal needs and obligations in addition to camp administration. It was certainly a full-time job and by full-time I don't mean eight o'clock to five o'clock, I mean full-time, when you may never go to sleep. That also marked the time when he had much less time to spend with old friends, kids. He had always been in charge, and I felt myself accountable to him or protected by him. He was the most important person in my life.

We younger people were now free and able to have time for amusements, to swim in the pool and enjoy the sun, to play soccer. There were dances and entertainment every Friday night. There were shows and musicals and operettas. There was some schooling in the town of Deggendorf with German faculty. We were curious, who were these people who were now our teachers? There wasn't much of a personal relationship; they were somewhat suspect at that time.

At this point, I was sixteen going on seventeen. I worked everyday in the commissary. I worked in food supplies. You had to have honesty in food supplies because food was currency. Later on in Deggendorf, we would get these Red Cross packages, and they had cigarettes, and cigarettes were worth more than any money you could find. So you had to have a fairly reliable group of people in charge of distributing the food. We had contracts with German bakers, stuff that we picked up and delivered. There wasn't really a shortage of food for us. We had plenty to eat, but food also could be used for barter with the German population.

I went to school, not every day, but I learned some English, started some French. I was engaged in that and then working, and then free time on weekends. I maintained relationships with peers. We lived in the same building, a hostel for young folks. Reinhard and I lived in the same place. Girls lived in another part of the building. I'm not quite sure who was in charge of that, but we were pretty well behaved. We listened to American music on the radio. The ballads of those days were so wonderful for learning English, because we learned the lyrics. It was very helpful. Army bands were playing constantly on the radio.

I found Deggendorf to be very fulfilling. I had good friends, a pretty girlfriend, I was working, people approved of me as a member of my community. But then there were the questions we asked: Where do we go from here? How do we get there? As director of the center, Louis's most important job was to maintain and build morale so people would have the sense that they were in motion towards some more ultimate destination.

And then there were all the detailed jobs that Louis had to attend to, for which he had some administrative help. He was corresponding a lot with people regarding immigration, regarding movement down to Italy to get to Palestine, to get there illegally through Italy. He was appealing to authorities in the United States for all of us who wanted to come to the States, and the same with Great Britain. He was dealing with UNRRA and that involved its own administration and bureaucratic requirements. We were purely dependant upon UNRRA's good will for food supplies and meeting any other basic needs, utensils, toiletries, all the stuff people need to get through the days.

The spirit in the center was really very high. I was really very optimistic that I would get to the States, not quite knowing when, but then, I've always been very optimistic by nature. I was optimistic. I realized that those older than I had experiences much more serious than mine. I was fortunate to be as young as I was. I'd been deprived of parental guidance that's true, but for those who had lost homes, spouses, children, they were in greater need of certainty than I was. They were as adults suspended in midair. They had reached a midpoint in their life. They had left one life, and how could they connect to a new life? They were suspended in midair and they had no control. Everything depended upon circumstances which they could not affect in anyway. It was very anxiety-provoking and frustrating. They were counting on good fortune when so much of their history had taught them that there was no such thing. They were more trouble to Louis than I. I knew my future was ahead of me and felt somehow that it would all work out. Living through the Holocaust didn't diminish my optimism.

Louis had to deal with discontented citizens, discontented because they needed certainty which he could not provide. He offered reassurance in the form of events, announcements in bulletin form, weekly reports to the public. Now, today, I am basically a psychotherapist. We have sessions when we listen to people's problems and anxieties. But Louis had to deal with hundreds of people's problems and anxieties on almost a daily basis. He was being harassed, I'm sure, because people always blame whoever

13. Vern Drehmel, Deggendorf Displaced Persons Center, ca. 1946. Photographer unknown. Courtesy of Edith Lowy.

is in charge when things don't go right. It must have been unbelievably straining, but Louis never talked to us about that.

He affected many people with his ideas. People knew they could trust his word. They knew that he would not promise something that he could not deliver. There was never any opposition to him as camp leader. There was never any effort to replace him.

Louis was reelected chairman of the Jewish Committee on February 18, 1946.[18] With the effective establishment of the Jewish self-government, Louis now understood the purpose of his work in the Deggendorf Center similarly to the purpose of social work, as he would later define it: "To deal with problems that people encounter with regard to their social function-ing, and beyond that to enhance human fulfillment and self-realization through active social participation. Social work is one of the social prac-tice mechanisms that intervenes in order to mediate tensions between society's imperatives and a person's needs, wants and expectations."[19]

Louis used his column in the *Deggendorf Center Revue* as a means for carrying out these goals. Part sermon and part political theory, his articles placed day-to-day problems in a larger context that reminded readers of their responsibilities to themselves, to the Deggendorf Center community, and to a greater social purpose: their preparation for the future. As Louis warned in "Kommende Sorgen" (Coming worries):

> We are so caught up in daily worries, but we mustn't forget the purpose of the Center—emigration. Look forward and be prepared for emigra-tion. Begin preparing now in daily life.... This life, so problematic, with so many scarcities, frustrates and embitters us, but these problems are different from those awaiting us. We can't make things right if all we do is scold and intervene and argue. We must prepare for a new free life in a free land.[20]

It was difficult for people to keep heart through the seemingly endless winter, and in "Die Insel" (The island), Louis dreamed of escaping from society altogether as with Daniel Defoe's *Robinson Crusoe* or Jean Jacque Rousseau's primitive man. If readers could not retreat to a desert island, then the Deggendorf Center offered its own opportunities for enjoyment:

> Why did *Robinson Crusoe* generate such excitement? He became a man of nature. He had no fear of others. He couldn't be a thief. He couldn't break rules. Laws are only needed when people live together, so he was unbound and free. On the island, he lived with nature, an ideal world for romantics, enthusiasts, and dreamers. Similarly Rousseau wrote of returning to nature. "Freedom," for Rousseau, was found by going back to nature, where it could be shouted with a full voice.
>
> Defoe, a poet, gave his description under the influence of his time. It wasn't Defoe's purpose to heal society. He had no way of knowing his book would have such an impact. And Rousseau, a thinker, prepared

the way for revolution. But even the dumbest people in Rousseau's day didn't go off into the woods to live like Adam and Eve!

A sad sign of our day is that people confuse democracy and anarchy. People don't place such value on culture. *Robinson Crusoe* has again become up to date. Wouldn't we think of him when we remember our recent suffering? Wouldn't we yearn to enjoy his freedom, to live as natural people? But that would be an absurd wish. Our culture would not allow it. . . .

At Deggendorf we are on ice. We wander about with our little pots for soup. We don't know much anymore about the world. Newspapers promise a great deal. Perhaps we will get some of it, but we don't know what will happen. We are not young people anymore, but we are not old either. There is not much sympathy for us. A youthful person warms the heart. For a youth, the war was a bad dream. Thanks to his elasticity he will have fewer after-effects.

Until now, we could not learn much, because we had no role models. But here office work makes possible learning the language of another country and possibly a second language. You need a language. If we have no skills with our hands, there is our nice tailor's room. We have a music hall standing open, a ping pong room, and a course for driving.[21]

Louis's efforts to develop the Jewish self-government in the Deggendorf Center were supported by the UNRRA team. From the day when Carl Atkin, the first UNRRA director, arrived in Deggendorf, Louis enjoyed a cordial working relationship with the UNRRA personnel. UNRRA respected the principle of self-determination for Jewish displaced persons, and the UNRRA team in Deggendorf served, in effect, as a civil service that helped implement the policies and plans of the elected Jewish Committee. When UNRRA personnel ended their tours of duty in the Deggendorf Center, their replacements transitioned seamlessly into their positions in the well-organized camp administration.

Some Jews in the Deggendorf Center would never lose their fears of people in uniform.[22] Even so, the UNRRA team earned the affection and trust of the Deggendorf Center community. In the *Deggendorf Center Revue,* tributes to Carl Atkin, the first UNRRA director of the camp, included a caricature of the swarthy uniformed figure, with a cigarette dangling from his mouth, and a baby, named "Center Deggendorf" in his arms.[23] A caricature of Miss Waters, the UNRRA nurse in the old-age home, showed her bespectacled profile in a heart-shaped frame with the heading, "She Stole Our Heart."[24] The roles of Mr. Buckhantz, the new UNRRA director, and the rest of the UNRRA team were gratefully described by Dr. Gutfeld, editor of the *Deggendorf Center Revue*:

The Empty Office

Today I went to the office of the UNRRA to see Mr. Buckhantz about some affairs connected with this newspaper. But he wasn't in; nobody was in except Miss Kitty. Instead I took the opportunity for a little chat with her about the members of the UNRRA Team. . . .

Outside the window I saw Miss Powers, our welfare officer, walking and talking with an elderly lady of the camp. Miss Powers promoted several welfare programs in the camp: Installation of the nursery, the organization of the various school classes and Kindergarten. She is also responsible for the camp housing and promotion of the recreation program. . . .

Miss Anne Kusta is the director's right hand. She gives her understanding and interpretation to many of our problems. Our former director, Mr. Atkin, had a great appreciation for her and I am sure she will get along well with the new director, Mr. Buckhantz. Miss Anne is working out the calorie value for our meals and knows how to manage it.

Being always short of writing paper for my editorial office, I asked Miss Kitty who would be most likely to help me out in this respect, but I don't tell you what she told me.

Then Dr. Tauber looked into the office. He had previously helped me with advice and prescription in connection with my ulcer treatment. Consequently, I knew him, and we shook hands. I admire his smiling patience in hearing the complaints of all our people. After Dr. Tauber left the office, my conversation naturally turned to our UNRRA nurses. Miss Elva Jane Waters (with the rank of first Lieutenant) . . . takes care of the *Altersheim* [old-age home] in every respect—sanitation, fuel, laundry, food, and many other items. She keeps busy from morning until night. Miss Erika Freundova has about the same functions in the hospital, and she is just as much appreciated by all who are there.

So we know all about Miss Powers, Miss Anne and all the others and their various tasks. They don't like to sit at their desks, but we see them running about busily attending to their affairs, and at the same time talking to everybody and listening to what they have to say like the good friends they wish to be to us.[25]

With an effective partnership in place between the Jewish self-government and the UNRRA team, Louis felt confident that the Deggendorf Center would be well administered even after the emigration of its first Jewish leaders. As he often advised in the *Deggendorf Center Revue,* Louis began to prepare for his own future. He had repeatedly refused offers to work in the new German government in Munich: "I wanted nothing to do with them! Absolutely nothing! I would go anywhere as long as we could get out of Europe." Once Ditta and her mother had located relatives in Boston, Louis and his small family decided to immigrate to the United States.

Louis enjoyed his work in the Deggendorf Center: "I had the greatest satisfaction because I saw things happen. There was something from nothing." In conversations with Miss Powers, the UNRRA social welfare officer, and with representatives from the American Jewish Joint Distribution Committee, he explored how to continue such work as his career:

I thought, "When I get to the United States, I don't know what I will be doing." There are two things I knew I wanted to do. One was to finish up school. I had gone to university, and I wanted to finish up the schooling. And second, I knew that the schooling I would want was no longer philology or philosophy. That was what I had been studying before the war. I would be glad to continue to study that, but I wanted to get into something practical such as the kind of work I was doing in Deggendorf: organizing, planning, developing, creating . . . I was becoming interested in seeing whether this can become professional. Are there schools where you can get trained to do these things? I remember asking the people from the Joint what they were doing. They were raising funds, helping people to emigrate, providing help to people in the United States.

My family had had contact with welfare workers in Munich, when we were in dire straits economically before the war. The welfare workers provided some money and some help to immigrate to Prague. They were what I would call case managers today. But the major side of social work for me was in community administration, community organization, community development, to use our lingo now, helping people to

UNITED NATIONS RELIEF AND REHABILITATION ADMINISTRATION
TEAM 55
APO. 757 U. S. ARMY

Deggendorf, 16th April 1946.

TO WHOM IT MAY CONCERN:

Re: Mr. Louis Löwy.

Mr. Louis Löwy has been a member of the Jewish Committee in Camp Deggendorf from July 1945 until April 15, 1946. The committee was an elected body and he served as chairman of the group during both terms of office. Mr. Löwy gave unstintingly of his time and energy and served the community well and willingly. Mr. Löwy was head of the ducational program in the camp. His command of English proved a very valuable asset. Mr. Löwy should be a valuable in many kinds of community problems. We wish him well.

U.N.R.R.A. Team 55.

14. Reference letter for Louis Löwy from W. V. Buckhantz, UNRRA Team 55, April 16, 1946. Courtesy of Edith Lowy.

help themselves. That was what interested me. That was what I thought was professional social work.

A New Harbor

Unfortunately, the United States was not ready to welcome Louis and other war refugees, particularly Jewish refugees, to its shores. Some Americans feared that displaced persons would become charges of the state or that they would gain passage on American ships in place of US service personnel who were waiting to come home.[26] In November 1945, legislation was pending in Congress to further restrict immigration from Europe even though only 10 percent of the year's quota for European immigrants had been filled.

From his perspective as commander in chief, however, President Harry S. Truman viewed "the immensity of the problem of displaced persons" as a security problem for the occupying US Army, and the need to relocate stateless or non-repatriable people into permanent homes was too urgent to be ignored. Determined not only to relieve suffering, but also to set an example to other nations, Truman used his executive powers to facilitate the immigration of displaced persons in the American zones of occupation "to the extent that our present immigration laws permit." On December 22, 1945, he issued a "Statement and Directive on Displaced Persons," famously known as the Truman Directive:

> Memorandum to:
> Secretary of State, Secretary of War, Attorney General, War Shipping Administrator, Surgeon General of the Public Health Service, Director General of UNRRA.
>
> The grave dislocation of populations in Europe resulting from the war has produced human suffering that the people of the United States cannot and will not ignore. This Government should take every possible measure to facilitate full immigration to the United States under existing quota laws. . . .
>
> The Secretary of State is directed to establish with the utmost dispatch consular facilities at or near displaced person and refugee assembly center areas in the American zones of occupation. It shall be the responsibility of these consular officers, in conjunction with the

immigrant inspectors, to determine as quickly as possible the eligibility of the applicants for visas and admission to the United States. . . .

Visas should be distributed fairly among persons of all faiths, creeds and nationalities. I desire that special attention be devoted to orphaned children to whom it is hoped the majority of visas will be issued. . . .

With respect to the requirement of law that visas may not be issued to applicants likely to become public charges after admission to the United States, the Secretary of State shall cooperate with the immigration and naturalization service in perfecting appropriate arrangements with welfare organizations in the United States which may be prepared to guarantee financial support to successful applicants. . . .

The Administration of the War Shipping Administration will make the necessary arrangements for water transportation from the port of embarkation in Europe to the United States, subject to the provision that the movement of immigrants will in no way interfere with the scheduled return of service personnel and their spouses and children from the European Theatre.[27]

Truman expected immediate action. As specified in his signing statement, "I hope that by early spring adequate consular facilities will be in operation in our zones in Europe, so that immigration can begin immediately upon the availability of ships."

And so it came to pass that the American Consulate in Munich began accepting visa applications from the Deggendorf Center in late March or early April 1946. As Louis recalled:

One night I went with Ditta to the movies. It was *The Devil and Daniel Webster* that was playing. But I hardly saw the movie because as soon as I arrived, somebody called out, "Hey, Louis, are you around? Buckhantz [the new UNRRA director] wants to see you immediately!"

"Damn it!" I thought. "I can't even have one night out at the movies!"

So I went back, and Buckhantz said, "Louis, the American Consulate has opened in Munich. They just requested that we submit a list of all the people who want to enter the United States. If we can prepare the listing in English and submit it within the next two or three months, then they will be considered."

So I worked translating and I got other people to work because we already had the information, the registrations in the Emigration Department, and this came in handy. Within a week, all these lists were in Munich.

And very soon, people were being processed. Physicians examined the people. All the things that had once gone on at Ellis Island went on in Munich. And then from there people, including ourselves—including myself, Ditta, and her mother—went to the Consulate and were examined, and we were granted our visas.

As Ditta remembered the story, once Louis was called out from the movies, she did not see him again for several days:

I can tell a very interesting thing about how the emigration came to pass. One night we went to the local movies. I still remember what it was; it was an American film, *The Devil and Daniel Webster,* a classic. And Louis was called out from the movie. And I thought it didn't seem terribly necessary to call him out in the evening! But they called him out to tell him that the American Consulate is opening up and he has to start processing all the applications for immigration, not just for him and myself and my mother, but for everybody in the camp who wanted to immigrate to the United States!

Now Louis had been very inventive always, keeping people busy in a positive way. Long before this occurrence, he had opened an emigration office. And all the volunteers, some people that had been secretaries or something, came, and people handed in their applications. He had made out a form. I don't even know if it was the official form yet. And people filled it in. So that gave people something to look forward to.

And when the consulate actually opened, he found himself buried under heaps of paper. He had to translate every single application. There was no one else who could do it. So I didn't see him for several days or longer! By doing it efficiently and quickly, he processed the list and got it to the consulate in Munich. I think it was one of the first lists to arrive from any of the DP camps because the people from the Deggendorf Center were on the first boat and on the second boat to the United States.

When the time came that we had to go to Munich to the consulate, I got deathly ill. I had some bronchitis or something, fever, coughing, miserable. We didn't have antibiotics, but my husband and my mother proceeded to give me a forced cure. They wrapped me in hot towels, wet towels, and covered me up with blankets, and I sweated it out. A day or two later we had to go, and I was better. I was young, and so I could withstand such a treatment. When we got to the consulate, they had American typewriters that didn't have the umlaut. We spelled it Löwy. So they said, well you just leave out the two dots; we don't have those dots. And that is how it became "Lowy."

In less than a week's time, Louis had submitted visa applications for more than two hundred prospective emigrants from the Deggendorf Center. It was his final accomplishment as chairman of the Jewish Committee. A few weeks later, as he prepared to leave, Louis wrote a heartfelt farewell for the *Deggendorf Center Revue:*

The winter passed and the hope of spring is starting to fulfill itself. Deggendorf and other camps will be emptier and people will begin to move. Let us hope that speed increases for everyone to reach their goals.

At this point I would like to thank all coworkers, colleagues of the Committee, heads of departments, and all who helped by building and forming our lives here. I express my heartiest thanks for the active support of our work by our members of the UNRRA teams. My sincerest thanks. Continue the work and don't forget the beautiful and difficult days in Deggendorf just as I will not.[28]

In the same issue of the *Deggendorf Center Revue,* Joseph Königer and the Jewish Committee offered parting words to *"Lieber Freund und Kollege Löwy"* (Esteemed friend and colleague, Löwy). A fitting tribute, the article expressed the optimism and civic pride that were, for Louis, the basis of community:

In the name of our entire Center, we feel called upon to send along with you, as you leave us, a few words. In these long months we have learned to know and value you as a fellow human being and as a comrade. . . . Perhaps the crowning achievement of your labors was the establishment of the Jewish Center Deggendorf, which under your leadership developed into the "Model Camp of the American Zone."

Now you are steering toward a new harbor, and we all, your fellow workers, wish that you may build up with just as much and even more energy a better future for yourself and for your family.[29]

Among the emigrants from the Deggendorf Center in the spring of 1946 were the small "band of wanderers" whom Louis had led across Europe. Reinhard Frank set off for Switzerland in search of his mother. He later immigrated to England after learning that his mother had died:

> I was one of the first people to leave Deggendorf in March 1946. There was one other person, a lady who later became a US diplomat. The two of us were transported in a US Army ambulance from Deggendorf to the Swiss border and dropped there, and then we crossed the border on foot.

Kurt Kohorn accepted a position with UNRRA in Paris before he immigrated to the United States. Gerhard Steinhagen, Georg and Heinz

15. Departing from Munich, April 1946. *Left to right:* Hilda Jedlinksy, Ditta Lowy, Kurt Kohorn. Photographer unknown. Courtesy of Edith Lowy.

16. Boarding train from Munich to Bremerhaven, April 1946. *Top row, left to right:* Ditta Lowy, Hilda Jedlinsky; *middle row, second from right:* Kurt Kohorn; *bottom row, center:* Louis Lowy. Photographer unknown. Courtesy of Edith Lowy.

Schindler, and Vern Drehmel were passengers on the first and second Liberty Ships that carried war refugees from Bremerhaven to New York City in May 1946.

It would take three more years, however, for all the Jews in the Deggendorf Center to find new homes. New arrivals from Eastern Europe outpaced opportunities for emigration, and by October 1948, the population had reached nearly two thousand, twice the size of the population during Louis's tenure as chairman. The foundation for self-government that Louis had laid continued to serve the growing community, and the Deggendorf Center was known as "an exceptionally active" center of Jewish cultural life until its dissolution on June 15, 1949.[30]

7

The Making of a Social Worker

ON THE LIBERTY SHIP in New York harbor, Vern Drehmel viewed the Manhattan shoreline with a combination of euphoria and dread. Now seventeen years old, he was traveling as a war orphan, and when he landed in America he would be separated from Louis for the first time since Auschwitz:

> I arrived on May 24, 1946. We came together on the same boat, Louis, Ditta, and me, but then on arrival we would need to be separated. Once we were anchored in front of the Statue of Liberty for the night, and I saw the lights of Manhattan, and I saw all the car lights in a long stream moving along the shore, I realized that I didn't know a soul there, realized that maybe I should have been more leery than I actually had been!

Vern recited to himself the Preamble to the United States Constitution, words that Louis had secretly taught him in a Terezín garret, and his usual optimism returned:

> Once again, it all worked out. Ditta and Louis went off to Boston. Ditta had relatives who were able to give the necessary financial assurances required by the government. I don't even remember saying good-bye to Louis and Ditta. Meanwhile we younger people were without definite destinations. We were sponsored by the US Committee for European War Orphans of the United Jewish Federation and the Jewish Family and Children's Services. We were all sent to a reception center that was located in the Bronx on Caldwell Avenue. It was a big brownstone house where you heard all languages. There were Jewish kids, also Catholic kids from Eastern Europe and the Baltic countries. The center became somewhat segregated according to our religious, ethnic identities. That's where I met Benji and Leila [two other Jewish war orphans].

I couldn't stand the chaos and the noise of New York City. Postwar Germany was in such ruin that nothing was moving. It was very peaceful and quiet! They had a very long funeral, I think, before industrial rebuilding after the Marshall Plan, which did not begin until 1948. I was used to bucolic peacefulness, seeing nature in the meadows and the woods, walking in the fresh air. In New York City, I could not take it.

One morning, I was called down and the social worker very kindly asked me where I would like to go in the United States. I was embarrassed because I wanted to get away from New York City. I said, "Boston. I have a friend in Boston, and there are good schools there, Harvard and MIT." When my interview was over, I said to Benji and Leila, "When they ask you where you want to go, say 'Boston.'"

So we were all sent to Boston on a sleeper train. After our experiences on freight trains, it was too much ritziness for us! Someone met the train from Jewish Family and Children's Services and drove us to their offices. Louis and Ditta came to greet us. The caseworker asked Louis and Ditta if they could take me in. They would have liked to, but they were rather busy keeping their noses above water!

But the Jewish Family and Children's Services had plans for us anyhow. They sent us to a summer camp in Maine [Camp Kingswood]. They put us on a Greyhound bus to Maine on that same day, and we were greeted by our teacher for the summer. He was a Jewish man from Chelsea; I can't remember his name. It was a Girl Scout camp, all outdoors. We had a cottage in the woods. We learned English and civics to prepare us to go to school in September.

This teacher worked us hard studying. We had to learn to write a new script. It was very exciting! We could go swimming in the lake. There was a swimming instructor from the Girl Scout camp, and we all learned to swim, and I got my lifesaving certificate. We worked hard at everything.

And then this teacher said, "Ok, I'm going to take you guys for haircuts. You need a crew cut!" This teacher had a crew cut [a very short razor-cut]. We had hair that was now a normal length. Our hair had grown out from being shaved by the Nazis.

We said, "Crew cut?"

He said, "Yeah, if you want to go to Harvard, you need a crew cut!"

I refused. The chief of casework was Mrs. Carter of Boston; she herself had been a refugee, a White Russian from the Russian Revolution, and she liked people who spoke up for their own rights. She sided with me. I knew that no one had the right to do something like that to me. I had learned that from Louis.

At the end of the summer, Jewish families from the Boston area were invited to Camp Kingswood to consider adopting the Jewish war orphans. Vern, at seventeen, was considered too old to be adopted, but he was taken in by a foster family, Helen and Harold Saftel, who offered Vern the choice of attending a public or a private school. Vern chose the public Brookline High School: "I wanted to go to public school. I had ideals about democracy, and so my foster family sent me to public school, and after two years, I ended up at Harvard."

Vern had found a new family, not only his foster family but also a family of fellow survivors. Vern, Benji, and Leila remained lifelong friends after their summer together, and Vern would always cherish his friendship with Louis and Ditta:

> People are very important to me. I spend a lot of time maintaining contact, holiday cards and letters. I've certainly learned that the most important thing we can do is to be connected to others. Louis considered every person very important, and so relationships, they're just life to me. The bonding is what Louis did for us. It's the most important food that you can give to people.

Beginning a Life

On their last night aboard the Liberty Ship, as Vern wondered about the future, Louis was making plans for the next day: "We arrived on the 24th of May, seeing the Statue of Liberty, and then we were anchored in the New York Harbor for a night, and in the morning we were out!" Ditta, meanwhile, waited anxiously to be reunited with her mother, who had traveled to the United States on an earlier ship. When Ditta and her mother had parted at the port of Bremerhaven, they were separated for the first time since the beginning of the war. Ditta recalled:

When we went to Bremerhaven, we were in quarantine. They kept us in quarantine in Bremerhaven because there was no more quarantine anymore at Ellis Island. So they kept us in quarantine for a while; I don't know how long it was. The American army was in charge, and they took away our blankets and everything to be disinfected, and we never got them back.

So coming then to this country, my mother was on the first boat, and we were on the second boat. When we were separated then, that was a very traumatic moment because we had never been separated throughout the whole war. It was traumatic. What if we don't get on the second boat? What if I never see her again? After all these years we had been together, and now we were separated on a very momentous enterprise, going to America!

Anyway, we got on the second boat about ten days later, and Louis asked the captain whether it was possible to send a telegram from our ship to the earlier ship, and we sent a telegram to my mother to say, "We are also on the way." Because my mother was very upset, too. She was suddenly all alone.

We were on a Liberty Ship run by the Merchant Marine. They treated us like dirt. If you were young and female on that ship, they treated you like a whore. They would say, "Would you like some more fruit? Want another orange?" One incident I remember that was really quite horrible: we went to the washroom. I don't think there were showers; we just washed. A big black man sat in there. I walked up to him, and with my faulty English, I said, "Would you mind leaving because we are washing?"

He said, "I mind my business and you mind yours!" And he wouldn't move.

This was not a good introduction! We were not prisoners. Today you hear about the abuse of prisoners. Well, it is not such an unusual occurrence that there is abuse of immigrants! So my husband eventually went to the captain and said that this kind of treatment of the passengers has to change. This is not acceptable.

Before we disembarked in New York, there was a lineup. They checked the papers and everything, they processed us on the ship, and then they said, "Good-bye." And there we were in New York! I remember that when we had started out in Bremerhaven, it was very cold, and when we arrived here, it was during a heat wave.

We arrived on the day when Truman had called out the National Guard about the railroad strike. There were no trains running. So we had to take a bus from New York to Boston. We got on the bus at two in the afternoon, and there were many stops along the way, and it took until midnight to reach Boston. There was no highway. There was no parkway at that time. And by the time we arrived in Boston at twelve midnight there stood my mother with my aunt welcoming us. She was already here! And that was the traumatic journey to this country.

When we arrived here, Louis and I went to my aunt's house in Hyde Park. Vern and another girl and boy, three of them, were taken over by the Jewish Family and Children's Services because they arrived as orphans. A few days later I got a telephone call: "I understand you know Vern Drehmel?"

I said, "Yes."

"Would you be interested in adopting him?"

I laughed. I said, "I would really like to, but I'm only two years older than he is and we arrived on the same boat!" So they realized that I wasn't a good prospect for that!

Then we stayed in some relative's house here in Hyde Park for a little while, and Louis immediately started working. Louis got a job, first a factory job and then a job in a warehouse as a bookkeeper. I was working in a small leather–goods factory. Pretty soon after that we got a little apartment in Dorchester. It was in a two-family house with the bathroom out on the landing. And my mother came with us.

My mother was a fine dressmaker, not a seamstress. She was a properly trained couturiere, and she was very, very talented. She started working on her own, from the apartment. Her customers came by word of mouth. Unfortunately, she only lived two years in this country. She died at the age of fifty-two. And the year when I turned fifty-two, it was a rough year; it was a rough year. I was afraid.

So pretty soon, Louis, still working as a bookkeeper, explored and started at Boston University. He had no papers to prove that he ever had gone to university, which he had in Prague. But they said, "He can take undergraduate senior courses, and then we will judge how he does, and we'll give him credit."

So he took Shakespeare and history, and he got A+. That poor professor of English, he was so proud. He thought everything that Louis knew he had learned from him! But they gave him sixty credits, two years of college, for the time he had gone to Charles University in Prague. So he finished up here and then he started at the [Boston University] School of Social Work. And after that, he got a PhD at Harvard.

In the Boston area, the agency responsible for providing resettlement services to Jewish war refugees was the Jewish Family and Children's Services. In Louis's experience, however, "They did not do very well. They were not prepared for the extent of the Holocaust." It was Louis rather than professional social workers who offered guidance to Vern's foster parents, and it was Vern's foster mother, Helen Saftel, who helped Louis find his way into the social work profession, as Louis recalled:

When I arrived here, the Jewish Family and Children Services contacted us and said, "You are immigrants here, and we're here to help you," which they really didn't do very well. But we were in an apartment. We were beginning a life. I was working in a factory, and then I was working as an inventory clerk in a warehouse on Sumner Street, Levinson warehouse, where they stored wool. I made forty bucks a week. I really didn't do much thinking about the future during that summer, but then the Saftels came into our lives, and I asked them, "What does one do?"

Vern was here in Boston. He came on the same boat as we did, and he was sent to Camp Kingswood. They sent many of these refugee kids up there so that "wealthy Jews," if you will, can go and adopt these children. And many went up, including the Saftel family, Helen and Harry Saftel, who were in real estate, and Vern was taken on by the Saftel family as foster parents. When the camp season was over, he went to the Saftels, and they wanted to know more about him, so they contacted us. We were his best friends living right here in Boston, and they came to visit us.

They came over every week to find out about Vern. We had an apartment in Dorchester, the Irish section of Dorchester, and they always came with the big Oldsmobile. These cars looked to us like boats, you know. All the people in the street wanted to know who are these people who are always getting visits from such rich people?

The Saftels came over, and they wanted us to give a background about Vern, as much as one could. They found consolation in talking with us. Helen Saftel was a voluntary social worker, a volunteer without being trained. She was at one time one of the directors of Hecht Neighborhood House [a Jewish settlement house]. And so she began to talk about Vern, and then I asked her about social work, and she said, "Look, Louis, you're a natural group worker from what I hear. You should become a social worker!" And she gave me a really good background. She said, "Why don't you see Saul Bernstein at Boston University?" And so Helen Saftel was really a major instrument in my life, unbeknownst at the time to her or to me!

I went in September to see Saul Bernstein, who had an office on Exeter Street at the School of Social Work, and he was very cordial and nice. He was not fully understanding my background, of course, and I don't blame him, but he explained to me what the possibilities were and how I could finish school: "Maybe you want to work at Hecht House as a group leader to see what it's like in America to work with groups!"

Although Boston University School of Social Work offered a concentration in social group work, the allied field of community organization "was the stepchild of the curriculum," in Louis's words. "It dealt mostly with fund-raising." As a result, when faculty members assessed Louis's aptitude for social work, they were more interested in his experience with youth groups in Terezín than in his leadership of the Deggendorf Displaced Persons Center. Nonetheless, Louis looked forward to studying social group work, and as always, he threw himself wholeheartedly into the effort. He volunteered at Hecht House for three nights per week from 1946 to 1949:

So I went over to Hecht House and I worked three evenings a week as a club leader. I had three groups, one group per night, with about twelve youngsters per group, and I did quite well. I studied their relationships. The first group called themselves "the 49ers" after the Gold Rush. They were very intrigued with me because I was a strange foreigner, and they taught me about American baseball. They were American Jewish youngsters, typical Jewish middle-class kids, and they were not very adventurous. They were fourteen and fifteen years old. I was twenty-six, twenty-seven. We went bowling and we had parties and we had a Purim carnival [a Jewish festival celebrating the Book of Esther]. Some of them recently [in the fall of 1990] had a telephone conversation with me. One became a social worker.

Louis was working full-time in the warehouse and volunteering at Hecht House when he entered Boston University as a part-time student in September 1947: "I learned American history and American literature; that's where I was deficient." After completing his bachelor of science degree in 1949, he was admitted with a full scholarship to the School of Social Work, where he earned his master's degree in social services in May 1951.

One of Louis's classmates was Ralph L. Kolodny, a World War II veteran who later would join the faculty of the School of Social Work. He remembered Louis "as slight of figure and always with a twinkle in his eyes":

We were students together at the School of Social Work shortly after the war, and I simply could not get over the liveliness, sense of humor, and warmth of someone who had been through the hell that he had lived through. I'm sure that all of my fellow World War II veterans felt the same way. No one was more ready than Louis to plan student parties and good times."[1]

Louis had special reason for the twinkle in his eyes. On April 15, 1951, Ditta gave birth to their first child, Susan Hilda, and on October 12, 1952, Peter Mark was born. Susan was named for Ditta's mother, and Peter for Louis's father, and, as Louis later explained, they formed "a link in the chain of a family that had ceased to exist but had to be created again."[2]

Louis continued to work with youth groups in his internships at Quincy Jewish Community Center and at Boston Children's Services: "Group work was almost confined and synonymous with children and youth." When he wrote his master's degree thesis, "Indigenous Leadership in Teenage Groups," Louis found that leadership is "a composite product of personality factors plus environmental aspects."[3] His conclusion reflected his own experiences as an indigenous leader during and after the war.

After taking all the courses that the School of Social Work had to offer in group work and in casework, Louis sought further clinical experience, and he accepted a postgraduate summer internship at Somerville Arlington Family Services. "I knew psychiatry from the European point of view which was linked with neurology. I knew Freud; I had read Freud in the original [German]. I knew that Erik Erikson had just come out with *Childhood and Society*." Louis soon discovered, however, that he found psychoanalytic theory more compelling than practice: "Waiting for clients to speak and all that, I found it very boring. I don't think I was the most skilled worker!"

Upon graduation from the School of Social Work in 1951, Louis looked for a position in a Jewish agency: "I wanted to become closer to Jews. I identified closely with Jewishness given my war experiences, but in a secular way, not in a religious way. The secular way just suited me very well." In addition, as he confided to Ditta, Louis had the longer-term goal of teaching in a school of social work: "I knew I needed a good deal of experience first."

Having worked for many years with children and youth, Louis was attracted by the opportunity to practice social group work with adults, and he accepted a position as director of adult activities at the Bridgeport Jewish Community Center in Bridgeport, Connecticut. "There is inherent in adult education a tremendous potential for the advancement of knowledge and skills, the gaining of an understanding of oneself and the community, and the dissemination of creativity and happiness," Louis believed, and placing his confidence in indigenous leadership, Louis empowered members of the community center to develop programs related to their interests.[4] Participants soon organized a Parents' Group, a Literary Group, a Cultural Group, and a Political Forum, with each program led by a membership committee, and with each committee transcending its stated purpose:

> Association with others will permit a person to test his feelings and may stimulate the individual to embrace new skills and competencies. He

can learn to be a leader as well as a follower; he can learn to appreciate art and assimilate this appreciation into other life experiences; he can learn to accept two sides of a story; he can learn new dance steps; and he can learn to broaden his social ability to 'make friends.'[5]

From the Terezín ghetto, to the Deggendorf Displaced Persons Center, to the Bridgeport Community Center, Louis was guided by the belief that personal fulfillment and social well-being arise out of the human capacity for learning throughout life:

> Adults have capacities and abilities to learn. Learning is a continuous process, not necessarily confined to the younger years of man's life or to any specific institution especially designed for learning. Learning begins as soon as the infant becomes aware of his environment and reacts toward it; it does not end until man loses consciousness forever. Lifelong learning is of especial importance in a democratic society because a democracy is built upon the assumption that its citizens have the knowledge and the judgment necessary to make intelligent decisions which benefit the common good. . . . Through adult education, people are able to become not only better-informed citizens but also better-acting citizens who participate actively to preserve and improve the democratic institutions.[6]

Cultural and educational groups would allow adults to explore their potential in the arts, in interpersonal relationships, and in civic engagement. In the Parents' Group, for example, parents would learn to express love for their children:

> How to give and accept love has been recognized as the central problem of human relations and the degree of maturity of a person is judged by the way he can receive love and offer it. . . . Parent education should stress the fact that mistakes are inevitable, that mistakes in the rearing of children do not lead to disaster if love and affection are the prime forces in the parent-child relationship.[7]

Beyond enhancing relationships within the family, however, the Parents' Group would encourage involvement in the community:

Parent education . . . has to move toward an awareness of the role as a parent, toward becoming interested in the community, and toward acting in the community to improve it constantly and to make it a better place to live in both for themselves and their children. A parent-education program not geared to community awareness and community participation is lacking its most potent ingredient.[8]

As the Adult Activities Program expanded, Louis sought a student intern, and he gained his first academic position as a field instructor for the University of Connecticut School of Social Work. Louis enjoyed building a professional network with social work faculty and with other social agencies in the region, and in 1952, several Bridgeport professionals called Louis's attention to a community need:

There was a social worker in the Department of Old Age Assistance in Bridgeport, I am forgetting her name; and there was a Mr. Applebaum, who was the leader of the Literary Group; and Mr. Schein, who was the leader of the Parents' Group; and a physician, Dr. Frank Northman, who was in general practice, and these people came to me. And Northman said, "Look, Louis, so many older people come to me as a physician, and I don't have time to talk to them. If they are sick, that's no issue, but they want to come and tell me about their children or their grandchildren or to complain that they never see their son. Wouldn't it be possible that the center does something for older people?

So I said, "I have an idea. Let's sponsor a panel on older people for the Political Forum." So we had a panel discussion, and Northman spoke about health issues of older people, and Schein talked about the relationships of children and older people, and Applebaum talked about the literary contributions of older people to world literature. And this forum ended very successfully, and as a result of it, these people came to me and said, "We want to be a committee to establish a lounge program for older people!" And so we went to Harold Lewis, who was my supervisor, and they said, "What do you think?"

And he said, "Wonderful idea! We'll set up a few bridge tables in the room downstairs," which had a separate entrance to the parking lot, "and the lounge will be there from three o'clock to five o'clock with Louis as counselor."

And out of this developed the older-adult program, the Leisure Lounge. Mrs. Dykler, an eighty-year-old woman became "the mother of the Leisure Lounge." She was president. Then we got them a television set because there were the McCarthy hearings, and they were glued to the television.

Ever vigilant against "capricious, arbitrary, and unjust decisions" by government officials, Louis joined the seniors in their fascination and fear of Senator Joseph McCarthy, who alleged that communists had infiltrated the State Department and the United States Army: "It was the McCarthy era, which frightened me to death, and I became interested in politics again."

It was easier to deal with the news, whether personal or political, when sharing it with others, and the Leisure Lounge became a popular gathering place for older members of the Bridgeport Community Center:

And then somebody said, "Look, Louis, in New York they have a center established only for older people. It is run by Harold Levine under the Department of Public Welfare. Why don't you talk to him?"

So I went to New York to talk to Harold Levine, who was running the first big senior center, the William Hodson Senior Center at Stewart Avenue. I went to New York to take a look at it. And from there, the people at the Hodson Center sent me to the Serowich Center near Bensonhurst, where they said, "The best thing you can do is to set up a five-day-a-week program, not a one-day program." And so that's what we did.

Then there was a woman in Bridgeport by the name of Mrs. Hirschkowitz. She was a lay person and a driving force in the Bridgeport Community Center. She really was the bane of Harold Lewis, my supervisor, and he always said, "Get her off my back!"

I said, "I will get her off your back. I'll make her chairman of the Older Adult Advisory Committee!"

And she loved it! She worked with me, in fact she went again to the Serowich Center in New York, and she brought back the idea of birthday parties, having parties for all the seniors. And before I knew it, there was a full-fledged operation! I made Cora Schetel the head of volunteers. She brought in volunteers, and I developed training sessions for them. And Bridgeport became a model senior center for the Jewish community centers. Ed Kadowitz was field secretary of the Jewish Community Centers. He came and I told him about it, and he told other centers in the New England area.

Of course, I could not help but see the policy implications of working with older people, implications for social security, for income security, for health care security. With my education in Europe, I saw the issues not as individual problems but as social responsibilities. Then Susan Kubie and Gertrude Landau came out with *Group Work with the Aged.*[9] Landau was one of the first group workers who established the senior center movement. And they became models for me.

Ever since his imprisonment by the Gestapo, Louis had had a horror of spending the days "with nothing to do," and he appreciated the vulnerability of older adults who were isolated in their homes: "The senior center movement appealed to me because here were older people who had lower incomes or who had nothing to do. Here were people who came close to the social work mission."

A Professor at Last

It was here, with memories of his political reawakening in the early 1950s, his founding of the Leisure Lounge, and his discovery of gerontology, that Louis Lowy's oral narrative came to an end. Louis had been recording his oral narrative through seven months, in sixteen hours and nine interview sessions with his colleague Leonard Bloksberg, when he grew too weak to continue. He had recalled his childhood in Munich and his education in London and in Prague; his efforts as a youth leader and teacher in the Terezín ghetto; his survival of the Auschwitz concentration camps; his escape with his students across Europe; his leadership of the Jewish self-government in the Deggendorf Displaced Persons Center; and finally his immigration to the United States, where he pursued a social work career. Although Louis did not record his whole life story, he succeeded in his purpose of telling that part of the story that he had never told before, the story of his professional formation as a social worker.

Louis knew that his writings and teachings would continue where his oral narrative left off. A prolific author, he had published nearly one hundred papers in English or in German, and twenty-two books, including *Adult Education and Group Work* (1955); *The Function of Social Work in a Changing Society: A Continuum of Practice* (1976); *Social Work with the Aging: The Challenge and Promise of the Later Years* (1979, 1985); *Social Policies and Programs on Aging: What Is and What Should Be in the Later Years* (1980); and *Why Education in the Later Years?* (with Darlene O'Connor, 1986).

The course of Louis Lowy's life and thought was documented not only in his publications, but also in his personal papers, in correspondence with colleagues and friends, and in hundreds of thank-you notes, meticulously saved, from former students, researchers, politicians, and policy makers from all over the world. As active in community education as in professional education, Louis wrote for community newsletters and trade bulletins, and he spoke frequently to local civic associations, community centers, and senior citizens' groups.[10] After giving a presentation for Family Day at the Hebrew Rehabilitation Center for the Aged in Boston, he received a thank-you letter typical of those accumulated throughout his career: "It was as though we had been waiting to hear what you had to say."[11]

Louis administered programs for older adults in the Bridgeport Community Center until 1955, when he was invited to return to Boston as assistant executive director of the Association of Jewish Centers of Greater Boston and as director of the Golden Age Council. With his growing expertise in gerontology and social welfare administration, he began teaching part-time at Boston University, and in 1957, eleven years after his arrival in the United States, he joined the faculty of the Boston University School of Social Work. At last he had realized his lifelong dream of becoming a university professor.

Louis remained at Boston University School of Social Work for the rest of his career, rising through the academic ranks from assistant professor (1957) to associate professor (1962) to professor (1966), to associate dean for curriculum (1977), to director of the Joint Doctoral Program in

Sociology and Social Work (1980), to professor emeritus (1985). Serving as principal investigator for research projects related to gerontology and health, he introduced and developed a gerontology concentration in the School of Social Work, and in 1977 he founded the interdisciplinary Boston University Gerontology Center, which later named its academic program in his honor: the Louis Lowy Certificate in Gerontological Studies.

Throughout his tenure at Boston University, Louis served on editorial boards and held leadership positions in national and international professional associations.[12] He evaluated international social welfare education programs for the United States Department of State, and his perspectives on social welfare policy in relation to health care and aging were sought by the Massachusetts Department of Public Welfare, the National Council on Aging, and the National Institute of Mental Health. Louis represented Massachusetts as a delegate to the White House Conference on Aging in 1961, 1971, and 1981.

When Louis earned his PhD from the Harvard University Graduate School of Education and Graduate School of Arts and Sciences in 1966, his dissertation research on the professional development of social work students, "Self and Role Clarification During Social Work Training: Study of the Incorporation of a Professional Role," examined the question that, twenty-five years later, he would ask about his own career.[13] Had he given his oral narrative a title, Louis might well have called it, "Self and Role Clarification During the Holocaust." Just as Louis had found that successful social work students "incorporate most aspects of social work role expectations, notably commitment to social values and preventive and promotional goals," so in his own life, Louis did not separate his personal and professional values or his private and public roles.[14]

"Teaching was Louis Lowy's life," in the words of several students, and Louis taught with respect for the dignity, self-determination, and lifelong capacity of people to learn and grow.[15] These were the values that guided Louis when he returned to Germany to help restore social work and social work education. As Ditta recalled:

> With Germany, he felt really that he had a mission. He felt that it was essential that he brought the knowledge, especially in his field of social

work, which is a field of acceptance, of accepting people as they are and what they are. This was very important to him. He never talked about his past there. It was sort of a tacit understanding not to talk about the past. He made sure for many years that he never wore short sleeves because he had a tattoo on his arm.

Return from the Holocaust

The Nazis had devastated the social work profession in Germany and Central Europe. Leading German social workers, many of whom were Jewish, had been exiled during the 1930s or imprisoned and killed during the war.[16] In the summer of 1946, an UNRRA survey revealed that social work was one of the smallest occupational groups among the "suviving remnant" of European Jews. Out of 50,071 Jewish displaced persons who were surveyed, only 24 were social workers.[17]

Louis himself would not have been counted as a social worker. Before the war, he had been a university student who had qualified as an elementary school teacher, and he had listed his occupation as "teacher" on his Deggendorf Center identify card. Once Louis had established himself professionally in the United States, however, he was prepared to contribute to social work education in Germany, and in 1964, he accepted an invitation from Dr. Teresa Bock, president of the German Association for Public and Private Welfare Service, to teach a course in social group work at the Academy for Youth Problems in Münster.

For the next twenty years, until 1984, Louis returned to Germany every summer as a visiting professor, consultant, and researcher. In universities and training academies throughout what was then West Germany, including those in Aachen, Bochum, Berlin, Cologne, Essen, Frankfurt, Freiburg, Hamburg, Mönchengladbach, Munich, Münster, Nuremberg, and Paderborn, he developed training institutes for social work faculty and practitioners on such topics as social group work, social work supervision, and adult education. Louis served on doctoral dissertation committees in social work and gerontology, and he introduced and taught curricula in gerontology for social workers and allied professionals.[18]

Louis's international activities as lecturer and consultant soon extended to universities in Austria, Belgium, France, Greece, Norway, and

Switzerland, and he consulted widely for international organizations such as the International Association of Schools of Social Work and the United Nations. In the words of Dr. Heinz J. Kersting, a professor of social work in the Niederrhein University of Applied Sciences in Mönchengladbach, Germany, Louis became a "bridge-builder across the Atlantic":

> Louis Lowy was a bridge-builder who connected continents, countries, generations and the most different people with each other. Thus he overcame innumerable borders. He did not work only in Germany but in many places in Europe, such as Lille, Gent, Athens, Vienna, Oslo, Roros in Norway, Luzern, Zürich and St. Gallen. He established close relationships among Europeans and organized a number of international conferences for social workers in Europe.[19]

Of all his international activities, however, it was Louis's work in Germany that had the greatest emotional significance for Louis and for his students. Heinz Kersting, who first studied with Louis in 1967 at the Academy for Youth Problems in Münster, remembered the experience as "a normative shock":

> Those of us who experienced Louis Lowy as a teacher remember that he was able to analyze complicated matters concisely and plausibly, and those were difficult, unusual matters based on even more unusual attitudes for us German social workers and teachers of social work. In the middle of the 1960s, German social workers were lagging far behind the international standard of social work knowledge. . . . Many things were new to us; some of them were even shocking, a "normative shock," Lowy called it.
>
> But confrontation was softened by his warm-heartedness, his being interested in his students and their lives. It was not our deficits that interested him. He worked with our resources. Learning from him and with him, we always had the feeling that the results of our learning were also the result of our own efforts, which had an extremely encouraging effect.
>
> Louis Lowy was a group worker, and he taught social work as a group worker. I have hardly ever experienced a scientist like Louis Lowy

whose message was identical with the way he conveyed this message. Louis Lowy lived his ideas in the way he taught: his respect for the clients' rights of self-determination, his orientation toward the clients' resources instead of their deficits, as well as his belief in the clients' competencies to learn to handle their problems themselves.

Today this form of teaching is quite common in Germany, but for those of us who belonged to an authoritarian period in time, it had been totally unusual. We had been used to teachers lecturing from behind a lecturer's desk. Older colleagues still had the unmistakable commanding tone in their ears. The self-determined thinking of learners had not been discovered yet. Self-determined adult education had not yet come into being. . . .

I remember my most important learning experience with Louis Lowy, which was a key experience to me, when Louis Lowy explained to us in a social group work training course the relativity of norms. I felt as if my whole world broke down. I was a Catholic priest at that time. I knew of course, that Lowy was not a Christian, much less a Catholic, for I had recognized him as being agnostic. Despite all good will, I was unable at that time to grapple with his way of thinking, which was so different from my firmly established and dogmatic conception of life. It was his high degree of humanity, however, which made it impossible for me to simply dissociate from his opinion. Today I know that the real shock had not been the scientific theory, but the fact that such a wise man—and I had experienced Louis Lowy as a wise man right from the beginning— was an unbeliever, an agnostic. Teaching was Louis Lowy's life.[20]

Louis had long ago rejected the principle of collective guilt. As he had explained in the *Deggendorf Center Revue,* the rule of law and the possibility of rehabilitation depend upon "the absolute value of any human being."[21] For Heinz Kersting and other students in Germany, it was Louis's friendship that exemplified his most powerful lesson:

Louis and his wife came to Germany year after year until shortly before his death, to the country of their torturers and the murderers of their relatives and friends. In Germany, they never talked publicly about how our fellow citizens, neighbours, perhaps even our parents and relatives had made them suffer. Louis Lowy talked about this horrible time only to very few people. Ditta and Louis Lowy never shamed us. They had acceptance, respect and empathy for us. They regarded us as likeable people, we who felt lost and injured after the war. They brought our resources to light and to some of us, who could have been children of their former persecutors, they gave the gift of their friendship.

Louis Lowy talked about his experiences in the concentration camps only if he was explicitly asked. It was only in his last curriculum vitae which he wrote shortly before his death that he mentions the years in Theresienstadt and Deggendorf as a part of his biography. Significantly, he refers to these years as a period of early professional activities. For many of us who knew about Louis' and Ditta's fate, meeting them was a symbol of forgiveness given to us.[22]

Teaching through the summers was physically exhausting for Louis, and when Ditta accompanied Louis on his travels through Europe, she often feared for his health:

As soon as school ended here in May, he packed up and went over there. Every summer, he taught for four weeks, for five weeks. He gave in that short time fully the hours and the content of a semester. I think he worked too hard. I think he overdid it, but once he committed to something, there was no holding back. He taught a full day, and at noon there was a break of maybe two and a half hours, and then it went on until dinnertime. And then, "One more question," that sort of thing. And he never said no. I think it was too exhausting after a whole year of teaching here to pick up and start four or five weeks of teaching all day, everyday!

He had such a sense of commitment that there was no question that he would do it. Once it happened in Switzerland that he got sick in the morning, and the lectures were in a building adjoined to a hospital. They put him in a bed for a few hours, and afterwards he went on!

Whatever the physical costs, Louis remained committed to teaching international social work as a "major instrumentality for human betterment,"[23] and by the time of his retirement from Boston University in 1985, he had received many awards for his work, including an honorary doctorate from Wheelock College and awards from Boston University, the Northeastern Gerontology Society, the Association of Higher Education in Gerontology, and the National Association of Social Workers.[24] In 1980, the Caritasverband, the German Catholic Social Service Organization, presented Louis with its highest honor, the Lorenz Werthman Medaille for voluntary social welfare service in the Federal Republic of Germany.

When Louis talked to others about retirement, he recommended trying something new. As he explained in an article for *New Findings Quarterly,* a newsletter for people who had retired from the shoe manufacturing industry:

> Retirement from one line of work, e.g. the shoe industry, can be viewed as an opportunity to engage in the pursuit of other activities and new engagements that offer novel interests, different outlooks and satisfactions, as well as the normal problems and crises of anything we do in this world. But this is life! This is being alive![25]

Louis offered this advice on retirement several years after he himself had retired. He never gave up his work. As professor emeritus, he continued writing, teaching, consulting, and corresponding with colleagues and professional associations throughout the world.[26] When Louis gave his final professional presentation to the Northeastern Gerontological Society on April 21, 1991, he recorded his remarks from his hospital bed and, in so doing, exemplified his view of the human condition: "Instead of viewing aging as a problem, we should view it as an opportunity for human fulfillment and a force for greater contribution toward a more humane society."[27]

Louis Lowy died of heart failure on May 22, 1991. As Ditta remembered:

> I think of every survivor, of every survival. Whenever there's hope, you go on. This was true of survival during the war, and it is true when people are very ill. Louis only wanted to reach seventy. That was his great

17. Louis Lowy's seventieth birthday, June 14, 1990. *From left to right:* Reinhard Frank, Louis Lowy, Kurt Kohorn, Vern Drehmel. Photographer unknown. Courtesy of Edith Lowy.

goal, and he reached seventy, but he couldn't reach seventy-one. He died a month before his birthday. I have seen that and I have experienced it myself: as long as there's a will to live, it's like a chemical running through your system contributing to living, to the life force. When that is gone, it's gone. The life extinguishes.

8

A Life's Work

THERE MAY NEVER HAVE BEEN A PROFESSION with as broad a purpose, as courageous a stance, or as fully realized a set of values as the field that Louis Lowy called social work. Louis presented his vision for social work in *The Function of Social Work in a Changing Society: A Continuum of Practice,* a monograph that he wrote in 1974 for newly created Swiss schools of social work:

> Since I have been conducting a series of seminars on social work practice with groups, supervision of social workers, adult educational approaches and methods, curriculum design and development in Germany, Switzerland, France, Belgium and Norway over the past ten years, I have become quite familiar with the problems and issues facing social workers and educators in their own countries. My activities overseas have certainly widened my perspective and sharpened my perceptions of social work that, in turn, have influenced my activities in practice and education in this country to a considerable extent. Recognizing the diversities of social programs and social work practice that are conditioned by different political, economic, social and cultural milieus, I have come to discover firsthand the commonalities and similarities that permeate our field and render it a common base. Yes, there is a unifying thread running through social work that gives it an identity all its own and creates a kinship among its practitioners all over the globe. . . .
>
> In these times when the justification for the existence of social work is being questioned again (as it has been so often in the past), I have come to the conclusion that without it many, many people in every country would be significantly deprived of a major instrumentality for human betterment. Or, to apply an old cliché: if social work did not exist, it

would have to be created. But since it exists, let us apply our energies towards keeping it continuously relevant to the demands of changing societies, the needs and aspirations of people and towards improving its capabilities of delivering quality services as a partner of social movements and social occupations which are mandated to enhance the conditions of life of all people.[1]

Social work for Louis Lowy was more than an occupation or a profession; it was the name that he gave to his life's work. Louis remembered his deportation to Terezín as the beginning of his social work career: "And so we marched off. And then began my career in Terezín as a social worker." At the time of his "early professional activities," however, Louis had little awareness of social work as a profession. Although he had become interested in social responses to poverty, particularly during his stay in London before the war, it would be many years before he learned about the origins of the settlement movement in London or the establishment of schools of social work in Europe or the United States.[2]

Louis's wartime activities were dangerous, and in later years his dedication to work sometimes endangered his health. He was motivated, as he explained, not by ambition or altruism, but by his will to survive. By the end of the war, Louis had emerged as a Jewish community leader who felt a sense of responsibility not only to the Jewish community but also to "the human community." In forming the Jewish self-government of the Deggendorf Displaced Persons Center, he was guided by the values of human worth, community self-determination, and the interdependence of generations, and he promoted human and social development by engaging people in social participation and lifelong learning. Louis immigrated to the United States with a purpose in search of a profession, and he found that he could express his purpose as a survivor in terms of the values and goals of social work, his chosen field:

At this juncture in the history of our profession we have little choice except to go forward with our heritage, filled with determination to work toward a better world. But the world will only be better if we work at it and use all our available resources. To be true to ourselves may involve us in occasional—possibly even frequent—conflicts with the very society that sanctions us and from which we seek approval. But because of our obligation to this same society, we have to advance our knowledge and skills to change it for the better, guided by basic values rooted in our belief in the worth of men.[3]

Human Worth and Self-Determination

A philosopher at heart, Louis was fascinated by the reciprocal yet often contradictory responsibilities of individuals and society.[4] Just as each person has an obligation to contribute to the common good, so society has an obligation to enhance the potential of every person. When the needs of the many conflict with the desires of a few, then a central problem in political theory becomes the basic function of social work—to mediate between individual and social needs: "If man would be the master of his destiny, then he must first recognize his destiny. To advance himself, he needs his own inner resources, which have to be discovered and put to creative use for the sake of himself and his fellow men. Society is a matter of give and take; we contribute to it and we receive from it. If we want to receive more, we must contribute more."[5]

In his own life, Louis had learned to identify his personal desires with his sense of social purpose. He first assumed leadership responsibilities when, at the age of fifteen, he left the safety of London to help his parents in their "great hopeful move" from Munich to Prague. Family experiences had prepared him for leadership, Louis believed. Whether he was teaching in the Terezín ghetto, guiding young men in their escape across Europe, or forming the Jewish self-government of the Deggendorf Displaced Persons Center, he upheld the values that he considered the legacy of Judaism: appreciation for the dignity and worth of every person, respect for the self-determination of individuals and communities, promotion of distributive social justice, and belief in people's potential to learn and grow throughout their lives.[6]

In the aftermath of the war, Louis sought the right of self-determination for the surviving Jewish community: "We want to become human beings again who contribute their shares in work and deed, who are no more objects but subjects deciding for themselves and their fate."[7] He advocated with the military authorities for the preservation of the Deggendorf

Center as a displaced persons camp for stateless and non-repatriable Jews, and he formed the Jewish self-government and the self-administered legal system of the Deggendorf Center on the basis of "the absolute value of any human being."[8] After being appointed by UNRRA as the leader of the Deggendorf Center, Louis insisted on a democratic election, and he arranged for a ballot box to be brought into the hospital so that the even most vulnerable people could vote. Joining with the leaders of other Jewish displaced persons camps, Louis participated in the Central Committee of Liberated Jews in the United States Occupied Zone of Bavaria, which represented the Jewish community to the military authorities and to the outside world.

Louis continued to promote the self-determination of individuals and communities throughout his career. As he stated in a 1959 address to the National Federation of Settlements and Neighborhood Associations, settlement houses have the responsibility to encourage communities to act on their own behalf:

> Today as yesterday we must give people a sense of participation in the determination of their needs, wants and interests. Many people still do not have the chance to participate in the determination of their own destiny in the community. The role of settlements has been to help people so that they can assume responsibility as citizens and as influence agents to guide their own destiny. . . . Settlements have to become again standard bearers for social change.[9]

As one of the founders of the senior center movement in the early 1950s, Louis empowered older members of the Bridgeport Community Center to establish the Leisure Lounge: "Continuing emphasis must be placed on the activation and involvement of older people themselves in shaping their present and future" as Louis explained,[10] and the senior center movement afforded older adults the opportunity to build their own community institutions:

> All older people . . . have three universal needs: material and physical security; social and psychological security; and group security, a sense of being linked with the community, with the young and the old. To

meet the first need is the function of our pension programs, insurance policies, social security and health programs. The second and third needs can only be met through provision of services at the community level. The Senior Center can be one of those institutions. It can become a major social institution for the elderly which is rightfully theirs, as much as all other age groups can claim social institutions as their own. Older people themselves are engaged in planning, directing, and carrying out such activities.[11]

The Interdependence of Generations

Louis Lowy was drawn to gerontology by his appreciation of the reciprocal needs and responsibilities of younger and older generations. He dedicated *Social Work with the Aging: The Challenge and Promise of the Later Years* to "the memory of my parents who were not allowed to grow old," and it was his deepest regret that he could not learn how to grow old from their examples.[12] What Louis had learned from his parents, however, was to respect the interdependence of generations. Younger and older people learn from one another and care for one another throughout their lives and throughout history. If the rise of National Socialism represented "a break in time,"[13] then social workers would help restore the course of civilization by engaging older people in social and political life:

Work with the aging can be exciting, whether it is in direct practice or through policy shaping and administration; whether with one person, with ten, or with hundreds; whether in a large bureaucracy or in a small informal agency; whether in an institution or in a community setting. In addition to the frustration and elation, the defeats and victories, the disappointing periods and the gratifying moments of all social work, one extra ingredient makes work with the aging uniquely exciting and rewarding: It brings together the past, the present, and the future in uniting us with people through time and space. We become aware of the march of generations, the continuity of history, and the unity of people, in spite of their uniqueness and variability. In their common heritage and destiny, we see a cosmic unity and a strength by which the human spirit continuously struggles to find an answer to the question, "Why survive?"[14]

Louis discovered at an early age that intergenerational relationships allow for personal and social development, family and community well-being, and the promise of historical and cultural purpose. Although he had become a man in Jewish law, he was still a child when, at the age of thirteen, he traveled to the safety of England in 1933. Throughout the long journey by train and by sea, Louis wore a cardboard sign with his name on it, and upon reaching his foster family's home in London, he cried with loneliness in his little room. In 1935, however, in responding to his mother's call for help, Louis returned to Munich as an adult with adult responsibilities. As he later taught, the developmental tasks of adulthood do not require leaving one's parents and families behind. Older and younger generations continue to need and to learn from one another throughout their lives, even as adult children assume greater responsibilities for their parents' care. In the developmental phase of *filial maturity,* Louis believed, adults redefine their relationships with their parents, assuming reciprocal caregiving roles: "Children become emancipated in order to be ready to help their own parents at a later stage in life and thereby learn how to be older themselves. In other words, we should help our children to learn greater interdependence rather than independence."[15]

When Louis and his family were deported to the Terezín ghetto, Louis discovered that communities as well as individuals and families require intergenerational care. The Jewish administrators in Terezín provided an old-age home and other services for elders, but at the same time, they benefited from the wisdom and skills of older people. Louis Lowy was among the youngest lecturers in the ghetto's famed adult-education series.[16] In the aftermath of the war, when Louis established the Jewish self-government of the Deggendorf Displaced Persons Center, he followed the patterns that he had seen in Terezín. He planned an old-age home with a special kitchen and other services for the aged, while also relying upon his elders for their political knowledge and expertise. Younger and older generations in the Deggendorf Center contributed to the development of educational and cultural activities, health care, and administrative services, and the participation of older people enhanced all aspects of social and political life:

Plato has already stated that the most appropriate response to the experiences of growing old is neither resignation nor continuation of middle-aged commitments but the adoption of values and activities different from those appropriate to the first periods in life. This view affirms that the "third age" makes possible the discovery of values and meanings different in character from those accessible during earlier periods. It affirms that the insights and values achievable in the later years are related to worldly needs and interests. Plato asserts that full participation of the old in the political arena and other areas of social responsibility is essential for the public good.

The "third age" is an integral stage of the whole life span. Our needs for survival, growth, and development and for achieving a sense of autonomy and meaning have to be met continuously. It is our task as social workers to infuse our values and beliefs about human dignity and social justice in working with the aging and their families and to utilize their resources and talents in making life better and more beautiful for everybody.[17]

As a survivor, Louis Lowy had tremendous empathy for the strengths and vulnerabilities of people in old age. As with displaced persons in the Deggendorf Center, older adults are survivors who have lost family and friends who loved them, work that sustained them, and roles and responsibilities that gave meaning to their lives:

To a large extent, our needs to belong, be rooted, and be accepted are based on our relationships with those we love—family and friends. As people grow older, close family members and friends depart and leave the older person alone in a world of yesterday. In earlier years, the loss of a loved one was traumatic enough; however, the younger person could still overcome the loss by replacement. For the aged person, isolation and loneliness gradually become a reality that did not exist before. The new surrounding world seems cold, unconcerned, and strange.

Where are the roots for belonging? This sense of aloneness and being deprived of family and peers engenders a feeling of irrelevance, mean-inglessness, and status anxiety unknown to the majority of younger people. It necessitates an emotional reorientation, for which many older people do not have so great a capacity, and also a new role adaptation, for example, as widower or widow, whose status and concomitant role definitions are at best ambiguous in our society.[18]

Just as the leaders of the Deggendorf Displaced Persons Center gave a sense of purpose to the Jewish community, so social workers have the task of instilling hope among older adults who have lost confidence in their ability to shape the future: "To move a group of aged toward effective action, the social worker needs not only to provide strategies and techniques for action, but to instill a new sense of confidence and dignity among them. Workers must convince the elderly that in spite of years of possible disappointment, something can be done."[19]

Applying the developmental goals of social work to his work with older people, Louis taught that social participation and learning help people cope with the losses of aging. Even as social workers serve older clients, they should respect them as community leaders and as educators of generations to come:

> There is a tendency among social workers and other professionals to view older people primarily as recipients of services. Contrary to this view, the elderly are also an important resource. . . . They are a source of support to spouse, children, grandchildren, siblings, and others. . . . As consumers and producers of goods and services, older people constitute an economic resource and in the political arena they are active citizens. They are teachers of oral history as they communicate their life experiences; they also transmit values and traditions to subsequent generations. They act as role models to the young on how to mature and grow older since they are living witnesses of past events who have endured and persevered throughout the economic, political, technological, cultural and social upheavals of this century.[20]

In Louis's view, the values of filial maturity and intergenerational caring were no less relevant to social welfare policy than to social work practice. As he explained in an article for *Advice for Adults with Aging Parents:*

> However we define family, the bonds which tie people together biologically, emotionally, spiritually, socially or culturally make it imperative

that we work towards private and public policies that are geared towards interdependence rather than one-sided care-giving, cooperation rather than competition, social justice rather than charity.[21]

In his last professional address, which he recorded from a hospital bed for the White House Conference on Aging Symposium in 1991, Louis affirmed the interdependence of generations as the basis for public policy and planning:

This conference has to affirm that there are intergenerational links, and not to fall into the trap of playing one age group or one sex group or one minority group or one needs group against the other. On the contrary, the more we establish the mutual dependency and reciprocity of the various age levels, the more we are likely to create a society that is all-inclusive. And only within an inclusive society will the specific problems that aging brings about be resolved or at least come closer to some solution.[22]

Social Participation and Learning

It was as a social worker and an educator that Louis tried to nurture a more humane world. When Louis traveled each summer to teach social work in Germany, some American Jews disapproved, as Ditta recalled:

He considered it his mission. And when somebody here aggressively asked him, "How can you go back to Germany to those people who did those horrible things to you?" His answer was, and I'll never forget it: "They've done bad things. If I want them to do better, I have to go there and teach them." That was his view.

Even as a child, Louis had coped with suffering by studying the causes of poverty, violence, and political turmoil that he observed around him. Neither imprisonment by the Gestapo nor deportation to the Terezín ghetto could dampen his need for learning. In the Pankcraz prison, Louis shared with cellmates his interests in the arts, theater, and the works of Sigmund Freud. In Terezín, he studied the approaches to community organization that were being tried by the Jewish ghetto administration. At the same time, for his own peace of mind, Louis looked for ways that he could be useful to others, and in his voluntary service as a youth leader and educator in Tererzín, Louis began to understand social participation and learning as the means for fulfilling not only his own potential but also the individual and social potential of others.

Louis's goals in Terezín and later in the Deggendorf Center ranged from solving and preventing problems to promoting "existential fulfillment and self-realization through social participation."[23] He later defined the function of social work as a *continuum of social work practice* that extended from curative, to preventative, to developmental goals:

> The developmental orientation, which now has become increasingly a part of the goals and practice of social work, particularly in the developing countries of the world, seeks to create conditions for people that allow them to fulfill themselves optimally, to comprehend the world of today and tomorrow, to find their place in it and to participate constructively and actively in their society as part of a larger world order. Fundamentally, this aspect of social work is learning.[24]

For Louis Lowy, education and adult education were as integral to social work as learning was to life. Those of Louis's pupils who survived Terezín were proud of their educational accomplishments there for the rest of their lives. The banners that they had strung across their room in L414 proclaimed that "knowledge is power," and Louis's belief that "truth must be sought out regardless where the search for it may lead" was a form of spiritual resistance.[25] His pupils in Terezín practiced English in confidence that they would live to see the Allies win the war. Similarly, the Jewish self-government of the Deggendorf Center sought to give people a sense of purpose by engaging them in educational, cultural, and political activities. Social participation and learning were the means for a grieving community to restore their heritage and to prepare for a new life.

When Louis entered Boston University in 1947, he had been living for many years by the values and goals that he would attribute to social work, and he found kindred spirits among social group workers who used educational and cultural activities as the means for promoting human dignity, self determination, and participation in a democracy. By the late 1950s, however, social group work as it had been practiced in clubs, settlements, and neighborhood centers was falling out of favor. Some social work educators wanted to distinguish social work from the fields of recreation, education, and adult education, and social work agencies had little place for indigenous community leaders and volunteers. If the function of social work was to mediate between individuals and society, then social workers increasingly emphasized the goals of individual adjustment and adaptation over social change and reform.[26] As Louis explained:

> It is understandable that during the period of its professionalization and search for status social work might have avoided a position which would disturb its acceptance by those forces in society which bestow status upon a profession. In other words, it has tended to conform to the dominant cultural values and viewpoints. One of these was the view that the individual's personality structure carries the major responsibility for the appropriate discharge of his societal role functions; while environmental factors deserve attention and may actually be responsible for dysfunction, the larger society and its value system is basically "sound" and does not require changes. Highest status has been accorded to professions which look at man's idiosyncratic functioning and try to restore his dysfunction within the basic premise of a "sane society."[27]

Although Louis did not share the premise of a sane society, he understood the conflicting values in social work as the inevitable consequence of a changing cultural and social environment: "Conflicting valuations and inconsistent beliefs abound in every society and social work value commitments are faced with equal conflicts and inconsistencies."[28] In his own writings and teachings, however, from his earliest columns in the *Deggendorf Center Revue* to his publications in social group work, social welfare policy, gerontology, and adult education, Louis presented a consistent view of social work values and goals. Far from distinguishing social work from allied occupations, he devoted his last book, *Why Education in the Later Years?* to identifying the commonalities between social work and adult education:

> Ultimately, both social welfare and education as fields and social work and education as occupations are philosophically oriented toward

enhancement, growth, development, and change of people within a social environment, in continuing transaction of persons-situations-milieu. By utilizing purposive change strategies with persons, groups, organizations, and communities, conditions can be maximized to enhance people's lives as members of their social network in their communities and can give them a meaningful place and role in society.[29]

From Terezín to the Deggendorf Center, Louis had performed some of his most significant work as an indigenous leader and an untrained volunteer, and he emphasized the importance of creativity as "a necessary condition for effective service to other people."[30] As with the interdependence of generations, Louis appreciated the reciprocal roles and responsibilities of professionals, paraprofessionals, and the people whom they serve, and he encouraged social workers to empower clients and volunteers as activists and leaders.[31] Devoting as much attention to community education as to professional education, he often wrote two versions of his papers, one for publication in academic or professional journals and another for newsletters and magazines that would be accessible to the general public.[32] He confronted the terrors of his day by writing and speaking against racism, prejudice, social and economic neglect, nuclear proliferation, and war:

> Here is a challenge for social work, not merely to pick up the pieces of mistaken or mismanaged social policies, but to assume leadership in extending the frontier of human endeavors in the service of a more equitable, just, and humane social order.[33]

Although he rarely talked about his past, Louis encouraged his students to incorporate the values and roles that he had assumed during the Holocaust into their identities as social workers. His goal as an educator was, above all, to prepare social workers who would carry on his work as agents of social change:

> When we think of a statesman, we have an image of a *political* leader whose experience and skill have given him a broad perspective which fosters wisdom in the discharge of his responsibilities. Statesmanship is an objective on the continuum of a political career.

In social work, statesmanship has not always been built into the career continuum. Social statesmanship has, in fact, received only passing attention in this country and has often implied a dichotomy of functions. On one hand was the clinically oriented social work practitioner who provided direct as well as indirect services to individuals, groups, and communities; on the other, a handful of social workers who by virtue of their positions in public or voluntary agencies administered large-scale social welfare programs and would participate in the formulation of large-scale social policies. In quite a few instances these individuals were "social statesmen" in theory as well as in practice.

If we accept, however, the premise of the dual function of social work . . . then we have to build the concept of social statesmanship into the career continuum of the social worker and make provisions to equip him for the possible achievement of such a goal. . . . Regardless of whether a social worker devotes his career to practice as a case worker, group worker, or community organizer; as administrator, researcher, or teacher, he should have a professional commitment to promote social change or reform. . . .

The development of attitudes, knowledge, and skill in effecting social change is basic and germane to *any* social work training program. This is not a question of training social welfare specialists, but a question of fundamental equipment for every social work practitioner who is to become fully committed to the "social" in social work and who sees the concept of social statesmanship as a desirable goal on the continuum of the social work career.[34]

An indefatigable social statesman, Louis Lowy continued writing, speaking publicly, and conferring with colleagues until the last days of his life. Today he is remembered in Europe as a social worker and social group worker, while in the United States he is best known for his contributions to gerontology and adult education. American policy makers increasingly accept the central principles of his work: that the basis for democracy and, therefore for social welfare policy in a democracy, is respect for the dignity, worth, and self-determination of individuals and communities; that community centers engage older people, including older immigrants, in education, creative arts, and intergenerational civic activities; and that social participation and learning contribute to the health and happiness of people of every age.[35]

According to his family and friends, Louis Lowy was a born educator. He remembered playing school as a young child in Munich, when he would gather his cousins around him to sing songs and to tell stories. Ever since his early professional activities in Terezín, when he traveled from room to room in L414 as an itinerant teacher and director of children's plays, he had a mission that transcended hardship and heartache. He lived with the knowledge of Auschwitz, yet, as his students believed, Louis Lowy enjoyed life because he had always loved his work:

> We need a heart and a head in social work. And we have to understand that we are part of a movement that has grown out of dedication. A basic commitment to human values, a belief in people as individuals and as neighbors, calls for vision, courage and conviction. It requires people who not only feel deeply but can articulate the feeling and have the courage to stand up and act. It requires people with grand ideas, dreamers, and at the same time people who are realistic and can deal with realities but have a goal of broad vision. If we do only what is possible, we will never achieve what is impossible. In a time of change, what we need is inner strength and security and conviction combined with courage, a willingness to experiment and a sense of adventure![36]

Although the Holocaust was a formative experience for Louis Lowy, it was his Jewish heritage that defined his life and thought. The Nazis identified Louis as a Jew whose birth to a Jewish parent determined the meaning and value, or lack of value, of his life. Louis identified as a Jew who found in his heritage the source of personal and professional purpose, even though he did not believe in God. In "Returning," his first article for the *Deggendorf Center Review*, Louis explained that it was the historical obligation of the Jewish people to realize the ideas of human progress, social and economic justice, and a new social order for "everybody living in the world."[37]

Louis's love of life, his sense of delight, and his efforts to instill hope for the future were consistent with Jewish religious teachings. The unifying values in his writings—human worth and self-determination, the interdependence of generations, and social participation and lifelong learning—were central values in Jewish history and culture. When Louis sought his first professional position as a social worker in the United States, he applied to Jewish communal agencies: "I wanted to become closer to Jews. I identified closely with Jewishness given my war experiences, but in a secular way, not in a religious way. The secular way just suited me very well."

Louis rarely spoke explicitly about Jewish subjects, however. Mindful of anti-Semitism and respectful of other people's cultural sensibilities, he talked about being Jewish only when he was addressing Jewish audiences. He had learned to be discreet during the war.

In the spring of 1945, after escaping from a death march, Louis had led a small band of followers eastward across Europe and away from the war. Early on, they took shelter in a deserted British POW camp, where they found a stash of British uniforms, generic khaki uniforms without insignias. After they had traded their concentration camp pajamas for British battle dress, Louis and his group were able to travel in relative safety through hostile and friendly populations without revealing who they really were.

Louis remembered surviving the Holocaust as the beginning of his social work career, but social work, for Louis, was like the British uniforms that he and his followers had found. Once he had assumed his role as a social worker, Louis could live by his values and realize his purpose without disclosing his past. He could lead generations of students through a precarious world even as they were learning to change it. Louis Lowy ultimately expressed his truest self in his dedication to social work, and social work was his name for living as a Jew.

Afterword

Social Work with Refugees and Displaced Populations

IT IS OFTEN THE SURVIVORS who first raise awareness of a catastrophe to the outside world. We learned after the Holocaust that eyewitness testimonies may be our primary sources of knowledge for months, for years, or even for generations after the event, and if we are to serve refugees and displaced populations effectively, we must begin by listening to them.

Jewish war refugees of the 1950s quickly learned not to talk about their pasts. Health and human services professionals, who rarely spoke the languages of the survivors, did not want to hear about their experiences during the war. In contrast to social workers of the postwar era, American social workers today are aware of genocide as a concept and as a reality, and we have better information about trauma, posttraumatic stress, resilience, and recovery. However, we are no more likely than our predecessors to speak a second language, let alone the particular languages of newly arriving populations, and we may be no better prepared to listen and to learn from the refugees and displaced populations whom we hope to serve.

As a survivor of the Holocaust, Louis Lowy taught his students to follow the guiding principles and values that he attributed to the social work profession: respect for human dignity, worth, and self-determination; appreciation for the interdependence of generations; and commitment to social participation and learning for people of every age. In recording his oral narrative, Louis Lowy gave further guidance to social workers of the future, with particular implications for social work practice with refugees and displaced populations. His testimony suggests that we will gain an orienting knowledge of displaced communities by listening with empathy, by respecting the meaning of *return,* by supporting cultural and educational activities, by empowering indigenous leaders, and by taking a critical and creative stance toward our profession.

An Orienting Knowledge

The need for *an orienting knowledge* was suggested to me by Maria Hirsch Rosenbloom, professor emerita of Hunter School of Social Work, who was one of the first social work educators to offer a course on the Holocaust.[1] Maria Rosenbloom had survived the war by living under a false identity. After her liberation, she worked with refugees and displaced populations in Germany, where she was employed by UNRRA and later by the American Joint Distribution Committee, a combined Jewish philanthropy known as "the Joint." As she remembered:

> I was assigned by the Joint to be the official escort of a shipment of refugees. I was to give every passenger ten dollars and get a receipt. I was told hundreds of times, I must get a receipt, and I got a receipt from everyone. It was September 21, 1947, around the Jewish holidays of 1947, and we celebrated Rosh Hashanah [the Jewish New Year] on the boat. It was a rickety boat, a military boat called the *Ernie Pyle*. It was a very miserable ride, seven days that you never forget. Many people got sick. One day, suddenly we heard a scream: "America!" And I can never say it without tears in my eyes. We suddenly saw land, and our sickness left us. The sight of America was an experience which sixty years later I cannot forget. It was the most meaningful experience of my life. It was true for all of us. The boat kept moving slowly towards the harbor and it circled or came in close distance of the Statue of Liberty. And this, too, I remember, how the most Orthodox Jews took off their hats–they don't do it, usually—to greet our lady, the Statue of Liberty. And this was 1947 and now it is 2007. This makes it sixty years ago, and I still cry when I talk about it. And I'm sure this is true for many of the passengers on that boat.
>
> Another moment that stays with me, that stays with most of us, is the moment that the boat started moving away from the land in Bremerhaven in Germany. That also was a moment that I will never forget. Most of us also felt that we would never go back to Europe because of what we left in Europe. Some of us did go back as tourists; I went, too, but Europe

was something that was terribly painful for us to have the memory of, to be connected with. So I remember distinctly the terrible moan that went out when the boat cut off from the anchor.

After arriving in New York City, Maria Rosenbloom was awarded a scholarship by the newly established Adelphi University School of Social Work, where she completed her master's degree in social work in 1952. She accepted her first professional position as a social worker in the Psychiatric Clinic of Beth Israel Hospital. Although most patients of the clinic were Jewish war refugees, they were never identified as such by the doctors or hospital staff:

> One of my first jobs after graduation was at the Psychiatric Clinic in the Beth Israel Hospital of New York. It was a very meaningful job. The majority of patients were survivors—very poor, very heartbroken, and very deprived of services because they spoke Yiddish, only. In that Jewish hospital in Manhattan, no psychiatrists spoke Yiddish. So they all were sent to me. Every survivor was sent to me, because the psychiatrists didn't speak Yiddish. It was very sad, but that's how it was. So it was my experience to get a lot of experience. I accumulated a lot of stories from survivors. They were telling me their life stories, their Holocaust stories, and I was very engaged emotionally with them, because it was so meaningful. It was a privilege to serve these people. When I think back about my career, I believe that it was the most meaningful job I ever had.

Americans charged with helping Jewish war refugees lacked an orienting knowledge. As Louis Lowy discovered, few Americans in the United States Army or in UNRRA spoke the languages of displaced populations under their protection. Carl Atkin, the first UNRRA director of the Deggendorf Displaced Persons Camp, did not speak German. In the United States today, language barriers continue to block access to effective health and human services for many populations.[2]

Beyond the language barrier, health and human services professionals did not cross the barriers of their own professional and cultural assumptions and beliefs. As recounted in chapter 7, Louis Lowy's friend and pupil Vern Drehmel remembered attending a summer program for Jewish war orphans, where a well-meaning teacher brought all the boys to the barber for crew cuts. The teacher had no idea that concentration camp survivors might object to having their heads nearly shaved. Throughout the world, Holocaust survivors faced ignorance and prejudice as psychiatrists and other experts made pessimistic predictions about their ability ever to live productive lives.[3] Louis Lowy later objected to similarly popular yet prejudiced assumptions about older adults, such as the "disengagement theory" that mistook loneliness for normative aging: "Social work, with an insecure knowledge base and a heavy value emphasis, has tended all too easily to latch on to theories that seemed to hold out great promise without always keeping a respectful distance and maintaining a willingness to wait for the evidence."[4]

In the absence of an orienting knowledge about the Holocaust, health and human services professionals took comfort in the conventional wisdom of their fields, and when their theories could not accommodate survivors' realities, then the survivors were silenced and their realities were ignored. Nonetheless, most survivors in the United States adapted successfully to their new lives. In his extensive longitudinal study, William Helmreich found that Holocaust survivors and their children fared comparably well to American-born Jews in the areas of family life, economic self-sufficiency, educational achievement, and civic engagement.[5] When they were met with indifference from helping professionals, survivors turned to one another for comfort, support, and mutual aid. Adult survivors typically married other survivors, and they formed social and philanthropic associations that continue to serve survivors and their descendants today. Some Jewish war refugees joined *Landsmanschaften,* societies for people from the same regions or towns in Europe. Here they could reminisce in their own language about life before the war, feeling a sense of connection to one another and to another time.

The Meaning of Return

Most Holocaust survivors were "stateless and non-repatriable Jews" who would never return to their prewar homes. When Louis Lowy visited Prague in 1945, and when Ditta and her mother visited Vienna, they found themselves in "living cemeteries" where everyone they were looking for was gone. Although visiting their hometowns was "terribly painful," as Maria Rosenbloom explained, survivors cherished their memories of family and community life before the war.[6] For Louis Lowy, Prague would always be the most beautiful city in the world.

Louis Lowy's first article for the *Deggendorf Center Review,* the newspaper of the Deggendorf Displaced Persons Center, had the intriguing title "Returning." Although his readers could not return to the lives they had known, they would return to a life of purpose: "Our small community here is in the midst of the hard struggle in finding the way back to life." Louis argued that the Nazi era had been "a break in time," the exception and not the norm. The Jewish people now had the responsibility to restore progress and the rightful course of history: "The history of mankind is a continuous fight for progress and the creation of humanity, the creation of a human community. Despots have always arisen who wanted to delay and to hinder the way. . . . Now we are again facing a break in time."[7]

Under the leadership of Louis Lowy, the Jewish community in the Deggendorf Center developed an array of cultural, religious, and educational activities that engaged people of all ages in civic life.[8] In order to believe in the future, the "surviving remnant" needed to remember its history, and according to Holocaust historian Jacqueline Giere, cultural activities in the Jewish displaced persons camps gave people a lifeline or, more precisely, a "timeline" to the irretrievable past.[9] Within six months of the war's end, the Central Committee of Liberated Jews in the United States Occupied Zone of Bavaria had established a Historical Commission to document prewar Jewish community life and, in so doing, to protect the timeline for an entire people.[10] After emigration, as Louis Lowy understood, younger and older survivors would face different challenges in building their new lives, but forgetting the past would never be an option. The Holocaust would become a part of their family heritage and history, of Jewish history, and of American history as well, as indicated by the establishment of the United States Holocaust Memorial Museum. Despite their initial reluctance to speak publicly about the Holocaust, many survivors eventually testified, and they continue to testify, as gestures of return.

Unlike survivors of the Holocaust, many refugees and displaced populations today hope to return to their countries of origin, if not during their own lifetimes then in future generations.[11] Whether or not they are able to return, however, they may never identify in the same way with their original homes. Memories of belonging—or of not belonging—to a place, a community, a culture, or a history define, in some essential way, one's sense of self. In his analysis of Holocaust testimonies, literary critic Lawrence Langer found that survivors struggle in vain to construct coherent life stories because they have no way to integrate "disruptive memories" of trauma with memories of their prewar and postwar lives.[12] According to psychoanalyst Dori Laub, "A home can never be a home again after trauma, and an erased relationship can never provide safety."[13] It is only through the empathy of a listener that survivors can bridge their unspeakable memories with words.

Empathy is more than a feeling. It is a communications skill. Empathic listeners communicate their full attention, humility, interest, and respect. Maria Rosenbloom communicated empathy to Holocaust survivors in Beth Israel Hospital, and they responded by trusting her with their stories. In Louis Lowy's narrative, as recounted in chapter 4, General Dwight D. Eisenhower communicated empathy in his tour of the newly established Deggendorf Displaced Persons Center on Yom Kippur in 1945. Louis was amazed by Eisenhower's respectful demeanor, by the way that he took off his hat and shook Louis's hand, by the firm insistence with which he asked: "Will you tell me what you people need?"

As supreme commander of the Allied Forces in Europe, Eisenhower did not need to tour the Jewish displaced persons camps. His staff had prepared detailed reports on the shortages of food, fuel, and medical supplies.[14] Eisenhower, however, sought an orienting knowledge. He wanted to meet and to listen to the Jewish war refugees in person, and he listened with such empathy that Louis Lowy, who had lost his parents and his entire family, found tremendous comfort in remembering their conversation: "He was like a friendly father talking."

Implications for Practice

The meaning of terms such as "refugees" and "displaced populations" changes with historical context. The United States Army originally coined the term "displaced person" in 1943 to define categories of war refugees who would be entitled to the protection of UNRRA, the newly formed United Nations Relief and Rehabilitation Agency. As often happens with technical language, however, the term "displaced person" had a poetic resonance that expanded its meaning over time. Today it is possible to think of many populations as *displaced,* including not only people who have fled large-scale disasters but also those who are living through more intimate disasters, such as homelessness, poverty, or domestic violence. People are displaced who have lost the safety of relationships with family or friends, the ability to trust in their health, the security of providing for basic needs, or the expectation of living with hope and meaning. Although Louis Lowy did not specifically write about social work with displaced populations, his descriptions of old people in nursing homes evoked the losses of survivors in displaced persons camps: "The new surrounding world seems cold, unconcerned, and strange."[15]

It is the goal of social work to help restore people's relationships with the social environment, which Louis Lowy believed was possible by engaging them in social participation and learning. In this sense, the testimonies of Louis Lowy and of other Holocaust survivors have particular implications for social work practice with refugees and displaced populations today, as well as wider applications in social work and related fields:

1. Seek *an orienting knowledge,* including knowledge that emerges across generations and over time, from refugees and displaced persons themselves. Listen with empathy—attention, interest, humility, and respect—and believe what people say. Show acceptance and patience with those who choose not to disclose their past.

2. Gain proficiency in more than one language. *Social work cannot be an international, human rights profession in English only.* Schools of social work and other health and human services professions should require second-language proficiency at the undergraduate level, when students have several years to begin learning a new language; at the master's degree level, when students can gain specialized professional vocabularies; and at the doctoral level, when students can use their language proficiencies in research.

3. Respect the meaning of *return* for refugees and displaced populations. Promote community self-determination and mutual aid by

supporting cultural, civic, and educational activities for people of every age and by accepting invitations to take part. In this sense, we will be returning ourselves to the social group work tradition.

4. Encourage and empower *indigenous leaders* as volunteers, as paraprofessionals, and as professionals, and open their access to professional education in social work and allied fields. It is indigenous leaders such as Louis Lowy and Maria Rosenbloom who will translate cultural values and beliefs about survival, health, healing, and return into knowledge for effective research and practice.

5. Take a critical and creative stance toward the social work profession in its changing cultural contexts. Question assumptions about knowledge, practice, and professional boundaries and roles in order to meet the expectations and needs of newly arriving populations.

In the years that I have been working on this book, I have been aware that I will never comprehend the Holocaust or the memories of its survivors. Nonetheless, my responsibility as a researcher has been to listen with empathy to Louis Lowy and to the other survivors who knew him. Social workers who serve refugees and displaced populations assume a similar task. Although we may never understand what survivors have lived through, we can listen with empathy, which is the beginning of an orienting knowledge.

NOTES

REFERENCES

INDEX

Notes

Preface

1. See, for example, Serena Woolrich, "Searches," *Together: The American Gathering of Jewish Holocaust Survivors and Their Descendants* 22, no. 1 (Apr. 2008): 22–23.

2. Jürgen Kalcher, "Social Group Work in Germany: An American Import and Its Historical Development," in *Growth and Development Through Group Work,* ed. Claudia J. Caron, Anna S. Fritz, Elizabeth Lewis, John H. Ramey, and David T. Sugiuchi (Binghamton, NY: Haworth, 2004), 51–71; Gisela Konopka, *Courage and Love* (Edina, MN.: Burgess Printing, 1988); Andrew Lees, ed., *Character Is Destiny: The Autobiography of Alice Solomon* (Ann Arbor: Univ. of Michigan Press, 2004); Blanca Rosenberg, *To Tell at Last: Survival Under False Identity, 1941–1945* (Chicago: Univ. of Illinois Press, 1995); Joachim Wieler, "Destination Social Work: Emigrés in a Women's Profession," in *Between Sorrow and Strength: Women Refugees of the Nazi Period,* ed. Sibylle Quack (Washington, DC: German Historical Institute and Cambridge Univ. Press, 1995), 265–82; and Joachim Wieler and Susanne Zeller, eds., *Emigrierte Sozialarbeit: Portraits Vertriebener Sozialarbeiter innen nach 1933* [Emigrant social workers: portraits of social workers who were exiled after 1933] (Freiburg, Germany: Lambertus, 1995), 217–32.

3. Wieler, "Destination Social Work"; Wieler and Zeller, *Emigrierte Sozialarbeit.*

4. Kalcher, "Social Group Work in Germany," 59; Heinz J. Kersting, "Lowy, Louis," in *Who is Who der Sozialen Arbeit* [Who's who in social work], ed. Hugo Maier (Freiburg, Germany: Lambertus, 1998), 371–73; and Louis Lowy, Curriculum Vitae, Oct. 1989.

5. Yehuda Bauer, "A Past That Will Not Go Away," in *The Holocaust and History: The Known, the Unknown, the Disputed, and the Reexamined,* ed. Michael Berenbaum and Abraham J. Peck (Bloomington: Indiana Univ. Press, 1998), 21; Raul Hilberg, "Sources and Their Uses," in Berenbaum and Peck, *Holocaust and History,* 5–11; and Dori Laub with Marjorie Allard, "History, Memory, and Truth: Defining the Place of the Survivor," in Berenbaum and Peck, *Holocaust and History,* 801.

6. Edith L. Holocaust Testimony (HVT-2868), Fortunoff Video Archive for Holocaust Testimonies, Yale Univ. Library, New Haven, CT, 1994.

7. Lorrie G. Gardella, "Millie Charles: Believing in the Mission," *Journal of Baccalaureate Social Work* 2, no. 2 (1999): 19–36; Lorrie G. Gardella, "Prime Mover: Pauline Roney Lang," *Journal of Baccalaureate Social Work* 1, no. 2 (1997): 22–42; Ruth Martin,

Oral History in Social Work: Research, Assessment, and Intervention (Thousand Oaks, CA: Sage, 1995).

8. Leo Eitinger, "Holocaust Survivors in the Past and Present," in Berenbaum and Peck, *Holocaust and History*, 767–84; William B. Helmreich, *Against All Odds: Holocaust Survivors and the Successful Lives They Made in America* (New Brunswick, NJ: Transaction Publishers, 1996); and Maria H. Rosenbloom, "What Can We Learn from the Holocaust?" *Occasional Papers in Jewish History and Thought*, no. 3 (New York: Hunter College Jewish Social Studies Program, Hunter College of the City Univ. of New York, 1994).

9. Eitinger, "Holocaust Survivors," 774.

10. Jewish Dispalced Persons Project, 2008, accessed on June 30, 2011, http://www .ushmm.org/museum/exhibit/online/dp/update.htm; Zeev W. Mankowitz, *Life Between Memory and Hope: The Survivors of the Holocaust in Occupied Germany* (Cambridge: Cambridge Univ. Press, 2002); and Judah Nadich, *Eisenhower and the Jews* (New York: Twayne Publishers, 1953).

11. Mankowitz, *Life Between Memory and Hope*.

1. A European Childhood

1. Louis Lowy, "Reflections on the Holocaust," paper presented at Temple Emmanuel, Newton, MA, May 5, 1978.

2. Louis Lowy, *Adult Education and Group Work: The Progress of Human Development Through Adult Education and Group Work* (New York: William Morrow, 1955), 13–14.

3. Rosenbloom, "What Can We Learn from the Holocaust?" 4; Maria H. Rosenbloom, "Implications of the Holocaust for Social Work," *Families in Society* 76, no. 9 (1995): 567–76.

4. Lowy, *Adult Education*, 27.

5. Unless otherwise attributed, quotations from Louis Lowy are drawn from an oral narrative testimony that he recorded from October 1990 through April 1991 at his home in Newton Highlands, MA.

6. Louis Lowy, "Group Participation: A Dynamic Force in the Senior Center," in *Senior Centers: An Environment for Group Service: Proceedings of the 11th National Conference on Senior Centers, Sheraton-Chicago Hotel, Chicago, IL, September 27–30, 1976*, ed. Bella Jacobs, 1–10 (Washington, DC: The National Council on the Aging, 1978), 6.

7. Lowy, "Group Participation," 6; Louis Lowy, *Social Work with the Aging: The Challenge and Promise of the Later Years*, 2nd ed. (Prospect Heights, IL: Waveland Press, 1985).

8. Louis Lowy, "Indigenous Leadership in Teenage Groups," *The Jewish Center Worker* 13, no. 1 (Jan. 1952), 15; and Louis Lowy, "A Social Work Practice Perspective in Relation to Theoretical Models and Research in Gerontology," paper presented the 19th Annual Meeting of the Gerontological Society, New York, Nov. 1966.

9. Lowy, *Adult Education*, 56; Lowy, "Group Participation"; and Louis Lowy, "Neighborhood Goals for Neighborhood Houses: A Summary," paper presented at the

Eastern Regional Conference, National Federation of Settlements and Neighborhood Centers, Lancaster, PA, Apr. 16–18, 1959.

10. Lowy, "Neighborhood," 28; Louis Lowy, *Social Policies and Programs on Aging* (Lexington, MA: Lexington Books, 1980); and Louis Lowy, *The Function of Social Work in a Changing Society: A Continuum of Practice* (Boston: Charles River Books, 1976).

11. Gordon A. Craig, *Europe Since 1815*, 3rd ed. (New York: Holt, Rinehart and Winston, 1971).

12. Lowy, "Neighborhood," 6.

13. Louis Lowy, "Adult Children and Their Parents: Dependency or Dependability?" *Long Term Care and Health Services Administration Quarterly* 1, no. 3 (Fall 1977): 244.

14. Lowy, "Adult Children," 245.

15. Lowy, "Neighborhood," 5.

16. Louis Lowy, "The Concept of the Social Environment in Social Group Work Practice," paper presented at the Boston Univ. Alumni Association of the School of Social Work, Boston, n.d.

17. Louis Lowy, "Curriculum Development in Social Work Education," paper presented at Boston Univ. School of Social Work, Boston, Feb. 5, 1982, 8.

18. Ruth Bondy, *Elder of the Jews: Jakob Edelstein of Theresienstadt* (New York: Grove Press, 1989); David Engel, *The Holocaust: The Third Reich and the Jews* (New York: Longman, 2000); and Ursula Pawel, *My Child Is Back!* (London: Vallentine Mitchell, 2000).

19. Bondy, *Elder of the Jews;* Martin Gilbert, "What Was Known and When," in *Anatomy of the Auschwitz Death Camp*, eds. Yisrael Gutman and Michael Berenbaum (Bloomington: Indiana Univ. Press, 1994), 539–52; and "Freud-Marle, Lilly," accessed July 24, 2006, http://www.perlentaucher.de/autoren/18791.html.

20. Engel, *The Holocaust.*

21. Bondy, *Elder of the Jews.*

22. Bondy, *Elder of the Jews.* See also "Theresienstadt," Center for Holocaust and Genocide Studies, accessed July 17, 2006, http://www.chgs.umn.edu; "Theresienstadt," *Holocaust Encyclopedia,* United States Holocaust Memorial Museum, accessed July 21, 2006, http://www.ushmm.org/wlc/en; and "Theresienstadt," Yad Vashem: The Holocaust Martyrs' and Heroes' Remembrance Authority, accessed July 19, 2006, http://www1 .yadvashem.org.

2. The Terezín Ghetto

1. Bondy, *Elder of the Jews.*

2. Bondy, *Elder of the Jews;* "Theresienstadt," Yad Vashem.

3. Lowy, *Social Work with the Aging,* 56.

4. Engel, *The Holocaust,* 119.

5. Bondy, *Elder of the Jews;* Gilbert, "What Was Known and When."

6. Bondy, *Elder of the Jews;* "Theresienstadt," CHGS; "Theresienstadt," USHMM; "Theresienstadt," Vad Yashem.

7. Bondy, *Elder of the Jews;* Pawel, *My Child Is Back!*

8. Pawel, *My Child Is Back!,* 52.

9. Lowy, *Adult Education,* 129.

10. Lowy, *Social Policies,* 214.

11. Lowy, *Adult Education,* 13–14.

12. Lowy, *Social Work with the Aging,* 291.

13. Lowy, *Adult Education,* 207; Lowy, *Social Work with the Aging,* 239.

14. Unless otherwise attributed, quotations from Edith Lowy are drawn from an oral narrative interview with the author on August 12 and August 19, 2004, in Lowy's home in Newton Highlands, MA.

15. Leo Hass, "The Affair of the Painters of Terezín," in *Seeing Through "Paradise": Artists and the Terezín Concentration Camp* (Boston: Massachusetts College of Art, 1991), 63–70.

16. Friedrich von Schiller, *Die Worte des Glaubens* [The word of the faithful], 1797, accessed Feb. 15, 2008, http://en.wikiquote.org/wiki/Friedrich_Schiller.

17. Friedrich von Schiller, "An Die Freude" ["Ode to Joy"], 1785, accessed Feb. 15, 2008, http://www.raptusassociation.org/ode1785.html.

18. Unless otherwise attributed, quotations from Vern Drehmel were drawn from an oral narrative interview with the author on January 11 and January 12, 2007, in Drehmel's home in Sea Ranch, CA.

19. Unless otherwise attributed, quotations from Reinhard Frank were drawn from an oral narrative interview with the author on November 4, 2006, in Frank's home in Cambridge, MA.

20. Erich Kästner, "Wert und Unwort des Menschen" [The worth and worthlessness of men], in *Der tägliche Kram Chansons und Prosa* [The daily stuff: poems and prose] 1945–1948 (Zurich: Atrium Verlag, 1949), 87. He is referring to *Emil und die Detektive* [*Emil and the Detectives*] (Hamburg: Cecilie Dressler Verlag, 1929).

21. Pawel, , *My Child Is Back!*

22. "Allgemeine Vorträge: Programm" [Program of general lectures], June 22, 1944, Terezín Memorial, Terezín, Czech Republic; Elena Makarova, Sergei Makarov, and Victor Kuperman, Victor, eds., *University Over the Abyss: The Story Behind 520 Lecturers and 2,430 Lectures in KZ Theresienstadt 1942–1944,* 2nd ed. (Jerusalem: Verba Publishers, 2004), 486.

23. Makarova, Makarov, and Kuperman, *University Over the Abyss,* 150.

24. Louis Lowy, "Educational Work in Terezín: A Sketch of a Study Program, June 22, 1944," in Makarova, Makarov, and Kuperman, *University Over the Abyss,* 150–51.

25. Markova, Markov, and Kuperman, *University Over the Abyss,* 150–51; and Klaus Scheurenberg, *Ich Will Leben: Autobiograph* [I want to live: autobiography] (Berlin:

Oberbaumverlag, 1982), as cited in Markova, Markov, and Kuperman, *University Over the Abyss,* 151.

26. Bondy, *Elder of the Jews;* Pawel; "Theresienstadt," USHMM.

27. Bondy, *Elder of the Jews,* 439.

28. Nili Keren, "The Family Camp," in Gutman and Berenbaum, *Anatomy of the Auschwitz Death Camp,* 439–40; and Laurence Rees, *Auschwitz: The Nazis and the 'Final Solution'* (London: BBC Books, 2005).

29. Bondy, *Elder of the Jews;* Rees, *Auschwitz;* and Miroslav Karney, "The Vrba and Wetzler Report," in Gutman and Berenbaum, *Anatomy of the Auschwitz Death Camp,* 539–52.

30. Bondy, *Elder of the Jews;* "Theresienstadt," CHGS; "Theresienstadt," USHMM; "Theresienstadt," Vad Yashem.

31. Vern Drehmel to Louis Lowy, June 14, 1990.

3. Escape from Auschwitz

1. "Auschwitz," *Holocaust Encyclopedia,* US Holocaust Memorial Museum, accessed Aug. 8, http://www.ushmm.org/wlc/article.php?lang=en&ModuleId=10005189; Yisrael Gutman, "Auschwitz—An Overview," in Gutman and Berebaum, *Anatomy of the Auschwitz Death Camp,* 5–33; Franciszek Piper, "The Number of Victims," in Gutman and Berenbaum, *Anatomy of the Auschwitz Death Camp,* 61–76; and Rees, *Auschwitz.*

2. "Subcamps of Auschwitz," Auschwitz-Birkenau Memorial Museum, accessed Feb. 28, 2008, http://www.auschwitz-muzeum.oswiecim.pl/html; Robert Van Pelt, "A Site in Search of a Mission," in Gutman and Berenbaum, *Anatomy of the Auschwitz Death Camp,* 93–156; and Rees, *Auschwitz.*

3. Rees, *Auschwitz;* Van Pelt, "Site in Search of a Mission."

4. Van Pelt, "Site in Search of a Mission," 131; Terrence Des Pres, *The Survivor: An Anatomy of Life in the Death Camps* (New York: Simon and Schuster, 1976).

5. Gutman, "Auschwitz—An Overview"; Primo Levi, *Survival in Auschwitz: The Nazi Assault on Humanity* (New York: Collier Books, 1986); and Rees, *Auschwitz.*

6. Rosenbloom, "Implications," 571; and Elie Wiesel, *Night,* rev. ed. (New York: Hill and Wang, 2006).

7. Rees, *Auschwitz;* David S. Wyman, "Why Auschwitz Wasn't Bombed," in Gutman and Berenbaum, *Anatomy of the Auschwitz Death Camp,* 569–87.

8. Shmuel Krakowski, "The Satellite Camps," in Gutman and Berenbaum, *Anatomy of the Auschwitz Death Camp,* 50–60; Piper, "The Number of Victims"; Rees, *Auschwitz.*

9. Krakowski, "The Satellite Camps"; Piper, "The Number of Victims."

10. Piper, "The Number of Victims"; Rees, *Auschwitz,* 180.

11. Rees, *Auschwitz,* 264.

12. Rees, *Auschwitz.*

13. Carl Zuckmayer, *Der Hauptmann von Köpenick* [The captain of Köpenick] (Berlin: Maerchen, 1931).

14. Reinhard remembers the route differently from Louis and Vern. In Reinhard's account, the group did not travel through Budapest until their return journey from Bucharest to Prague.

15. Louis Lowy, "Of Enduring and Curing, of Caring and Daring," paper presented at the Hooding Ceremony, Boston Univ. School of Social Work, Boston, May 21, 1979.

4. The Social Statesman

1. Louis Lowy, "Returning," *Deggendorf Center Revue,* no. 1 (early Nov. 1945): 1.

2. Mark Wyman, *DP: Europe's Displaced Persons, 1945–1951* (Philadelphia: Balch Institute Press, 1989).

3. Bondy, *Elder of the Jews;* "Theresienstadt," CHGS; "Theresienstadt," USHMM; "Theresienstadt," Yad Vashem.

4. Bondy, *Elder of the Jews,* 447.

5. Tereza Štěpková, Terezín Initiative Institute, http://www.terezinstudies.cz/eng/main, e-mail message to author, June 4, 2008.

6. Jewish Displaced Persons Project, 2008, accessed on June 30, 2011, http://www.ushmm.org/museum/exhibit/online/dp/update.htm; George Vida, *From Doom to Dawn: A Jewish Chaplain's Story of Displaced Persons* (New York: Jonathan David Publishers, 1967); and Zorach Warhaftig, *Uprooted: Jewish Refugees and Displaced Persons after Liberation* (New York: Institute of Jewish Affairs of the American Jewish Congress and World Jewish Congress, 1946).

7. Supreme Headquarters Allied Expeditionary Force, "SHAEF Administrative Memo No. 39, 1944," United States Holocaust Memorial Museum, accessed May 12, 2008, http://www.ushmm.org/museum/exhibit/online/dp/menu.htm; and Vida, *From Doom to Dawn.*

8. Jewish Displaced Person Project; United Nations Relief and Rehabilitation Administration, *Operational Analysis Papers, No. 13: U.N.R.R.A. Displaced Persons Operation in Europe and the Middle East* (London: UNRRA European Regional Office, Division of Operational Analysis, Dec. 1946); and Mark Wyman, *DP.*

9. Dwight D. Eisenhower to President Truman concerning Jewish Displaced Persons, Sept. 18, 1945 (letter, 3 pages), the Eisenhower Presidential Library and Museum, accessed April 16, 2008, http://www.eisenhower.archives.gov/dl/holocaust/holocaustpage.html.

10. Earl G. Harrison, "Mission to Europe to Inquire into the Condition and Needs of Those among the Displaced Persons in the Liberated Countries of Western Europe and in the SHAEF Area of Germany—with Particular Reference to the Jewish Refugees—Who May Possibly Be Stateless or Non-Repatriable," August 1945 (11 pages), Eisenhower Presidential Library and Museum, accessed April 16, 2008, http://www.eisenhower.archives.gov/dl/holocaust/holocaustpage.html; and Judah Nadich, "After Liberation the Jews Had Old

and New Problems," in *Rabbi Judah Nadich, Writings,* Oct. 17, 2007, accessed May 16, 2008, http://judahnadich.com/2007/10/17/after-liberation-jews-had-old-and-new-problems.

11. Harrison, "Mission to Europe," 9; Jewish Displaced Person Project; UNRRA, *Operational Analysis.*

12. Yosef Grodzinsky, *In the Shadow of the Holocaust: The Struggle Between Jews and Zionists in the Aftermath of World War II* (Monroe, Maine: Common Courage Press, 2004), 118.

13. Harrison, "Mission to Europe," Judah Nadich, *Eisenhower and the Jews;* Vida.

14. Harrison, "Mission to Europe."

15. Nadich, *Eisenhower and the Jews,* 34.

16. Harrison, "Mission to Europe," 1–2.

17. Harrison, "Mission to Europe," 3; Nadich, *Eisenhower and the Jews;* Nadich, "After Liberation."

18. Jewish Displaced Persons Project; Harrison, "Mission to Europe"; Nadich, *Eisenhower and the Jews;* Nadich, "After Liberation"; Leo W. Schwarz, *The Redeemers: A Saga of the Years 1945–1952* (New York: Farrar, Straus and Young, 1953); Vida, *From Doom to Dawn;* and Warhaftig, *Uprooted.*

19. Harrison, "Mission to Europe," 7.

20. Dwight D. Eisenhower to President Harry Truman Concerning the Harrison Report and Jewish Displaced Persons, Sept. 14, 1945 (telegram, 2 pages), the Eisenhower Presidential Library and Museum, accessed Apr. 16, 2008, http://www.eisenhower.archives.gov/dl/holocaust/holocaustpage.html.

21. Nadich, *Eisenhower,* 39–40.

22. Dwight D. Eisenhower to President Truman Concerning Jewish Victims of Nazi Persecution, Oct. 8, 1945 (letter, 4 pages), Eisenhower Presidential Library and Museum, accessed Apr. 16, 2008, http://www.eisenhower.archives.gov/dl/holocaust/holocaustpage.html, 3; Eisenhower to President Truman, Sept. 18, 1945; Nadich, *Eisenhower and the Jews.*

23. Harrison, "Mission to Europe," 4.

24. Eisenhower to President Truman, Sept. 14, 1945.

25. Nadich, *Eisenhower and the Jews.*

26. Nadich, "After Liberation."

27. "Winzer," DP Camps in Germany, accessed May 16, 2008, http://www.dpcamps.org/dpcampsGermanyW-Wi.html.

28. Josef Königer, "Lieber Freund und Kollege Löwy" [Esteemed friend and colleague, Löwy], *Deggendorf Center Revue,* no. 11 (Apr. 15, 1946): 1.

29. Ruth Gay, *Safe Among the Germans: Liberated Jews after World War II* (New Haven, CT: Yale Univ. Press, 2002), 95–96.

30. Gay, *Safe Among the Germans;* Nadich, *Eisenhower and the Jews;* and Schwarz, *The Redeemers.*

31. Nadich, *Eisenhower and the Jews.*

32. Gay, *Safe Among the Germans;* Nadich, *Eisenhower and the Jews;* Schwarz, *The Redeemers;* and Warhaftig, *Uprooted.*

33. "Verzeichnis der Einwohner des D. P. Centers Deggendorf (Stand vom I. I. 1946)" [Registry of the inhabitants of the Deggendorf Displaced Person Center (from Jan. 1, 1946)].

34. Nadich, *Eisenhower and the Jews,* 194.

35. Nadich, *Eisenhower and the Jews,* 193; UNRRA, *Operational Analysis,* 20.

36. "Neuwahl des Jewish Comittees Unseres Centers" [New election of the members of the Center Jewish Committee]. *Deggendorf Center Revue,* no. 1 (Nov., 1945): 4.

37. "Displaced Persons: Administration," *Holocaust Encyclopedia,* United States Holocaust Memorial Museum, accessed April 7, 2008, http://www.ushmm.org/wlc/article.php?lang=enandModuleI=10005418; Mankowitz, *Life Between Memory and Hope;* "The Central Committee of Liberated Jews, 1945 to 1950." Jewish Virtual Library, accessed May 16, 2008, http://www.jewishvirtuallibrary.org/jsource/Holocaust/central comm.html.

38. Nadich, *Eisenhower and the Jews.*

39. "Displaced Persons: Administration"; Jacqueline Giere, "We're On Our Way, But We're Not in the Wilderness," in Berenbaum and Peck, *Holocaust and History,* 699–715; Mankowitz, *Life Between Memory and Hope;* Nadich, *Eisenhower and the Jews;* "Central Committee of the Liberated Jews."

40. Louis Lowy, "Zum Farewell" [Farewell to you]. *Deggendorf Center Revue,* no. 11 (Apr. 15, 1946): 1.

41. Doris L. Bergen, "The 'Volksdeutschen' of Eastern Europe, World War II, and the Holocaust: Constructed Identity and Real Genocide," *Yearbook of European Studies* 13 (1999): 70–93.

42. Nadich, *Eisenhower and the Jews;* Nadich, "After Liberation."

43. Nadich, *Eisenhower and the Jews.*

44. Eisenhower to President Truman, Sept. 14, 1945; and Eisenhower to President Truman, Sept. 18, 1945.

45. Louis Lowy, "Besinnung" [Reflection], *Deggendorf Center Revue,* no. 3 (early Dec. 1945): 2.

46. "Neuwahl," 4.

47. "Neuwahl"; and Schwarz, *The Redeemers,* 69–70.

48. Schwarz, *The Redeemers,* 69.

49. "Neuwahl," 4.

50. "Neuwahl," 4.

51. Louis Lowy, "Social Work and Social Statesmanship," *Social Work* 5, no. 2 (1960): 97–104.

52. Lowy, *Social Work with the Aging,* 55.

5. Louis and Ditta

1. Woolrich, "Searches."

2. Helmreich, *Against All Odds*, 121; and Henry F. Holocaust Testimony (HVT-2442), Fortunoff Video Archive for Holocaust Testimonies, Yale Univ. Library, New Haven, CT, 1992.

3. Edith L. Holocaust Testimony.

4. Gertrude Schneider, *Exile and Destruction: The Fate of Austrian Jews, 1938–1945* (Westport, CT: Praeger, 1995).

5. Edith L. Holocaust Testimony.

6. Lawrence L. Langer, *Holocaust Testimonies: The Ruins of Memory* (New Haven, CT: Yale Univ. Press, 1991), 2.

7. "Hochzeit Louis Löwy" [The wedding of Louis Lowy], *Deggendorf Center Revue,* no. 3 (early Dec. 1945): 7; Simon Schochet, *Feldafing* (Vancouver: November House, 1983); and Mark Wyman, *DP.*

8. "Hochzeit Louis Löwy."

9. Lowy, "Besinnung," 2.

10. Königer, "Lieber Freund und Kollege Löwy," 1.

6. Deggendorf Displaced Persons Center

1. Giere, "We're On Our Way"; Samuel Gringauz, "Jewish Destiny as the DP's See It," *Commentary* 4, no. 6 (Dec. 1947): 501–9, accessed June 3, 2008, http://www.commentary magazine.com/viewarticle.cfm/jewish-destiny-as-the-dps-see-it-466; Mankowitz, *Life Between Memory and Hope;* and Schwarz, *The Redeemers.*

2. Giere, "We're On Our Way," 703.

3. Gringauz, "Jewish Destiny," 501.

4. Lowy, "Returning," 1.

5. "Jüdische Selbstverwaltung im Jewish Center Deggendorf" [Jewish self-government in the Jewish Deggendorf Center], *Deggendorf Center Revue,* no. 10 (Mar. 30, 1946): 4.

6. Alexander Gutfeld, "The Empty Office," *Deggendorf Center Revue,* no. 4 (late Dec. 1945): 6; and Nadich, *Eisenhower and the Jews.*

7. Mankowitz, *Life Between Memory and Hope,* 133; Nadich, *Eisenhower and the Jews,* 193–95; and Schwarz, *The Redeemers,* 42.

8. "Jewish Displaced Persons, 1945–1951."

9. Kurt Buchenholz, "Cultural Life in Our Center," *Deggendorf Center Revue,* no. 1 (early Nov. 1945): 4.

10. "Verzeichnis der Einwohner des D. P. Centers Deggendorf."

11. Lowy, "Zum Farewell," 1.

12. Berenbaum and Peck, *Holocaust and History,* 693; see also Giere, "We're On Our Way," 699–715.

13. Konopka, *Courage and Love;* Rosenberg, *To Tell at Last;* and Pawel, *My Child Is Back!*

14. Mark Wyman, *DP.*

15. Louis Lowy, "Rehabilitation," *Deggendorf Center Review,* no. 2 (mid-Nov. 1945): 1.

16. Jacob Biber, *Risen from the Ashes* (San Bernardino, CA: Borgo Press, 1990); Harrison, "Mission to Europe"; Kathryn Hulme, *The Wild Place* (Boston: Little, Brown, 1953); Nadich, *Eisenhower and the Jews;* Schochet, *Feldafing;* Schwarz, *The Redeemers;* Vida, *From Doom to Dawn;* and Mark Wyman, *DP.*

17. Harrison, "Mission to Europe"; Gay, *Safe Among the Germans;* and Mark Wyman, *DP.*

18. Ihre Herzlich, [Title illegible], *Deggendorf Center Revue,* no. 8 (Feb. 28, 1946): 4.

19. Lowy, *Social Work with Aging,* 51.

20. Louis Lowy, "Kommende Sorgen" [Coming worries], *Deggendorf Center Revue,* no. 5 (Jan. 12, 1946): 4.

21. Louis Lowy, "Die Insel" [The island], *Deggendorf Center Revue,* no. 6 (Jan. 26, 1946): 2.

22. Dina G. Holocaust Testimony (HVT-264), 1982, Irene F. Holocaust Testimony (HVT-2404), 1992, and Lore, L. Holocaust Testimony (HVT-946), 1987, Fortunoff Video Archive for Holocaust Testimonies, Yale Univ. Library, New Haven, CT.

23. Annemarie Durra, "Das Ist Unser Pappi Carl Atkin" [This is our daddy Carl Atkin], drawing, *Deggendorf Center Revue,* no. 7 (Feb. 15, 1946): 7.

24. Annemarie Durra, "Miss Waters: She Stole Our Heart," drawing, *Deggendorf Center Revue,* no. 12 (May 18, 1946): 8.

25. Gutfeld, "The Empty Office," 6.

26. Harry S. Truman, "President Truman's Statement and Directive on Displaced Persons, Dec. 22, 1945," World War II Resources, accessed July 24, 2008, http://www.ibiblio.org/pha/policy/post-war/index.html.

27. Truman, "President Truman's Statement and Directive."

28. Lowy, "Zum Farewell," 1.

29. Königer, "Lieber Freund und Kollege Löwy," 1.

30. "Deggendorf," *Holocaust Encyclopedia,* United States Holocaust Memorial Museum, accessed June 24, 2006, http://www.ushmm.org/museum/exhibit/online/dp/camp13.htm; Gay, *Safe Among the Germans;* Nadich, *Eisenhower and the Jews;* and Schwarz, *The Redeemers.*

7. The Making of a Social Worker

1. Ralph Kolodny, letter to author, Oct. 11, 2004.

2. Lowy, "Reflections."

3. Lowy, "Indigenous Leadership," 13.

4. Lowy, *Adult Education,* 27.

5. Lowy, *Adult Education,* 63.

6. Lowy, *Adult Education,* 206–7.

7. Lowy, *Adult Education,* 126.

8. Lowy, *Adult Education,* 160.

9. Susan Kubie and Gertrude Landau, *Group Work with the Aged* (New York: International Universities Press, 1953).

10. Louis Lowy, "Family Caregiving for the Elderly," *Advice for Adults with Aging Parents* 2, no. 1 (Feb.–Mar. 1987): 5–7; Louis Lowy, "Why Education in the Later Years?" *New Findings Quarterly: A Special Publication for Shoe People Age 55 and Over,* Apr. 1987, 4–5.

11. Lowy, "Adult Children."

12. Lowy, Curriculum Vitae.

13. Louis Lowy, "Clarification of Self and Role Perceptions in Social Work Students During Training: A Study of Incorporation of a Professional Role," PhD diss., Harvard Univ., Cambridge, MA, 1965; Louis Lowy, "Toward an Educational–Human Service Linkage Model for People in their Later Years" (unpublished paper, 1989).

14. Lowy, "A Social Work Practice Perspective," 6.

15. Heinz J. Kersting, "Lowy, Louis"; and Heinz J. Kersting, "Louis Lowy: Bridge-Builder Across the Atlantic and Important Teacher of German Social Workers" (unpublished paper, n.d.).

16. Kalcher, "Social Group Work in Germany"; Konopka, *Courage and Love;* Lees, *Character Is Destiny;* Rosenberg, *To Tell at Last;* Wieler, "Destination Social Work"; Wieler and Zeller, *Emigrierte Sozialarbeit.*

17. UNRRA, *Operational Analysis.*

18. Kersting, "Lowy, Louis"; Kersting, "Louis Lowy: Bridge-Builder"; Lowy, Curriculum Vitae.

19. Kersting, "Louis Lowy: Bridge-Builder," 7.

20. Kersting, "Louis Lowy: Bridge-Builder," 2–3.

21. Lowy, "Rehabilitation"; and Lowy, "Group Participation."

22. Kersting, "Louis Lowy: Bridge-Builder," 8.

23. Lowy, *Function of Social Work,* v–vi.

24. Lowy, Curriculum Vitae; Alban Scherzinger, "Louis Lowy," in Wieler and Zeller, *Emigrierte Sozialarbeit,* 217–32.

25. Lowy, "Why Education?" 5.

26. For example: Louis Lowy, *An Assessment-Survey Report of Indigenous Social Work Literature of Social Work Methodology* (Boston: Boston Univ. School of Social Work and International Association of Schools of Social Work, 1988); Louis Lowy, "Human-Services Professionals: Their Role in Education for Older People," in *Growing Old in America,* ed. Beth B. Hess and Elizabeth W. Markson (New Brunswick, NJ: Transaction Publishers,

1991), 557–68; Louis Lowy, "Social Consciousness and Social Causes: Impulses for Social Reform at the Turn of the Century in Berlin," in *Views of Berlin,* ed. Gerhard Kirchoff (Boston: Birkhauser, 1989), 47–54; Louis Lowy, "Toward an Educational–Human Service Linkage"; and Louis Lowy and Darlene O'Connor, *Why Education in the Later Years?* (Lexington, MA: Lexington Books, 1986).

27. Louis Lowy, "Remarks to the White House Conference on Aging Symposium," paper presented by audio-recording at Northeastern Gerontological Society, New Haven, CT, Apr. 21, 1991; Lowy, *Social Work with the Aging,* xviii.

8. A Life's Work

1. Lowy, *Function of Social Work,* v–vi.

2. Katherine A. Kendall, *Social Work Education: Its Origins in Europe* (Alexandria, VA: Council on Social Work Education, 2000); Lees, *Character Is Destiny;* and Lowy, "Social Consciousness."

3. Lowy, "Social Work and Statesmanship," 102.

4. Lowy, "Returning"; Lowy, "Rehabilitation"; Lowy, "Die Insel"; Lowy, *Function of Social Work.*

5. Lowy, *Adult Education,* 27.

6. Lowy, "Returning," 1; Lowy, *Function of Social Work,* 29; Lowy, *Social Work with the Aging,* 598.

7. Lowy, "Returning," 1.

8. Lowy, "Rehabilitation," 1.

9. Lowy, "Neighborhood," 8–9.

10. Lowy, *Social Work with the Aging,* xiv.

11. Lowy, "Group Participation," 6.

12. Lowy, *Social Work with the Aging,* dedication.

13. Lowy, "Returning," 1.

14. Lowy, *Social Work with the Aging,* xviii.

15. Lowy, "Adult Children," 244.

16. Makarova, Makarov, and Kuperman, *University Over the Abyss.*

17. Lowy, *Social Work with the Aging,* xvi.

18. Lowy, *Social Work with the Aging,* 288.

19. Lowy, *Social Work with the Aging,* 353.

20. Lowy, "Toward Educational–Human Service Linkage," 24.

21. Lowy, "Family Caregiving," 16.

22. Lowy, "Remarks."

23. Lowy, *Function of Social Work,* 30.

24. Lowy, *Function of Social Work,* 31.

25. Lowy, *Function of Social Work,* 29.

26. Albert S. Alissi, "The Social Group Work Tradition: Toward Social Justice in a Free Society," *Social Group Work Occasional Papers* (West Hartford: Univ. of Connecticut School of Social Work, 2001); Gisela Konopka, "The Significance of Social Group Work Based on Ethical Values," *Social Work with Groups* 1 (1978): 123–31; Gisela Konopka, "Perspectives on Social Group Work," in *Social Work with Groups: Proceedings 1979 Symposium,* ed. Sonia Abels and Paul Abels (Louisville, KY: Committee for the Advancement of Social Work with Groups, 1981), 111–16; Harry Specht and Mark E. Courtney, *Unfaithful Angels: How Social Work Has Abandoned Its Mission* (New York: Free Press, 1994); Harleigh B. Trecker, *Group Work Foundations and Frontiers* (New York: Whiteside, 1955).

27. Lowy, "Social Work and Statesmanship," 98.

28. Lowy, *Function of Social Work,* 29.

29. Lowy and O'Connor, *Why Education in the Later Years?,* 169.

30. Lowy, *Social Work with the Aging,* 56.

31. Lowy, *Function of Social Work,* 35; Lowy, "Adult Children"; and Louis Lowy, "Volunteers in Programs for the Older Citizen," in *The Citizen Volunteer,* ed. Nathan E. Cohen (New York: Harper Brothers, 1960), 156.

32. Lowy, "Why Education?"; Lowy, "Family Caregiving."

33. Lowy, *Social Work with Aging,* xviii.

34. Lowy, "Social Work and Statesmanship," 99–100.

35. Janice Blanchard, "As the Pendulum Swings: A Historical Review of the Politics and Policies of the Arts and Aging," *Generations* 30, no. 1 (2006): 50–56; Julian Chow, "Multi-Service Centers in Chinese Immigrant Communities," *Social Work* 44, no. 5 (Sept. 1999): 70–81; Gay Hanna, "Creativity Matters: New Partnerships Build Momentum for Arts and Aging," *Aging Today: The Bimonthly Newspaper of the American Society on Aging* 29, no. 6 (Nov.–Dec. 2008): 7–9; Nancy Morrow-Howell and Marc Freedman, eds., *Civic Engagement in Later Life: Generations* 30, no. 4 (Winter 2006–7); Barbara L. Nicholson and Diane M. Kay, "Group Treatment of Traumatized Cambodian Women: A Culture Specific Approach," *Social Work* 44, no. 5 (Nov. 1999): 470–80.

36. Lowy, "Neighborhood."

37. Lowy, "Returning," 1.

Afterword: Social Work with Refugees and Displaced Populations

1. Unless otherwise attributed, quotations from Maria Hirsch Rosenbloom are drawn from an oral narrative interview with the author on February 27, 2008, in Rosenbloom's home in Manhattan.

2. Hispanic Health Council, *A Profile of Hispanic Health in Connecticut: The Case for Change in Policy and Practice* (Hartford: Hispanic Health Council, 2006); Mel Gray, John Croates, and Tiani Hetherington, "Hearing Indigenous Voices in Mainstream Social Work," *Families in Society* 88, no. 1 (2007): 55–66; Priska Imberti, "Who Resides

Behind the Words? Exploring and Understanding the Language Experience of the Non-English-Speaking Immigrant," *Families in Society* 88, no. 1 (2007): 67–74.

3. Helmreich, *Against All Odds;* Eitinger, "Holocaust Survivors."

4. Lowy, "A Social Work Practice Perspective," 540.

5. Helmreich, *Against All Odds.*

6. Rosenbloom, "What Can We Learn from the Holocaust?" See also Rosenbloom, "Implications."

7. Lowy, "Returning," 1.

8. Buchenholz, "Cultural Life in Our Center," 7.

9. Berenbaum and Peck, *Holocaust and History,* 693; Giere, "We're On Our Way."

10. Mankowitz, *Life Between Memory and Hope.*

11. Diane Drachman and Ana Paulino, eds., *Immigrants and Social Work: Thinking Beyond the Borders of the United States* (Binghamton, NY: Haworth, 2004); and Miriam Potcoky-Tripodi, *Best Practices for Social Work with Refugees and Immigrants* (New York: Columbia Univ. Press, 2002).

12. Langer, *Holocaust Testimonies,* 174.

13. Laub, "History, Memory, and Truth," 799.

14. Eisenhower to President Truman, Sept. 18, 1945; Nadich, *Eisenhower.*

15. Lowy, *Social Work with the Aged,* 288.

References

Archives

Auschwitz-Birkenau Memorial and State Museum, Oświęcim, Poland. http://
www.auschwitz-muzeum.oswiecim.pl/html.
Eisenhower Presidential Library and Museum, Abilene, KS. http://www.eisen
hower.archives.gov/dl/holocaust/holocaustpage.html.
Fortunoff Video Archive for Holocaust Testimonies, Yale Univ. Library, New
Haven, CT.
Terezín Initiative Institute, Prague, Czech Republic. http://www.terezinstudies
.cz/eng/main.
United States Holocaust Memorial Museum Photo Archives, Washington, DC.
http://www.ushmm.org/research/collections/photo.

Books and Articles

Alissi, Albert S. "The Social Group Work Tradition: Toward Social Justice in a
Free Society." *Social Group Work Occasional Papers.* West Hartford: Univ. of
Connecticut School of Social Work, 2001.
"Allgemeine Vorträge: Programm" [Program of general lectures]. June 22, 1944.
Terezín Memorial, Terezín, Czech Republic.
Bauer, Yehuda. "A Past That Will Not Go Away." In *The Holocaust and History:
The Known, the Unknown, the Disputed, and the Reexamined,* edited by
Michael Berenbaum and Abraham J. Peck, 12–22. Bloomington: Indiana
Univ. Press, 1998.
Berenbaum, Michael, and Abraham J. Peck, eds. *The Holocaust and History: The
Known, the Unknown, the Disputed, and the Reexamined.* Bloomington:
Indiana Univ. Press, 1998.
Bergen, Doris, L. "The 'Volksdeutschen' of Eastern Europe, World War II, and
the Holocaust: Constructed Identity and Real Genocide." *Yearbook of Euro-
pean Studies* 13 (1999): 70–93.

Biber, Jacob. *Risen from the Ashes*. San Bernardino, CA: Borgo Press, 1990.

Blanchard, Janice. "As the Pendulum Swings: A Historical Review of the Politics and Policies of the Arts and Aging." *Generations* 30, no. 1 (2006): 50–56.

Bondy, Ruth. *Elder of the Jews: Jakob Edelstein of Theresienstadt*. New York: Grove Press, 1989.

Buchenholz, Kurt. "Cultural Life in Our Center." *Deggendorf Center Revue*, no. 1 (early Nov. 1945): 4, 7.

"Central Committee of Liberated Jews (1945–1950), The." Jewish Virtual Library. Accessed May 16, 2008. http://www.jewishvirtuallibrary.org/jsource/Holocaust/centralcomm.html.

Chow, Julian. "Multi-Service Centers in Chinese Immigrant Communities." *Social Work* 44, no. 5 (Sept. 1999): 70–81.

Craig, Gordon A. *Europe Since 1815*. 3rd ed. New York: Holt, Rinehart and Winston, 1971.

"Deggendorf." *Holocaust Encyclopedia*, United States Holocaust Memorial Museum. Accessed June 24, 2006. http://www.ushmm.org/museum/exhibit/online/dp/camp13.htm.

Des Pres, Terrence. *The Survivor: An Anatomy of Life in the Death Camps*. New York: Simon and Schuster, 1976.

"Displaced Persons: Administration." *Holocaust Encyclopedia*, United States Holocaust Memorial Museum. Accessed April 7, 2008. http://www.ushmm.org/wlc/en/article.php?ModuleId=10005418.

Drachman, Diane, and Ana Paulino, eds. *Immigrants and Social Work: Thinking Beyond the Borders of the United States*. Binghamton, NY: Haworth, 2004.

Durra, Annemarie. "Das Ist Unser Pappi Carl Atkin" [This is our daddy Carl Atkin]. Drawing. *Deggendorf Center Revue*, no. 7 (Feb. 15, 1946): 7.

———. "Miss Waters: She Stole Our Heart." Drawing. *Deggendorf Center Revue*, no. 12 (May 18, 1946): 8.

Eitinger, Leo. "Holocaust Survivors in the Past and Present." In *The Holocaust and History: The Known, the Unknown, the Disputed, and the Reexamined*, edited by Michael Berenbaum and Abraham J. Peck., 767–84. Bloomington: Indiana Univ. Press, 1998.

Engel, David. *The Holocaust: The Third Reich and the Jews*. New York: Longman, 2000.

"Freud-Marle, Lilly." Accessed July 24, 2006. http://www.perlentaucher.de/autoren/18791.html.

Gardella, Lorrie G. "Millie Charles: Believing in the Mission." *Journal of Baccalaureate Social Work* 2, no. 2 (1999): 19–36.

———. "Prime Mover: Pauline Roney Lang." *Journal of Baccalaureate Social Work* 1, no. 2 (1997): 22–42.

Gay, Ruth. *Safe Among the Germans: Liberated Jews after World War II.* New Haven, CT: Yale Univ. Press, 2002.

Giere, Jacqueline. "We're On Our Way, But We're Not in the Wilderness." In *The Holocaust and History: The Known, the Unknown, the Disputed, and the Reexamined,* edited by Michael Berenbaum and Abraham J. Peck, 699–715. Bloomington: Indiana Univ. Press, 1998.

Gilbert, Martin. "What Was Known and When." In *Anatomy of the Auschwitz Death Camp,* edited by Yisrael Gutman and Michael Berenbaum, 539–52. Bloomington: Indiana University Press, 1994.

Gray, Mel, John Croates, and Tiani Hetherington. "Hearing Indigenous Voices in Mainstream Social Work." *Families in Society* 88, no. 1 (2007): 55–66.

Gringauz, Samuel. "Jewish Destiny as the DP's See It." *Commentary* 4, no. 6 (Dec. 1947): 501–9. Accessed June 3, 2008. http://www.commentarymagazine.com/viewarticle.cfm/jewish-destiny-as-the-dps-see-it-466.

Grodzinsky, Yosef. *In the Shadow of the Holocaust: The Struggle Between Jews and Zionists in the Aftermath of World War II.* Monroe, ME: Common Courage Press, 2004.

Gutfeld, Alexander. "The Empty Office." *Deggendorf Center Revue,* no. 4 (late Dec. 1945): 6.

Gutman, Yisrael. "Auschwitz—An Overview." In *Anatomy of the Auschwitz Death Camp,* edited by Yisrael Gutman and Michael Berenbaum, 5–33. Bloomington: Indiana Univ. Press, 1994.

Hanna, Gay. "Creativity Matters: New Partnerships Build Momentum for Arts and Aging." *Aging Today: The Bimonthly Newspaper of the American Society on Aging* 29, no. 6 (Nov.–Dec. 2008): 7–9.

Hass, Leo. "The Affair of the Painters of Terezín." In *Seeing Through "Paradise": Artists and the Terezín Concentration Camp,* 63–70. Boston: Massachusetts College of Art, 1991.

Helmreich, William B. *Against All Odds: Holocaust Survivors and the Successful Lives They Made in America.* New Brunswick, NJ: Transaction Publishers, 1996.

Herzlich, Ihre. [Title illegible]. *Deggendorf Center Revue,* no. 8 (Feb. 28, 1946): 4.

Hilberg, Raul. "Auschwitz and the 'Final Solution.'" In *Anatomy of the Auschwitz Death Camp*, edited by Yisrael Gutman and Michael Berenbaum, 81–92. Bloomington: Indiana Univ. Press, 1994.

———. "Sources and Their Uses." In *The Holocaust and History: The Known, the Unknown, the Disputed, and the Reexamined*, edited by Michael Berenbaum and Abraham J. Peck, 5–11. Bloomington: Indiana Univ. Press, 1998.

Hispanic Health Council. *A Profile of Hispanic Health in Connecticut: The Case for Change in Policy and Practice*. Hartford: Hispanic Health Council, 2006.

"Hochzeit Louis Löwy" [The wedding of Louis Lowy]. *Deggendorf Center Revue*, no. 3 (early Dec. 1945): 7.

Hulme Kathryn. *The Wild Place*. Boston: Little, Brown, 1953.

Imberti, Priska. "Who Resides Behind the Words? Exploring and Understanding the Language Experience of the Non-English-Speaking Immigrant." *Families in Society* 88, no. 1 (2007): 67–74.

"Jewish Displaced Persons Project." The United States Holocaust Memorial Council and the Second Generation Advisory Group, the United States Holocaust Memorial Museum. Accessed June 30, 2011. www.ushmm.org/museum/exhibit/online/dp/update.htm.

"Jüdische Selbstverwaltung im Jewish Center Deggendorf" [Jewish self-government in the Jewish Deggendorf Center]. *Deggendorf Center Revue*, no. 10 (Mar. 30, 1946): 4.

Kalcher, Jürgen. "Social Group Work in Germany: An American Import and Its Historical Development." In *Growth and Development Through Group Work*, edited by Claudia J. Caron, Anna S. Fritz, Elizabeth Lewis, John H. Ramey, and David T. Sugiuchi, 51–71. Binghamton, NY: Haworth, 2004.

Karney, Miroslav. "The Vrba and Wetzler Report." In *Anatomy of the Auschwitz Death Camp*, edited by Yisrael Gutman and Michael Berenbaum, 539–52. Bloomington: Indiana Univ. Press, 1994.

Kästner, Erich. *Emil und die Detektive* [*Emil and the Detectives*]. Hamburg: Cecilie Dressler Verlag, 1929.

———. "Wert und Unwort des Menschen" [The worth and worthlessness of Men]. In *Der tägliche Kram Chansons und Prosa, 1945–1948* [The daily stuff: poems and prose, 1945–1948], 85–89. Zurich: Atrium Verlag, 1949.

Kendall, Katherine A. *Social Work Education: Its Origins in Europe*. Alexandria, VA: Council on Social Work Education, 2000.

Keren, Nili. "The Family Camp." In *Anatomy of the Auschwitz Death Camp,* edited by Yisrael Gutman and Michael Berenbaum, 428–40. Bloomington: Indiana Univ. Press, 1994.

Kersting, Heinz J. "Louis Lowy: Bridge-Builder Across the Atlantic and Important Teacher of German Social Workers." Unpublished paper, n.d.

———. "Lowy, Louis." In *Who is Who der Sozialen Arbeit* [Who's who in social work], edited by Hugo Maier, 371–73. Freiburg, Germany: Lambertus, 1998.

Königer, Josef. "Lieber Freund und Kollege Löwy" [Esteemed friend and colleague, Löwy]. *Deggendorf Center Revue,* no. 11 (Apr. 15, 1946): 1.

Konopka, Gisela. *Courage and Love.* Edina, MN.: Burgess Printing, 1988.

———. "Perspectives on Social Group Work." In *Social Work with Groups: Proceedings 1979 Symposium,* edited by Sonia Abels and Paul Abels, 111–16. Louisville, KY: Committee for the Advancement of Social Work with Groups, 1981.

———. "The Significance of Social Group Work Based on Ethical Values." *Social Work with Groups* 1 (1978): 123–31.

Krakowkski, Shmuel. "The Satellite Camps." In *Anatomy of the Auschwitz Death Camp,* edited by Yisrael Gutman and Michael Berenbaum, 50–60. Bloomington: Indiana Univ. Press, 1994.

Kubie, Susan, and Gertrude Landau. *Group Work with the Aged.* New York: International Universities Press, 1953.

Kugelman, Cilly. "The Identity and Ideology of Jewish Displaced Persons." In *Jews, Germans, Memory: Reconstructions of Jewish Life in Germany,* edited by Michal Y. Bodemann, 65–76. Ann Arbor: Univ. of Michigan Press, 1996.

Langer, Lawrence L. *Holocaust Testimonies: The Ruins of Memory.* New Haven, CT: Yale Univ. Press, 1991.

Laub, Dori, with Marjorie Allard. "History, Memory, and Truth: Defining the Place of the Survivor." In *The Holocaust and History: The Known, the Unknown, the Disputed, and the Reexamined,* edited by Michael Berenbaum and Abraham J. Peck, 799–812. Bloomington: Indiana Univ. Press, 1998.

Lees, Andrew, ed. *Character Is Destiny: The Autobiography of Alice Solomon.* Ann Arbor: Univ. of Michigan Press, 2004.

Levi, Primo. *Survival in Auschwitz: The Nazi Assault on Humanity.* New York: Collier Books, 1986.

Lowy, Louis. "Adult Children and Their Parents: Dependency or Dependability?" *Long Term Care and Health Services Administration Quarterly* 1, no. 3 (Fall 1977): 243–48.

———. *Adult Education and Group Work: The Progress of Human Development Through Adult Education and Group Work.* New York: William Morrow, 1955.

———. *An Assessment-Survey Report of Indigenous Social Work Literature of Social Work Methodology.* Boston: Boston Univ. School of Social Work and International Association of Schools of Social Work, 1988.

———. "Besinnung" [Reflection]. *Deggendorf Center Revue,* no. 3 (early Dec. 1945): 2.

———. "Clarification of Self and Role Perceptions in Social Work Students During Training: A Study of Incorporation of a Professional Role." PhD diss., Harvard Univ., Cambridge, MA, 1965.

———. "Die Insel" [The island]. *Deggendorf Center Revue,* no. 6 (Jan. 26, 1946): 2.

———. "Educational Work in Terezín: A Sketch of a Study Program, June 22, 1944." In *University over the Abyss: The Story Behind 520 Lecturers and 2,430 Lectures in KZ Theresienstadt 1942–1944,* 2nd ed., edited by Elena Makarova, Sergei Makarov, and Victor Kuperman, 150–51. Jerusalem: Verba Publishers, 2004.

———. "Family Caregiving for the Elderly." *Advice for Adults with Aging Parents* 2, no. 1 (Feb.–Mar. 1987): 5–7.

———. *The Function of Social Work in a Changing Society: A Continuum of Practice.* Boston: Charles River Books, 1976.

———. "Group Participation: A Dynamic Force in the Senior Center." In *Senior Centers: An Environment for Group Service: Proceedings of the 11th National Conference on Senior Centers, Sheraton-Chicago Hotel, Chicago, IL, September 27–30, 1976,* edited by Bella Jacobs, 1–10. Washington, DC: The National Council on the Aging, 1978.

———. "Human-Services Professionals: Their Role in Education for Older People." In *Growing Old in America,* edited by Beth B. Hess and Elizabeth W. Markson, 557–68. New Brunswick, NJ: Transaction Publishers, 1991.

———. "Indigenous Leadership in Teenage Groups." *The Jewish Center Worker* 13, no. 1 (Jan. 1952): 10–15.

———. "Kommende Sorgen" [Coming worries]. *Deggendorf Center Revue,* no. 5 (Jan. 12, 1946): 4.

———. "Rehabilitation." *Deggendorf Center Review,* no. 2 (mid-Nov. 1945): 1.

———. "Remarks to the White House Conference on Aging Symposium." Paper presented by audio-recording at Northeastern Gerontological Society, New Haven, CT, Apr. 21, 1991.

———. "Returning." *Deggendorf Center Revue,* no. 1 (early Nov. 1945): 1.

———. "Social Consciousness and Social Causes: Impulses for Social Reform at the Turn of the Century in Berlin." In *Views of Berlin,* edited by Gerhard Kirchoff, 47–54. Boston: Birkhauser, 1989.

———. *Social Policies and Programs on Aging.* Lexington, MA: Lexington Books, 1980.

———. "Social Work and Social Statesmanship." *Social Work* 5, no. 2 (1960): 97–104.

———. *Social Work with the Aging: The Challenge and Promise of the Later Years.* 2nd ed. Prospect Heights, IL: Waveland Press, 1985.

———. "Toward an Educational–Human Service Linkage Model for People in Their Later Years." Unpublished paper, 1989.

———. "Volunteers in Programs for the Older Citizen." In *The Citizen Volunteer,* edited by Nathan E. Cohen, 141–56. New York: Harper Brothers, 1960.

———. "Why Education in the Later Years?" *New Findings Quarterly: A Special Publication for Shoe People Age 55 and Over.* Apr. 1987, 4–5.

———. "Zum Farewell" [Farewell to you]. *Deggendorf Center Revue,* no. 11 (Apr. 15, 1946): 1.

Lowy, Louis, and Darlene O'Connor. *Why Education in the Later Years?* Lexington, MA: Lexington Books, 1986.

Makarova, Elena, Sergei Makarov, and Victor Kuperman, eds. *University Over the Abyss: The Story Behind 520 Lecturers and 2,430 Lectures in KZ Theresienstadt 1942–1944.* 2nd ed. Jerusalem: Verba Publishers, 2004.

Mankowitz, Zeev W. *Life Between Memory and Hope: The Survivors of the Holocaust in Occupied Germany.* Cambridge: Cambridge Univ. Press, 2002.

Martin, Ruth. *Oral History in Social Work: Research, Assessment, and Intervention.* Thousand Oaks, CA: Sage, 1995.

Morrow-Howell, Nancy, and Marc Freedman, eds. *Civic Engagement in Later Life: Generations* 30, no. 4 (Winter 2006–7).

Nadich, Judah. "After Liberation the Jews Had Old and New Problems." In *Rabbi Judah Nadich, Writings,* Oct. 17, 2007. Accessed May 16, 2008. http://judahnadich.wordpress.com/2007/10/17/after-liberation-jews-had-old-and-new-problems/.

———. *Eisenhower and the Jews.* New York: Twayne Publishers, 1953.

"Neuwahl des Jewish Comittees Unseres Centers" [New election of the members of the Center Jewish Committee]. *Deggendorf Center Revue,* no. 1 (Nov. 1945): 4.

Nicholson, Barbara L., and Diane M. Kay. "Group Treatment of Traumatized Cambodian Women: A Culture Specific Approach." *Social Work* 44, no. 5 (Sept. 1999): 470–80.

Pawel, Ursula. *My Child Is Back!* London: Vallentine Mitchell, 2000.

Piper, Franciszek. "The Number of Victims." In *Anatomy of the Auschwitz Death Camp,* edited by Yisrael Gutman and Michael Berenbaum, 61–76. Bloomington: Indiana Univ. Press, 1994.

Potcoky-Tripodi, Miriam. *Best Practices for Social Work with Refugees and Immigrants.* New York: Columbia Univ. Press, 2002.

Rees, Laurence. *Auschwitz: The Nazis and the 'Final Solution.'* London: BBC Books, 2005.

Rosenberg, Blanca. *To Tell at Last: Survival under False Identity, 1941–1945.* Chicago: Univ. of Illinois Press, 1995.

Rosenbloom, Maria H. "Implications of the Holocaust for Social Work." *Families in Society* 76, no. 9 (1995): 567–76.

———. "What Can We Learn from the Holocaust?" *Occasional Papers in Jewish History and Thought,* no. 3. New York: Hunter College Jewish Social Studies Program, Hunter College of the City Univ. of New York, 1994.

Scherzinger, Alban. "Louis Lowy." In *Emigrierte Sozialarbeit: Portraits vertriebener Sozialarbeiter/innen nach 1933* [Emigrant social workers: portraits of social workers who were exiled after 1933], edited by Joachim Wieler and Susanne Zeller, 217–32. Freiburg, Germany: Lambertus, 1995.

Scheurenberg, Klaus. *Ich Will Leben: Autobiograph* [I want to live: autobiography]. Berlin: Oberbaumverlag, 1982. As cited in *University Over the Abyss: The Story Behind 520 Lecturers and 2,430 Lectures in KZ Theresienstadt 1942–1944.* 2nd ed. Edited by Elena Makarova, Sergei Makarov, and Victor Kuperman, 151. Jerusalem: Verba Publishers, 2004.

Schneider, Gertrude. *Exile and Destruction: The Fate of Austrian Jews, 1938–1945.* Westport, CT: Praeger, 1995.

Schochet, Simon. *Feldafing.* Vancouver: November House, 1983.

Schwarz, Leo W. *The Redeemers: A Saga of the Years 1945–1952.* New York: Farrar, Straus and Young, 1953.

Specht, Harry, and Mark E. Courtney. *Unfaithful Angels: How Social Work Has Abandoned Its Mission.* New York: Free Press, 1994.

"Subcamps of Auschwitz." Auschwitz-Birkenau Memorial Museum. Accessed Feb. 28, 2008. http://www.auschwitz-muzeum.oswiecim.pl/html.

Supreme Headquarters Allied Expeditionary Force. "SHAEF Administrative Memo No. 39, 1944." United States Holocaust Memorial Museum. Accessed May 12, 2008. http://www.ushmm.org/museum/exhibit/online/dp/menu.htm.

"Theresienstadt." Center for Holocaust and Genocide Studies (CHGS). Accessed July 17, 2006. http://www.chgs.umn.edu.

"Theresienstadt." *Holocaust Encyclopedia,* United States Holocaust Memorial Museum (USHMM). Accessed July 21, 2006. http://www.ushmm.org/wlc/en.

"Theresienstadt." Yad Vashem: The Holocaust Martyrs' and Heroes' Remembrance Authority. Accessed July 19, 2006. http://www1.yadvashem.org.

Trecker, Harleigh B. *Group Work Foundations and Frontiers.* New York: Whiteside, 1955.

Truman, Harry S. "President Truman's Statement and Directive on Displaced Persons, Dec. 22, 1945." World War II Resources. Accessed July 24, 2008. http://www.ibiblio.org/pha/policy/post-war/index.html.

United Nations Relief and Rehabilitation Administration (UNRRA). *Operational Analysis Papers, No. 13: U.N.R.R.A. Displaced Persons Operation in Europe and the Middle East.* London: UNRRA European Regional Office, Division of Operational Analysis, Dec. 1946;

Van Pelt, Robert. "A Site in Search of a Mission." In *Anatomy of the Auschwitz Death Camp,* edited by Yisrael Gutman and Michael Berenbaum, 93–156. Bloomington: Indiana Univ. Press, 1994.

Verzeichnis der Einwohner des D. P. Centers Deggendorf (Stand vom I. I. 1946) [Registry of the inhabitants of the Deggendorf Displaced Person Center (from Jan. 1, 1946)].

Vida, George. *From Doom to Dawn: A Jewish Chaplain's Story of Displaced Persons.* New York: Jonathan David Publishers, 1967.

Warhaftig, Zorach. *Uprooted: Jewish Refugees and Displaced Persons after Liberation.* New York: Institute of Jewish Affairs of the American Jewish Congress and World Jewish Congress, 1946.

Wieler, Joachim. "Destination Social Work: Emigrés in a Women's Profession." In *Between Sorrow and Strength: Women Refugees of the Nazi Period,* edited by Sibylle Quack, 265–82. Washington, DC: German Historical Institute and Cambridge Univ. Press, 1995.

Wieler, Joachim, and Susanne Zeller, eds. *Emigrierte Sozialarbeit: Portraits Vertriebener Sozialarbeiter innen nach 1933* [Emigrant social workers: portraits of social workers who were exiled after 1933]. Freiburg, Germany: Lambertus, 1995.

Wiesel, Elie. *Night.* Rev. ed. New York: Hill and Wang, 2006.

"Winzer," DP Camps in Germany. Accessed May 16, 2008. http://www.dpcamps .org/dpcampsGermanyW-Wi.html.

Woolrich, Serena. "Searches." *Together: The American Gathering of Jewish Holocaust Survivors and Their Descendants* 22, no. 1 (Apr. 2008): 22–23.

Wyman, David S. "Why Auschwitz Wasn't Bombed." In *Anatomy of the Auschwitz Death Camp,* edited by Yisrael Gutman and Michael Berenbaum, 569–87. Bloomington: Indiana Univ. Press, 1994.

Wyman, Mark. *DP: Europe's Displaced Persons, 1945–l951.* Philadelphia: Balch Institute Press, 1989.

Zuckmayer, Carl. *Der Hauptmann von Köpenick* [The captain of Köpenick]. Berlin: Maerchen, 1931.

Index

Italic page numbers denote photographs or illustrations.